W9-AUU-467

MY CHANGELESS FRIEND

2 Volumes—Vol. II

My Changeless Friend

By

FRANCIS P. LEBUFFE, S.J.

Arranged for Daily Meditations
Throughout the Liturgical Year

VOLUME II—PENTECOST TO ADVENT

THE APOSTLESHIP OF PRAYER
NEW YORK 58, NEW YORK

Volume II

First Printing 10,000

Imprimi potest John J. McMahon, S.J.
Nihil obstat John M. A. Fearns, S.T.D.; Censor Librorum.
Imprimatur Francis Cardinal Spellman, D.D. Archbishop, New York.

PRINTED IN U.S.A.

PENTECOST

PENTECOST

TALKING TELLINGLY OF GOD

We have heard them speak in our own tongues the wonderful works of God.

Acts 2:11.

IT was the first Pentecost of the New Law and down from high Heaven the Holy Ghost had come with the noise of a mighty wind and the lightning of tongues of fire. It was upon a group of poor, ignorant, frightened men He came, and He changed them into fearless preachers of His word. Straightway Peter arose and led them forth to begin that great levying of souls which still goes on. Jerusalem was filled with men and women from all parts of the known world, strange folk from North and East and South and West, yet they heard Peter and the other Apostles speaking to them in their own tongue and they drank in unto their own conversion the glad tidings of great joy that meant redemption for them one and all. That day the Church of God was formed because each man heard them speak in his own tongue the wonderful works of God.

What a lesson for us all! The Church had its first birthday because St. Peter and the Apostles spoke to men in their own tongue of the wonderful works of God. That was the way the Church was born and that is the way the Church has been perpetuated and that is the way each soul is brought to know and love and serve God better.

It is not enough for us to know God and to tell men of His love, but we must learn to tell them of God in their own tongue, to talk of Him to them in their own way. We must search out their thoughts, their ways, their moods, and show them God and all His love in the way that will appeal to them best. He is infinite and so His limitless attractiveness can draw each heart, no matter how strange its desires may be, no matter how wayward its cravings may be.

But there is one language all can understand, and that is the language of deeds. If by our ways and our works we speak of God to men, we shall win them to Him. To those in sorrow we must come, touching their bruised souls most tenderly and lifting up their bowed heads gently, as a mother would, until they look up once more to God. The sin-soiled souls will come with all the reek of life upon them and we must pity them and hold out a helping hand that they may slip no more, but begin again to mount the stairs that lead upward through this darkened vale of tears to God's throne. To the proud and rebellious, who petulantly hurl back their grievances against God, we must be gentle with a patience that knows no end and will not give way to sharp retorts and scoldings, even though these be well deserved—and the proud will learn to hate their own petulancy and think more kindly and more lovingly of their God who sends them such a friend.

It is good to talk of God, yes, very good, but the way to speak loudest of Him and most persuasively is to live His ways and through our lives tell of His wonderful works. At home, at work, at play, in school, or out in the public ways of men, the one loud cry that attracts each human being is the eloquent voice of a life that is led with God. Then men will understand us, for we shall be speaking to each in his own tongue.

Dear Jesus, there is nothing nearer my heart than the strong desire to bring souls to You. I sometimes dream of preaching eloquently about You to all, dream of drawing countless souls to You by written or spoken word—and yet this often cannot be. So let me learn the vital lesson of telling men of You in the way I always can and in the way they understand best. Let me grow—I say it reverently—let me grow to be Your double that men may see me and seeing me may know You. Thus shall I tell them most persuasively in their own tongue of upright deeds, of the greatness of Your love and of the wonderful things of God.

PENTECOST MONDAY

LIFT UP YOUR HEARTS!

Lift up your hearts! We have lifted them up to the Lord.
Preface of the Mass.

EACH morning as he stands on the inner threshold of the great Sacrifice the priest, with uprising arms, cries out as though in warning of the sacrilege of inattention, when God is coming down anew to dwell among us: "Lift up your hearts!" And quick upon his cry comes the answer of the attendant folk voiced by the altar-server: "We have—unto the Lord." Thus it was at early morn many hundred years ago; thus it is each day we call "today"; thus it will be unto the end.

Yet let us pause and ask ourselves: Can I each morning from my heart make answer as does the altar-boy?

"Lift up your hearts!" What strange memories of yesterday that brings! Yes, we lifted up our hearts. A trifling joy there was and we laid full hold on it and we lifted up our hearts to catch a bit of the rainbow that was bending down on us passingly. A new-won prize for which we had striven hard made our hearts leap, when we found it within our grasp. A kind word from this friend, a bit of approval from another, and our hunger for sympathy was met and we were buoyed up with freshened courage. We caught the little things that please—most of us have few big things—and we pressed from them each ounce of cheer—but then? Did we think of the Giver? Did our minds ever once turn to the "Father in Heaven from whom all good things descend"? It is so easy—and yet so unmannerly—to snatch the gift and never once say "Thank you" to the Giver.

"Lift up your hearts!" "We have lifted them up to the Lord." When love comes from those nearest and dearest to us, we must look through it and above it and beyond it to that infinite love of which it is the veriest spark. When comfort and encouragement come from friends who know how rightly to feed new strength into our hearts, we must remember Him who sent the "Comforter" to give us of the seven-fold gifts and make us "strong and perfect Christians and soldiers of Jesus Christ." When another stands near us in time of trial and shores us up lest we fall, we must remember that it was our changeless Friend who bore our iniquities and died for our sins and now dwells always on our altars to help us.

And how good it will be to "lift our hearts up to the Lord"! It will not rob us of the passing joys. It will not steal from them the least bit of their sweetness. Nay, rather will it add thereto. Love, sanctified by being linked to infinite love, must needs be truest love; courage linked to Omnipotence will know no fear; encouragement blessed by the Comforter will gain immeasurably.

Indeed, we must lift up our hearts. The shadows fall too often and the clouds gather too fast at times and they may darken our lives too much and make us see only gloom. But back of the cloud there is sunshine, and the shadow itself always comes because of light, and so we must learn to travel around to the back of the cloud and through to the end of the shadow, where brightness begins. That we do, when we lift up our hearts to the Lord.

Dear Jesus, I am so apt to catch the little joys of life and center my heart thereon, and to let the shadows of life cast their darkness too lingeringly. I ought to lift up my heart, but I ought, too, always to lift it up to You. Thus it will stay lifted up; for, then, whether joys come or go, stay long or speed quickly away, deep down in my heart will be the peace which lifts up our hearts unfailingly to You, the "God of peace and all consolation."

PENTECOST TUESDAY

FRIENDS AREN'T KEPT WAITING

Behold, I stand at the gate and knock.
Apocalypse 3:20.

IT is impolite to keep anyone waiting, above all a friend. Custom, sanctioned by the best instincts of man, teaches us thus, and when it is one we love and who reciprocates our love, then there must be no delay in hearkening to his wish. Let but the cheering accents of his voice be heard, let but his distant footfall sound upon our path, and we are quick to lessen the space that holds us apart.

Now Christ stands at our door and knocks, not at the door of our earthly home, for that sweet pleasure is denied us, but at our hearts. Jesus, our God, friend from long ago before an earthly friend had loved us, stands asking that we let Him come and find rest within. Nor comes He once or twice as our life is spun away, but daily and hourly this strong Lover of souls would gain admittance to the deepest love we have. He asks it as though He could not claim the right thereto, He pleads for it as lover has ever pleaded for another's love. Yet hour after hour, or day after day, or maybe year after year, we keep our Friend a-knocking at our hearts. Oh! He may be there already by His sanctifying grace, which we have tried to keep these many years, but there is an inner gateway of our heart wherein He would gain entrance. Long, long ago by His kind grace we have given Him a welcome into our love and He indeed has entered and has supped with us, and we with Him, and we have known the joy of having such a guest. A share of our love He has, but has He all? Is there not a corner, perhaps a large corner of our hearts, that we fear to yield to Him? He asks of faithful parents to give Him of their little ones to fill His cloister-homes and maybe He finds a hesitancy in their giving. He asks again the sacrifice of a friend who, though not bad, is leading us just a bit aside from our truest Friend, and sometimes we seem to feel there might be room for choice! And in the lesser ways, we keep the Lord and God of all a postulant at our door. A bit of selfishness here has laid long claim to our hearts, an unordered quest for ease or learning has won unholy conquest there, again a too close clinging to the things of time—these are what keep our Lord from out His full possession.

Trifles, yes, made gewgaws that break and fade, but not trifles when they make us impolite to God!

Jesus, most relentless Lover our human hearts have ever known, I must not, will not, filch from You the love You crave so deeply. My heart is Yours from this hour on, Yours whole and undivided, and there will be no rapine in the holocaust. Yet, dearest Lord, because I know my truant self, I beg Your mighty grace that, when You ask the sacrifices that must always be, You will not ever find me wanting.

"Take and receive, O Lord, my liberty,
Take all my will, my mind, my memory;
Do Thou direct and govern all and sway
Do what Thou wilt, command and I obey.
Only Thy grace and love on me bestow,
Possessing these all riches I forego."

PENTECOST WEDNESDAY

NO LOCK-STEP

And they were all filled with the Holy Ghost, and they began to speak with divers tongues, according as the Holy Ghost gave them to speak.

Acts 2:4.

CAN you beat that, Father! Here we started to do a bit of Catholic Action and to distribute Catholic literature, and to help the poor, and, and——" "Well, what's gone wrong, Bill?" "Gone wrong—well, there is the crowd from St. N—'s and they're starting in, too, but in a different way. What's the idea? Why can't we all be the same, and do the same, and——" "Wait a minute, Bill, wait a minute. Did you ever read the story of the first Pentecost? Did all the Apostles say and do the same thing? Just read: 'And they were all filled with the Holy Ghost, and they began to speak with divers tongues, according as the Holy Ghost gave them to speak.' Heaven save us, Bill, from a lock-step Church in which all Catholics must do exactly the same thing in every line! I hope I die before that happens."

Bill's flare-up was not unusual. We must agree in matters of Faith and morals, but diversity of viewpoints and differences of activity are natural, and yet so often friction results. Isn't the world big enough and wide enough to allow for this?

Within the family mother becomes irritated because father drops his shoes just where she thinks the shoes should not go; and father gets angry because mother does not put back the newspaper where he has decided it properly belongs; and between parents and children friction grows because a healthy difference of opinion on trifling things is outlawed by either or both.

In societies, even of the most pious sort, much good is offset because some domineering prefect or president will tolerate no plan of action which she has not thought out or decided to be *the* one. Other suggestions are ignored or "steam-rollered" under, until the paralyzing force of disgust or lethargy numbs all into peaceful stagnation.

Each of us differs much in our personality, and all of us, for that very reason, work best when we have freest scope and swing. Inevitably there will be much give-and-take and much subordination of personal views will be asked of us that our activities may harmonize gracefully with the activities of others. But to be so intolerant of others that when we stamp our foot all others must dance, and when we clap our hands they must rise, and when we say "no," all must count the question as infallibly settled—well, that is the height of sad nonsense. That was not the way God began His Church. He left many points of discipline to be decided by His Apostles, and—we say it with reverence—it were well for us to take a cue from God. And that is not the way the Church has been run down through the centuries in matters not pertaining to revealed truth and morals—and, by and large, the Church has been the outstanding success of history. It would be a drab, unthrilling world were it filled with "yes-men." We must be strongminded enough to have our own definite opinions, and broadminded enough to see that there are other viewpoints, and tolerant enough to give full play to all that is right and true. After all not all people like chocolate ice-cream, nor does every one like potato salad.

Dear Jesus, make me big enough to see life and all life's activities as a whole. Naturally, I have my own views and my own ways of doing things; and, quite naturally, they seem to me to be the best ways. But let me remember that others too have their own ways of thinking and of acting which appear to them of at least equal worth with mine. Give me the grace to be properly tolerant of others at all times, especially in matters of Your service.

PENTECOST THURSDAY

RUDE TO GOD

And grieve not the Holy Spirit of God, whereby you are sealed unto the day of Redemption.

Ephesians 4:30.

THE last thing a decent man or woman wants to do is to insult a guest. That is a primary dictate among all who have the least desire to be polite and who have even the minimum of regard for friends. To invite a man into my house, to have him sit at my table and chat away familiarly, and then to do something that pains him—that is unthinkable.

Yes, unthinkable among human friends and human acquaintances—but not when dealing with our Heavenly Guest, the Holy Ghost. By reason of sanctifying grace, I became the temple of the Holy Ghost, and God resides within me in a special way. He is more truly and intimately my guest and I His host than could ever be between earthly friends. He is with me at early morn, across the noon-day hours, at evening time, and He abides with me during the unconscious lapse of the night hours. He is within me at home and when I am abroad; He is within me when I pray or when I while away the time playfully; He is within me when all is bright and when clouds lower. He is within me always—protecting me "unto the day of Redemption," when I shall be His guest for all eternity.

"Grieve not the Holy Spirit of God." And yet we do grieve Him when we follow lowered ideals and hearken to the call of the world. For it truly grieves Him to be the guest of earthly-minded folk. And if we pamper ourselves and yield to sensuality, letting the demands of ease and comfort hold sway, we grieve Him then, for He is a pure Spirit and would win us to loftier seeking. If we are unkind and hurt another, we grieve Him there, for He loves the one we hurt just as much as He loves us. And if I pray and let my mind wander afar, and pay little attention to Him when I speak with Him, that impoliteness grieves Him much.

That is all true—but with our dim faith we do not realize it. In fact, it hardly ever dawns on us that by our sins, even the slightest, we are positively rude to our Heavenly Guest. If we but had faith!

Dear Jesus, I am sorry that I have been so rude in the past, but I had not really thought of it all in just that light. I dislike being rude to anyone —much less being rude to God. And so I now beg pardon of You and of God the Father and of the Holy Ghost whom I have grieved—and I promise to try not to be rude again.

PENTECOST FRIDAY

GOD WANTS TO BE LOVED

And because you are sons, God hath sent the Spirit of His Son into your hearts, crying: Abba, Father.

Galatians 4:6.

YOU know, I almost came to hate God. Every time my teacher spoke of God, it was: 'God will punish you if you do that.' If the priest gave a sermon, it was filled with hell and sin and God's wrath. If I asked for a prayer for some intention, I was told I might get it '*if* it is God's holy will'; I was warned to expect refusal; I never once was told to pray expectant of an answer. Oh, Father, that doesn't get you anywhere; that doesn't make you feel like working for God; there's no love in that; there's—"

Quietly the old priest spoke:

"No, Ellen, there isn't. And it's all quite the wrong way to look at God. I couldn't serve God either if that were all I knew about Him. God is more than that."

Long they sat and talked, until the love of God warmed a heart that had almost been turned against Him. And as night fell, Ellen went forth with a light and joy in her heart it had never known before.

Why should we always talk of God as though He were some big policeman just waiting to catch us doing wrong? Why should all our talk be of sin and hell and God's punishments? Of course God hates sin; of course He punishes sin. But that is not the side we ought to stress. Life is hard enough and its burdens weigh us down sufficiently without our darkening it all with a cringing fear of God. God is our *Father;* we are His *children;* Christ is our *brother;* we "are no longer strangers and foreigners, but . . . fellow-citizens of the Saints and members of the household of God." Why can we not dwell on that? Love drives out fear; and love drives us on to hardest things with a song on our lips; and love makes all things easy.

God *is* love, and He *does* love me. He loved me from eternity and drew me out of nothing, giving me existence in preference to myriads of others that He might have created in my stead. He has loved me every moment of my existence, upholding me by His omnipotence lest I fall back into my native nothingness. He has so loved me that He came down from Heaven and suffered and died for me to save me from sin. He has so loved me that when I sinned again and again, each time He forgave me my sins and gave me back His friendship, which I had spurned. He loves me so much that He has become my Food times without number, and He dwells within me as in His tabernacle.

Love—love—love—that is what is written largest across all the dealings of God with me. Then why not write it boldly across all my dealings with Him? Of course we should never lose our filial fear of God any more than a loving son forgets his respectful reverence for a devoted father. This is not the servile fear of a slave for its task-master. If God wished me to fear Him with a servile fear and stand in dread of Him, would He have acted as He has? If He wished me to fear Him thus, would He have been born a lovable Babe at Bethlehem or have called to Himself all that "labor and are burdened"? If He wished me to fear Him thus, would He have told me that He was "meek and humble of heart" and that "the bruised reed He shall not break; and the smoking flax He shall not extinguish"?

It just doesn't all make sense! And so many do thus fear and dread God; and many talk and write and preach of Him as though He were some tyrant gloatingly waiting to cheat us of what we want, hungrily watching to trap us in wrongdoing. What an injustice to the God of love! What a parody of the Babe of Bethlehem!

Fear cramps and numbs and repels; love opens the heart wide and spurs on and unites lover with loved one. Life's road is hard enough without making it harder, harder than God ever intended it to be. Love makes it easy, or at least easier; and it is my love that God wants: "Thou shalt *love* the Lord thy God"; if you *love* Me, keep My commandments"; Simon . . . *lovest* thou Me?" "By this shall all men know that you are My disciples, if you have *love* one for another."

Dear Jesus, teach me this secret of loving You. I know that You are just and that You hate sin and that You will punish it. But that is only when I force You to it. The one thing You have done is to show Your *love* for me, far back from all eternity down to this very moment. I wish to love You, and I know You wish to be served in a spirit of love. And that's the only decent way to serve You, isn't it?

PENTECOST SATURDAY

REPAYING GOD

Is this the return thou makest to the Lord, O foolish and senseless people? Is He not thy Father that hath possessed thee, and made thee, and created thee?

Deuteronomy 32:6.

MOSES is about to die and in his last talk to the people of Israel he chides them much for all their stubbornness and stiffneckedness. Despite all that God had done for them, despite the manna and the quail in the desert, despite the living waters that gushed forth from the rock miraculously, despite the fact that, though they had been forty years journeying through the desert, their garments were not worn out, neither were the shoes of their feet consumed with age—yes, despite it all, again and again they rebelled against God and disobeyed His strict command and jumped at every slight pretext to murmur against Him. No wonder the old leader so near death cried out in bitterness: "For I know thy obstinacy, and thy most stiff neck. While I am yet living and going in with you, you have always been rebellious against the Lord. . . . Is this the return thou makest to the Lord, O foolish and senseless people? Is not He thy Father that hath possessed thee, and made thee, and created thee?"

We are apt to be very harsh in our condemnation of the Jewish folk, but what of ourselves? Our own record of grateful loyalty to God is perhaps just as sorry a one. God was good to the Jews, but He has been far better to us.

He has given me the priceless gift of Faith and all the Sacraments with their plentiful graces. And yet I may be almost ashamed of that Faith, quite apologetic about professing it, eager to be known as a "broad-minded" Catholic. Maybe I am quite careless, and act as though the Sacraments were never intended for me. In the goodness and largeness of His Sacred Heart, He is daily immolated on our altars and always present in the Tabernacle. He wants to come to each and all of us frequently, yes, daily, in Holy Communion. Yet what devotion have I to Holy Mass, even when I do attend it? And how do I treat Him, when He comes to me?

It may be that He has granted the wedded love of man and woman to take concrete living form in little ones, who are to be taught to know and love Him as their Heavenly Father. Yet would these children ever learn this from the lives of father and mother? All the instructions and exhortations in the world are worthless, if father and mother contradict them in their lives. God has given them these little ones to be given back to Him one day, and yet perhaps they are sent to schools—for fashion's sake—where snobbish parents are willing to have any and every name mentioned except the name of our Father who is in Heaven. Is this a proper return?

To me in my individual life God has given many graces that I may be perfect as He is perfect: the ordinary graces of each day, and frequently very unusual ones. Yet what kind of spiritual specimen am I? Little better, perhaps, than a spiritual Tom Thumb, who has never grown up to man's stature in the way of God. Can a dwarfed soul make proper return to God?

Dear Jesus, I have little to pride myself on, when I think of the return I have made to You for all that You have given to me. Daily at Mass the priest asks: "What shall I return to the Lord for all that He has given to me?" What shall I return? My best, of course; for even that is poor enough. Yet that is precisely what I have not given. So give me grace now, please, that I may be no longer foolish and senseless, making scant return for all You have lavished on me.

TRINITY SUNDAY

PLEASE DON'T LEAVE ME ALONE!

Behold, I am with you all days, even to the consummation of the world.

St. Matthew 28:20.

PRAY hard for me and please, please, don't leave me alone!" were the words that came speeding across the country, straight from the heart of one who found the fight of life hard. Years of slight ups and hard downs had at length brought home a rightful distrust of self and, as the daily pressure of temptation closed in on him and he saw the same old sins so frighteningly near, the call came pleadingly. The battle must not be lost, and yet to feel that no human help was nigh, which would make God's inner help of grace quite visible, would spell defeat, even as it had spelled it many a time before. "Pray hard for me," the letter read, but something more poignantly human was added: "Please, please, don't leave me alone!"

That was the cry from one human heart; but is it not the great wail that goes up to the throne of God from each one who has his own soul's safety constantly in mind? "Please, please, don't leave me alone!" An open danger is here, a hidden snare there, a tugging allurement elsewhere, and, even when these are gone, within us are the old cravings of mind and heart and body, to follow which would mean far waywardness from God. Man's life is truly a warfare and lustily must we fight, but we cannot fight alone.

And why? Oh, just because it is hard to push ahead, whether through open spaces or wooded slope, when there is no one at your side; just because it is hard to give and take manfully in the grueling game of life and never have anyone to tell you, "Well done!"; just because it is hard to wipe away the tear, and wear a deceiving smile, if no one has seen the tear fall and no one pierces beneath the mask; just because it is hard to walk through the valley of the shadow of death and know that, if in a moment of slipping we were to reach out our hand for help, it would fall back untouched to our side.

"It is not good for man to be alone," is as true today, as it was of old, when the first man walked in Eden in single majesty. Deep down within us is the yearning for some one who will guide and guard us, some one who will shore us up when we lean heavily, some one who will lift up our drooping eyes, that see too much of earth and its lowering appeal, until we can see again "the mountains whence cometh help." Yes, in our heyday of power, when the wine of life runs full and strong, and the music of life is sweet with harmony, the passing joys dull the consciousness of this craving. The merrymaking of the moment and the power to do and dare, when and how and what we please, intoxicate us and make us forgetful that we are but frail and failing men.

But let the music be hushed, and let the shadows fall and let the friction of life wear through our thin robes of power, the old gnawing is there again in full consciousness. We have been at the festive board of life, "where some sit seldom and few sit long," and now—we are alone. No, not unless we would wilfully have it so.

For no matter where we are, no matter when this need of help is felt, there is One to whom we can turn, One whose very nearness robs the vastest desert of its loneliness, whose absence would make a throng of milling thousands an utter isolation. He is ever ready and most willing to take us by the hand and help us over the rough places and through the gathering darkness; to protect us against danger "from the morning watch even unto the night," whether it fronts us openly or lies hidden to strike more surely. But we must call upon Him and we must ask His help;

for thus He has willed that we ourselves should show a care for our souls. We must school ourselves from youngest years in morning and in evening prayers, at noon, in places of work and of pleasure, to cry to Him: "Please, please, don't leave me alone!"

Dear Lord, I need You much in this brief struggle we call life. I really want to win the fight and be a credit to the saving power of Your grace. But You know how weak I am, and I know it, too. My own past makes me rightly afraid of myself, afraid, too, "of the arrow that flieth in the day, of the business that walketh about in the dark; of invasion and of the noon-day devil." And so I beg You now, and I ask You, to give me much grace that in every hour of need I may cry from my heart—and please hearken always quickly to my cry—"Please, please, don't leave me alone!"

TRINITY MONDAY

DOING THE THINGS OF GOD

And why call you me, Lord, Lord, and do not the things which I say?

St. Luke 6:46.

THE people were all gathered about our Lord on the plain in Galilee and they were being told plain truths. One charge after another was laid on them, kindly but firmly, and then, as though summing up the whole situation, our Lord said plainly: "And why call you me, Lord, Lord, and do not the things which I say?" He knew that the poor folk followed Him, all a-hungered for a leader; He could not help hearing their many protestations of loyalty and devotedness; yet He has but one straightforward answer to it all. Words are cheap; words, though well-meant, are passing things that cost little. Deeds tell; for they cost. Solid proof of loyalty lies in deeds, not in words.

Our Lord spoke those words long, long ago, but He meant them for each and every one of us. We all call Him "Lord, Lord"; but do we do the things that He says? No matter in what sphere our lives are cast, God's will is written large thereon. And if we neglect the known will of God, or fail to search for it if we are in doubt, then all our cries of love, and all our protestations of devotedness, are sounding brass and tinkling cymbals.

Father and mother have clear, definite duties to each other and to their little ones. If these are neglected—no matter how holy the pretense

—all the extra prayers and activities in pious associations are but cries of "Lord, Lord" with the fact-proofs of love wanting.

Children, too, owe much to parents, and if these duties are left unfulfilled, all other good works, all holy practices are vain delusions . . . for the essentials of their state of life are absent.

So, too, in the business world. It is all well and good to be generous with the money we have made. But have we earned it justly? It is a vain cry of "Lord, Lord", when our money goes ostentatiously to help the starving, if that same money has been made off other starvelings, to whom we sell our products or whom we employ at a beggar's pittance.

Teachers, too, and all those who have charge over others have much here about which to challenge themselves. Long prayers are excellent; but have class-assignments been prepared well and has class work been corrected? Much spiritual work outside of class with students is good, but is the ordinary, humdrum, colorless routine-work done aright? The "Lord, Lord" of these "extras" is good enough; but are we doing the routine things, the essential things which He wants, and which are demanded if good work is to be done?

Dear Lord, I know myself and what strange notions can and do come to me. When I think of sanctity and of serving You well, at once my mind runs off into extra prayers, and extra work, and extra activities. I am so prone to stress the unusual, and to forget that real love of You is shown first of all and principally in doing what You want me to do and when You want me to do it. This is mostly so colorless and so lacking in thrills that instinctively I reach out for the unusual. And yet I must learn this fundamental lesson, and learn it soon. So give me grace, of course, to say "Lord, Lord," but at the same time to show You that I mean it by doing the things which You say.

TRINITY TUESDAY

PLAYING OUR OWN PART

Saul was exceeding angry, and this word was displeasing in his eyes, and he said: They have given David ten thousands, and to me they have given but a thousand.
1 Kings 18:8.

THE grass is always greener, Mary, you know, in the other fellow's yard" was the only answer that could be made to the petulant outpourings of jealousy that came so spitefully from quivering lips. "Some other part in the play should have been given to me—that's all." "Well, suppose it should! Why let that make you botch the part you have? Why be so green-eyed as to make yourself all out of sorts and so unmannerly? Be a good young lady and stop stamping your feet in anger and look to your own task and do that well. You know what I said—'the grass is always greener—' "

Poor fools that we are at times! Instead of trying to manage what we have, instead of measuring up to tasks assigned or bearing the crosses that have been placed on us, we fasten envious eyes on others, and keep repeating to ourselves: "Oh! if only I were like that!"

A young man and woman stand at the altar of God and, having tested out their love, plight it to each other to take, hand in hand, whatever the years may bring, and then, as time swings by, and others reap more plentifully of the fruits of the world—money, honors and pleasures—they feel a tugging at their hearts and maybe bitterness grows apace. They fail to count up the favors God has bestowed upon them, they forget to total up the good things He has given them. "The grass is greener" over there, and they spoil the part God would have them play in life.

Here is one who had ambitioned highly, who fain would have stood out before all men ranking foremost among them for attainments and success in the chosen task of life, yet God for His own reasons may have sealed the doors fast shut and denied all entrance there. Of course it is hard to make a great detour in life and come out far away from our self-plotted path. But if God wants it so, are we going to be forever gazing elsewhere than at the tasks assigned us here and now? Shall we childishly pout and stamp wilful feet because we cannot do what we want?

The tasks of life await us daily, hourly, and it were very wise in an adult way to take them as they are. They might have been otherwise! Yes. And being otherwise they would have been more to my liking! Decidedly. But what of that? A hundred years from now what jot or tittle of difference will it make whether I have stood high or low, whether I did big things or the very little things that form the web and woof of most men's lives? I know the answer. And I know quite as well that, whereas then it will not matter at all what I did, the manner of my having done it will mean everything. Then it will not be the "what" but the "how" of my life that will count—and that alone.

Dear Jesus, You know what a jealous thing I am. I am always wanting to be otherwise, always grieved because I am not called to play the part in life that others play. This is so very childish, but it is the truth, hurt as it does for me to admit it. So please let me learn to stop this yearning to play another's part and give me sense to attend to myself and to my own affairs and to use all my energy to play my own part well.

TRINITY WEDNESDAY

HELP THEM HOME!

Suffer the little ones to come unto Me.
St. Mark 10:19.

OUR Lord, as is the way with friends, is wont to talk with us of those He loves. Often He tells of those great men and women who are now at home with Him amid the adoring Angels, loyal soldiers, when yet they tarried in this foreign land. Sometimes, too, He speaks to us of comrades in arms who need our prayers, as the fight goes hard with them and the crown of victory seems to fall from out their grasp. Again we hear His pleading voice tell of the holy souls who tarry in the purging flames, souls perhaps of our own dear dead, souls all of them of His own dear dead.

Long years have we heard the Church's mournful cry, "Eternal rest grant unto them, O Lord," and today as we kneel before Him, our Lord joins in that mournful plaint for souls and intercedes for those He loves. He reaches out to us helpless hands, helpless because He willed to be dependent on our charity, because it is His good pleasure to be "Omnipotence in bonds." "Suffer the little ones to come unto Me. They have spent their mortal days—and spent them well. Yet the dust and stain of struggling years are yet upon them and keep them from My presence. Souls redeemed by My precious Blood, souls for whom I died as no man died, souls whom I love, as only I can love, are kept from Me. My friends are held from Me—and 'there in hope the lone night-watches keep.' How I long to bring them home with Me, that where I am there also My little ones shall be! How I long to have My friends safe by My side forever! And you alone, My brethren, you alone can restore them to Me, you alone can unite Me to My own. Not Angels nor Saints now robed in glory can ransom them from 'the holy house of toll, the frontier penance-place.' Oh, man, powerful in your weakness, give back to your God the souls He made!"

Can we listen to that pleading of our Friend and not hearken to His cry? Can we go our unremembering way and forget the "prisoners of the King," to whose prison we alone hold the key? A little extra prayer as the hours of the day pass by, a little extra care to blunt our sharpened tongue, a little extra thought to soothe the cares of saddened hearts—and by such works we shall unlock the captive's cell and bring Christ's friends back to Him. "Before the mountains were made or the earth and the world was formed, from eternity to eternity" He has looked forward to that meeting. Shall we not hasten the coming of that joy? Shall we not do for God what we would do for an earthly friend?

Lover of souls, O Lord, I hearken to Your cry! Succor and aid will I bring to those You love; freedom and joy will I hurry to those dear souls, whose coming You so desire. Little can I do for You, few are the favors You ask. Surely this little will I do with all my heart. Never shall morning wear to evening but I shall think me of Your captive friends; think of them that their bonds may be loosed, pray for them "that all feet may come to the Everlasting Home." Then if one day, dear Lord, Your waiting be for me, may someone in that hour speed my coming to Your arms!

CORPUS CHRISTI (TRINITY THURSDAY)

PLEASE VISIT ME

Remember me and visit me.

Jeremias 15:15.

THESE words, meant to be the cry of man to God, may well be turned into the pleading of our sacramental God. "Child of man, remember Me and visit Me." It is the age-old cry for love from the intensely human Heart of Christ our Lord. As of old on the moon-lit slope of Olivet He tottered in His agony to the side of the Apostles, if haply He might find comfort in their sympathy, so now from out the tabernacle the Sacred Heart of Jesus pleads for a companion, pleads for one to come aside and break His isolation. When the dying thief looked over the tangled wreckage of his lawless days, his poor wild heart begged for remembrance and the Master of life and death heard his sharp cry. Now that same loving Master asks us to remember Him, yes, pleads for our poor company and the fitful love of our truant hearts.

The cry of a strong man is a woeful, frightening thing to hear, and this is the cry of the strongest of men, the infinite appeal of the God-man. "Remember Me and visit Me." Can we refuse Him? If our nearest and dearest in the midst of pain and sorrow call for us and yearn to see us, does distance or expense keep us from their side? What now that God calls for our companionship! Today and every day the Prisoner of nineteen hundred years, pained by the sins of myriad faithless souls, saddened by the infidelity of those who should serve Him best, is waiting patiently, waiting expectantly for our footfall on the vacant pavement of His prison. Alone He watches, oh so often! "I am become like to a pelican of the wilderness: . . . I have watched, and am become as a sparrow all alone on the housetop." "Remember these things, O Jacob, and Israel, for thou art My servant. I have formed thee, thou art My servant, Israel, forget me not." God is lonely—what a thought!—lonely and we, and none but we, have the stupendous privilege of visiting Him. Men and not Angels are the callers He desires.

Jesus, my God, how I have neglected You! How many a time I have heard but not hearkened to those words of Thine, "I am become a stranger to My brethren . . . . and I looked for one that would grieve together with Me, but there was none: and for one that would comfort

Me and I found none." "I was . . . in prison and you did not visit Me." Yes, You have been a stranger to me. So near and yet I have time upon time passed Your door and never stopped to speak a word to You to break the long monotony of Your solitary vigil. To other friends I have gone; but to You—! But this is the past, Lord Jesus, and pardon it in Your mercy. Forgive the many years of thoughtlessness and from this day on make my heart find its keenest pleasure in Your company. Lord, that I may love "the beauty of Your house and the place where Your glory dwelleth."

"Oh, shame, Lord, for me to weary,
Weary of giving to Thee,
Whose Heart was but weary of waiting
To suffer and die for me."

FRIDAY WITHIN OCTAVE OF CORPUS CHRISTI

YOU'RE HUNGRY

In those days there was a very great famine.
1 Machabees 9:24.

THE street car was speeding down Broadway; in the seat behind me two women were carrying on a running chatter. Above the jangle of the car and the roar of the street noises their high-pitched voices carried every word into my ear. One woman was very querulous, and after repeated curt remarks her companion said, kindly but firmly, "Do you know what's the matter with you? You're hungry."

"The matter with you is that you're hungry." And as I looked out on blatant Broadway, on its night-club "ads," its burlesque notices, its flaming electric signs over moving-picture houses and legitimate-stage theaters, there flashed across my mind the thought: "Poor men and women! The matter with you is that you're hungry—very hungry. That is why you are restive and always on the go. That is why you draw out your revelries into the waking hours of the dawn. That is why you keep feeding yourselves more and more pleasure. You're hungry, not with a physical hunger that you can and do assuage with the good things of life, but with a ceaseless, gnawing hunger of the soul. And the husks of pleasure only make you hungrier. You're hungry—for God."

"You're hungry." Long, long ago Saint Augustine cried: "Our souls are made for Thee, O God, and they are restless till they rest in Thee." Not all the pleasant things of life are bad, nor are they worthless. But they simply cannot give ultimate satisfaction. A stick of candy pleases a child for a while; a rattle amuses him for the moment. A dance can bring real pleasure while it lasts, and a party can speed the hours away quite merrily. But these things are passing; and when they are gone, our souls are hungrier than ever.

That is why from our earliest years the Church tries to tell us of God and of His love for us. That is why she points to the pleasant things of earth too, and blesses them; yet, even as she blesses the very food we eat and the journeys that we take, she gives us her motherly warning that these things are good only because they are intended to lead us to something better. She blesses man and maid with the great Sacrament of marriage and hallows the lawful pleasures thereof, but she lifts the eyes of man and wife beyond the world of sense and focuses them on Christ and His Church, of which union their marriage union is a symbol. She takes young children into her classrooms and instructs them in the fundamentals of knowledge and in the arts and the sciences, but she tells them all the while of God who is truth itself and in whom all lesser truths find their meaning. She knows her children are hungry, and, good mother that she is, she does her best to satisfy that hunger lastingly.

Dear Jesus, my soul is often a puzzle to me; it is so restless at times and reaches unwisely for the baubles and pleasures that are about me. Some of them I need; and some of them I can rightly have. But even when I have enjoyed them lawfully to the full, they leave me wanting something else. Sometimes, too, the call of the world of sin is loud and its forbidden pleasures are blatant in their appeal. Stand by me then, dear Lord, and make me clearly see that all such earthly foods will always leave me hungry.

SATURDAY WITHIN OCTAVE OF CORPUS CHRISTI

WE FEEL SECURE

Why have the Gentiles raged, and the people devised vain things? The kings of the earth stood up, and the princes met together against the Lord, and against His Christ.

Psalm 2:1, 2.

THERE is a completeness of satisfaction and a robust sense of security in every true Catholic, which is a surprise to our non-Catholic brethren. God forbid that we should be proud, unworthy heirs, as we are, of the great Catholic legacy, but our view of time and of eternity is so adequately correct, our beliefs are so perfectly squared off with the doctrines left two thousand years ago by the Son of God Himself, our faith is so permanent, lasting even "unto the consummation of the world," that there must inevitably be a sturdy sureness in all our ways. The storms of twenty centuries have wasted their fury against Christ's Church, and we, its latest inheritors, know that it will stand unmoved until the day-dawn when the Church Triumphant will alone chant forth God's mercy in a song that is ever new. With the Psalmist we are forced to cry out in very joy: "The measuring-lines are fallen for me in pleasant places; yea, mine inheritance is fair with me."

We do possess our souls in peace, and most so, when we come into the presence of our Sacramental Lord, who has watched these many hundred years, "while Gentiles raged, and the people devised vain things." Here against Him in His Sacrament of love have their vainest plots been laid and yet have been always foiled. Masses in caves and in catacombs, Masses in peat-bogs and in wildernesses, Masses in dungeons and in hidden garrets —that is the story of land after land that once knew Christ. But there has always been the day of our Lord's returning, always the time of the second spring.

What a wondrous heritage is our Catholic Faith and I am one of the heirs! I may come and kneel before the same Lord Jesus, made fugitive so often and yet abiding with us still. I may come and pay that homage others paid and for it were flung to beasts or still more ravening men. I may come and find Him in His proper home, not hid away, lest other Herods should discover Him. I *may*—but do I? My faith is strong and, God willing, I would die for it—but am I living it? If Christ, my best of friends, be but a bit of the way down the street from me, why does He find me so seldom in His home? If He be really Emmanuel, "God-with-us," why do I not make Him my confidant, first and foremost before any earthly friend He may have given me? His real presence is the centre and heart of our whole faith, the richest gift of our Christian heritage. Do my actions, and not my words alone, show that I treasure it as such? Suppose tomorrow persecution would rob our blessed Lord of all His tabernacle-homes, would we really miss Him? Would there be moments of each day we would have to fill in otherwise than we fill them now? As we would pass His former home among us, would our feet instinctively turn aside to rest a while with Him? Is our Lord's real presence a vital, strong fact in our every-day life, or must He, too, be classed among forgotten friends?

Dear Jesus, how strangely incompetent I seem to grasp what Your sacred presence with us means. My noble ancestry of Saints realized it well and made Your home their trysting-place with You. Their appreciation was so strong, so deep, so true—and mine! Jesus dear, I know I am a witless, senseless child of holiest folk and ill deserve to have You with me, but pardon my heedless past, and from this moment on, let me learn to find my happiest hours with You.

SUNDAY WITHIN OCTAVE OF CORPUS CHRISTI

SELFISH TOWARDS GOD

Is it time for you to dwell in ceiled houses, and this house lie desolate?

Aggeus 1:4.

THE Babylonian exile was over. For sixty years the exiled Jews had been awakened by the hiss of the lash to a new day's thankless task, which they had well merited by their forgetfulness of God. But the penalty of their sin had now been paid and their Captor-King's edict had gone forth. Across the desert they had retraced their way and climbed the hills of Moab and mounted the steep ascent from Jericho to Jerusalem, and on the slopes of Sion and Ophel had rebuilded for themselves comfortable homes. All the while, however, the house of God was left in its ruins. Then the lash of the word of God's prophet fell more biting on their souls than ever the scourge of the slave-masters of Babylon upon their bodies: "Is it time for you to dwell in ceiled houses, and this house lie desolate?" The newly awakened echoes of Cedron and of Hinnom had scarcely fallen back into their long undisturbed silence before the house of God was being rebuilt by busy hands; and God's prophet saw that his words had not fallen on deaf ears.

Gone is the link which bound the Chosen People of God. Gone is the Temple wherein God dwelt in symbol and in sign. But into their inheritance we, the newer folk of God, have come, and in the midst of us stand many temples, wherein the Man-God dwells in the awful reality of His hidden presence. These homes of Jesus Christ are built on highways and by lonely roadsides, in crowded cities where men, shoulder to shoulder, fight the ever-thickening fight for the goods of this world, and far out on the slopes of the country hillsides, whereon His sunshine lies in undarkened brightness. But these throne-rooms of our King must be kept in neatest splendor and the lamp that tells of His presence must be ever well trimmed and brightly burning, and the sacred vessels of the altar and the varied vesture of His priest must be ever such as become the Lord of all. So to us as to the older race of God the prophet's words come loud and strong: "Is it time for you to dwell in ceiled houses, and this house lie desolate?"

Is it time to dwell in our comfortable homes with all the ease of modern life, and the church be an unfit habitation for our God? Is it time for us to be clothed in satins and in silks and the priest to be liveried in a way unworthy of the King of Heaven? Is it time for us to sit at our well-laden tables and the sacred vessels of God's altar to stand in need of repair? Some can give of their abundance, and others must stint their poverty to share their widow's mite. Some can give gold, and others' gifts must be the work of deft fingers and tireless hands. The call has come and Jesus Christ has deigned to stand in want of our help. Shall our best Friend find us failing Him in His need?

Hidden King, my Lord and my God, how graciously You deign to stand in need of my assistance, that by succoring You in Your want, I may win a nearer place to You in Heaven! I thank You for this privilege and I mean to do what in me lies to make Your home fit resting place for God. What I have may be small indeed, but that I give to You. Just take it, Lord, and make my heart full happy in the taking.

MONDAY WITHIN OCTAVE OF CORPUS CHRISTI

CHRIST IS ALWAYS NEAR

Wheresoever the body shall be, thither will the eagles also be gathered together.

St. Luke 17:37.

BUT a few short days with the Saints of God show us whence they draw their strength. They, the great eagles of the Church militant, are ever gathered wheresoever the saving Body of their God is. In the days when the memory of the swift, visible visit of our Lord was still fresh in all men's minds and the world's anger against His followers was still young, the hunted Roman folk, hid deep beneath the shielding earth, knelt about the Body of their murdered King and nerved their hearts to run the race through death to glory. The stalwart missionaries of old journeyed afar into the twilight lands of heathendom to the peoples that sat in darkness, and single-handed led the captives of Satan back to Christ. And their strength? It was won at the altar of God whereat they stood and drank the Blood that inebriated their souls with the unconquerable love of the living Christ.

But we need not go to former days. Look around us upon those saintly men and women who are fighting shoulder to shoulder the great fight of life. In the dim light of morning when the East is scarce fringed with the dawn, their footfalls ring upon the vacant pavement as they hurry to greet their sacramental God in Holy Communion. While the world is yet asleep they keep the "watches of the saints" and feast upon the Bread that sinews their arms and strengthens their hearts to battle on in this sin-stained world. Look at those silent forms: a father, whose fingers are gnarled and bent with toil but in whose eyes shines the light of another world; a mother, strong in the strength of her saintly will to teach her little ones to love the Lord she loves so well. Young men and women too are there, whose grace-lit faces tell of souls kept clean and pure amid the world's foul atmosphere.

Where, too, does that great host of priests and religious, our brethren in our Lord, staunch pillars of their God's own Church, gain courage and might to win Heaven, not for themselves alone, but for myriads of weak, fainting souls? Ask the young teacher whose patience is strained to the breaking at the persistent ignorance of giddy youth; ask the aged porter whose hands have grown hard and whose steps have tottered unto weariness answering those who knock at the door of God's servants; ask the many silent forms that flit about upon noiseless errands of study or household work, ask them one and all what makes their life worth living. And for answer? Go to the chapel at break of day, at the high noon, at the closing hours of even-tide and see the eagles gathered about the Body of their God. Life without the sacramental presence of our God would be life without light, life without joy, life without meaning.

Oh, dear Lord Jesus, what an unworthy companion of the Saints am I! How hard do I not find it to make Your home my home! I grow weary of Your Sacred Presence and tire of Your gentle company. Oh, I cannot hide it from Your eyes! But weary not of my childish restlessness. For I love You, Lord, even as fretful child loves gentlest mother. And did ever mother bear with childish whims as You?

"Give me, O priest, my daily bread,
  And fill for my lips the cup;
For famished my soul till I seem as dead!
  Good priest, let me eat and sup.

Give me, O priest, my Heavenly Food,
  And the journey I will not dread;
What if tomorrow He bring my rood,
  When tonight He hath broke me Bread?"

TUESDAY WITHIN OCTAVE OF CORPUS CHRISTI

ENDING THE DAY WITH CHRIST

Stay with us, because it is towards evening and the day is now far spent.

St. Luke 24:29.

EVENING is come and the troopers of Christ, the men and women, the girls and boys of every Catholic home, like valiant soldiers, kneel to salute their Captain before they pitch the tents to sleep. All day long the noise of battle has rolled and their souls are tired of the strife. Strong men have toiled away from home, shoulder to shoulder with a sinful, godless world. Frail women have tried hard during the lagging hours of a hidden life to make their home like unto Nazareth's and to bring up little ones even as Mary reared the little Christ. Young men and young women with arms yet new to the fight have struggled fearlessly to keep their soldier's robe of grace untarnished by the foul missiles which an abandoned society hurls daily at the clean of heart. Now, as darkness closes round the plain and the dead hush falls, all the goodly soldiers of Christ bend low and whatever may have been the fortunes of the day, they pledge once more a soldier's fealty.

And with them, the men-of-the-line in Christ's army, also kneel the great corps of His officers, holy priests and cloistered religious, who marshal in this valley of tears the hard-pressed legions of their unconquered God. With knightly hearts they draw near once more to where their Leader tabernacles in their midst and tell Him once again that they mean to lead His troops to victory.

Thus we kneel at even-tide, but our ranks are thinned. Not all who heard the clarion call at morn are with us now, for many a fellow man-at-arms has fought this day his "last, dim, weird battle of the west." God rest their soldier-hearts!

O Jesus, our hearts are full, for the war is hard and short rest comes with the quiet of the night. Here, Lord, I kneel beneath the flickering rays of the tiny altar light and cast myself before You as a soldier bivouacing for the night. "Taps" has sounded, Christ my Captain, and on bended knee Your soldier, wearied with the warfare of the day, asks pardon of You for the many times he has failed since reveille. Lord Jesus, at times we have lowered our banner; at times we have failed to front our foes; but ah! thanks to You, we have never lost our flag, never suffered it to be trampled in the dust. And now evening is come. Tarry hard by us, dear Lord. Like the valiant general, guard Your sleeping host, "for the night cometh when no man can work." Guard us until another morrow lights us to new battle for Your sacred Name. Tarry with us, Lord!

"When the sun ascends each day—
When it sinks, and day is o'er—
Stay with me, good Jesus, stay,
Dwell with me forevermore."

WEDNESDAY WITHIN OCTAVE OF CORPUS CHRISTI

FOOD OF THE BRAVE

I have food to eat you know not.
St. John 4:32.

OF old gathered about the buried altars of the catacombs, while famished beasts were made hungrier for their coming, the hunted children of a hunted Saviour fed their souls on the marrow of the "Lion of Juda," and Rome on her firm-set hills shook in wonder and dismay when these frail sons and daughters of Adam stood still against the shock of gnashing teeth and rending claws. Rome had never knelt with them in darkness around sunken altars in pit and caves and tunneled quarries, had never seen them eat of the Bread which was really God, and Rome, till then unconquered, grew afraid.

That was long ago, yet down the lapsing years the story of unknown courage has been retold, and now comes fresh again these latest days. "I have food to eat you know not," is the answer we, like our hero ancestors before us, hurl back to a world that cannot understand the manner of our lives. Each child of God's own good Church is a giant in this world of pigmies, for his strength is as the strength of ten, because his heart is pure," fed with the Bread of Angels.

"I have food to eat you know not" is on the lips of sainted father and mother as they walk away with firm, sure step from the parting with the child they have given to God's high service. "God takes our child, but God gave that child to us, and God may have it, yes, may have them one and all, if so His blessed will demands." Those hearts may bleed, those eyes may redden with burning tears—for they are human—but there is no weakness, there is no repining. Their souls are fed unto unyielding power by a Food in the strength of which they have walked to the mountain of sacrifice.

At the same banquet of the early morning young men and women kneel to break their fast with the Bread of Life, to inebriate their souls with the wine that will keep them pure in the midst of a sinful world. By their side mere infants lift their tiny hands in loving expectation of the child's best Friend and, all day long, at school, at play, at home, Heaven seems to laugh from out those faces, kissed so visibly by the sunshine of God's grace.

Far withdrawn from the ways of men the cloistered leaders of God's army, summoned to council with their Captain before the dawn has broken the eastern night, receive the Body of the King of kings, and nerve their hearts to lead once more God's men-of-the-ranks against the ancient foe. Their lives men cannot understand. Their self-forgetfulness, their self-control, their other-worldliness are puzzles to a world long deeply darkened by the night of sin.

The heroism of Catholic lives is one of the standing miracles God has deigned to give to a fallen world. Explain it you cannot, unless you know the Blessed Sacrament, unless you know that love of God which brought Him and still brings Him to our altars. Catholicism is the biggest riddle of the world as long as the consecrated Host is merely bread to it.

"I have food to eat you know not," O world, and cannot know, and that is why my heart is strong. That is why I can bear the smart of pain, the shock of shattered nerves, the agony of bruised and battered limbs, with a playful word upon my shrunken lips; that is why poverty has no sting and riches no siren call; that is why I can kneel beside the bed of dying loved ones, and with trembling fingers close their eyes in sleep that knows no waking, and yet go back to life with the same old smile of joy; that is why, when Christ, my Captain, calls, I can leave the world and turn my back upon its fleeting baubles, and bind my life with triple vow to serve my King.

OCTAVE OF CORPUS CHRISTI

UNAPPRECIATED PRIVILEGES

Who will give me in the wilderness a lodging-place of wayfaring men and I will leave My people and depart from them? . . . For they have proceeded from evil to evil, and Me they have not known, saith the Lord.

Jeremias 9:2, 3.

UNAPPRECIATED privileges are usually withdrawn. At school, in the walks of business life and in the ways of the professions, when a granted favor is markedly unnoticed, the recall is usually swift and absolute. We do not wish to throw pearls before swine, and a mistaken judgment in the bestowal of favors proves a lesson to us. We proceed more cautiously in the future with our largesses.

Suppose, however, Christ our Lord acted as is our wont. How long would He then remain upon our altars? His residence there behind the locked tabernacle door is a privilege that no creature would have dared ask God to grant. I know that Christ is a neighbor on the same street with me, or may be a dweller in the same house as I, yet do my actions show my faith? Is His house to me as a stranger's house that I hurry by and never have the least desire to enter? Or, if I do at times cross His threshold, are my visits as frequent as they would be to a dear, but merely human, friend who dwelt as near?

Again, what of my care for kneeling at the altar-step and carrying thence away God as my bosom's Guest? Privilege! The word is beggared of all meaning, even when we picture Mother Mary herself at the altar-rails. Yet what of my appreciation? Do I really feed my soul on God as frequently as I may? Or again, if I do, what of my prayer, my acts of thanks, my adoration while my Heavenly Guest is within me? Is the daily breakfast of my soul less hungered after than the daily breakfast of my body? Or if partaken of, has it grown to be scarcely more to me than the food that crosses my lips a short while afterwards?

Oh, as Christ our Lord remembers the ways of men with Him, and thinks how Angels would have acted, had they been privileged as we, what are His thoughts? Were He not God, would He not be fain to recall the boon He had granted and leave us orphaned of a Friend for whom we showed such little love? Can we not hear Him in His unappreciated loneliness amid the crowded cities of men, cry out as He did to the faithless citizens of Jerusalem thousands of years ago: "Who will give me in the wilderness a lodging-place of wayfaring men, and I will leave My people and depart from them? . . . For they have proceeded from evil to evil, and Me they have not known."

O Jesus, I am truly sorry for the way I have left You all alone, and the poor, scant thanks I have returned You for Your wondrous gift. Were You to treat me as I deserve, You would not tarry another hour upon the altar nor come again a single time to be my Guest! But, Jesus dear, do not, I beg of You, regard my faults and waywardness nor all my slights. Do not, I beg of you, take away this miracle of love. Just give me grace to love You more and then the past will be quite righted.

SACRED HEART (FRIDAY AFTER OCTAVE OF CORPUS CHRISTI)

IN SPITE OF IT ALL

If your sins be as scarlet, they shall be made as white as snow; and if they be red as crimson, they shall be white as wool.

Isaias 1:18.

YES, Father, that is all true, every single word of it. He is mean; he is selfish; he is untruthful. Gratitude has no least place in his make-up and politeness and consideration are unknown to him. He has treated me shamefully and has no use for the children. Yes, Father, that and much more is all true—but in spite of it all I love him."

Thus from her deepest heart spoke the frail, tired, little woman: "But in spite of it all I love him."

Wonderful, we say. Yes, it is, but there is an even more wonderful love than that in this world. It is the love of God for our wayward, self-centered hearts. "Can a woman forget her infant, so as not to have pity on the son of her womb? And if she should forget, yet will not I forget thee. Behold I have graven thee in My hands." That is the story of God's dealings with mankind; that is the story of His dealings with each soul; that is the story of His dealings with my own soul. Despite my past with all its high-heaped negligences, and its oft-repeated sins, our Lord cries out to me: "In spite of it all I love you."

Strange Sacred Heart! Our past is one long record of transgressions. Scarcely had we come to know of the gift of our Baptismal innocence than we began to use our newly-won reason to flaunt His law. Our "own sweet will" was very sweet to us, far more enticing than the strict way of His commandments. Childish wilfulness soon grew into youthful self-seeking and a grosser disregard of much that He would want was written larger upon our lives. Then, when the years had brought us into full maturity, though they took away with them the outward manner of children, there still remained rebellion against God's law. With regard to Him alone, childhood's undisciplined ways still prevailed.

Maybe there have been few mortal sins in our lives, but what a mess of self-seeking, and petty vanities and lack of decent respect for the reasonable wishes of others! Maybe we did kneel each morning and each evening in prayer, but what scant regard for politeness, when it was God with whom we spoke! To church we went, quite frequently, perhaps, but did we pay as much attention as we did when we went to the theater? Yet again, it may be that we have all too frequently violated God's law most seriously. Perhaps sin has come into our lives such as we thought could never soil our soul, such as to cause the blood to mantle to our cheeks in veriest shame. Perhaps the story of the prodigal has been rewritten in our waywardness, and we have tried to feed our souls on the husks of swine, far from our Father's home.

Yet, be the past what it may, be it as foul and as loathsome as human waywardness can make it, as we turn to our Lord we hear Him cry: "In spite of it all I love you." In spite of it all! Why? Because He made us from utter nothingness and called us into being "in His own image and likeness"; because He redeemed us, paying our ransom with His own Precious Blood; because He has sanctified us, time and time again, whenever we gave Him the chance to draw us unto Him. In spite of it all! Because He sees all the good we can do—for ourselves—for others—for Him, and He is quite too big to be done with us and let us have our wilful way in spoiling things.

Dear changeless Friend, how wonderfully insistent You are in Your love for me! I do not deserve it at all. I have done enough to spoil any love for me, yes, any love except Yours. My past is enough to disgust any one with me, if it were known as You know it. But not so with You. "In spite of it all I love you." Dear Lord, too long, too very long, have You been forced to put it that way. So now I beg You, please give me much grace that soon, very soon, You may drop those words: "In spite of it all."

SATURDAY WITHIN OCTAVE OF SACRED HEART

IT'S MY FAULT

Jerusalem, Jerusalem, thou that killest the prophets, and stonest them that are sent unto thee, how often would I have gathered together thy children, as the hen doth gather her chickens under her wings, and thou wouldst not?
St. Matthew 23:37.

THERE was one thing the Jews could never say with any truth, and that was that Christ did not try to win their love. Time and time again He insisted that it was to them first He must preach the Kingdom of God. It was in their towns that He had cured the sick and the lame and the blind. It was on their lake He had stilled the storm and swept the fishes miraculously into their nets. To Jerusalem He had come again and again, teaching in its streets, crying out in its Temple. Pleading He had come, scolding He had come, with a whip of cords He had come—but Jerusalem would have none of it: "Jerusalem, Jerusalem . . . how often would I have gathered together thy children . . . and thou wouldst not!"

Jerusalem could not truthfully blame our Lord—neither can I. If I am not holier today than I am, the fault is all my own. His grace has been plentiful in my life, and He has never once denied me any least grace that I needed. Jerusalem killed the prophets, and stoned them that had been sent by God as bearers of His message, and Jerusalem murdered them despite God's plentiful graces given her children to understand and hearken to His call. I, too, may have sinned, yes, sinned grievously and frequently and most defiantly. This I did despite the grace He gave me at every moment of my life. It was my own wilfulness that caused my sin "through my fault, through my fault, through my most grievous fault." The sin was mine, and I fell, rejecting the grace which came plentifully into my soul.

And after I had sinned, again He pleaded with me for my love, even as after all the murders of Jerusalem, Christ would have gathered together her children with all the care and solicitude that a mother hen has for her little brood. If I did not give Him my love, it was *I* who refused Him.

No, I can never blame our Lord. He has been very, very good to me. And I? To put it on the lowest level, I have been grossly impolite, refusing to open the door of my heart when He stood there knocking.

But that is the past, and mean as it is, ungrateful as it is, it must not discourage me. Of course, I ought to be ashamed; of course, I ought to be thoroughly sorry; but discouraged—no. For He forgives and forgets; and now, right now, He is pleading for my love just as though I had never treated Him as I have.

Dear Jesus, I am thoroughly ashamed of myself for the way I have treated You. Never a day has come and gone but Your grace came plentifully, too. Yet, I have quite steadily refused to give You my love, and when I did give it, I gave it quite grudgingly. It is all so mean and so ungrateful that it would discourage me did I not know that You love me still despite it all. I am sorry, but not discouraged; and with Your grace, I will do better in the future.

SUNDAY WITHIN OCTAVE OF SACRED HEART

TOO BIG TO BE REFUSED TO GOD

I will not offer to the Lord my God holocausts free cost.
2 Kings 24:24.

THE crippled old man sat at the window and watched the darling of his latest days hurry down the street to return no more. Long he peered—immovable; for his child had left him to go behind cloister walls to serve her God alone. Gladly he gave her up but, oh, the tugging at the old man's heart, as the sunshine went from out his life! Long he looked and lovingly, and now, when distance had swallowed up her whom he was never to see again, he turned to his wife with quiet poise and utter resignation: "Dearest, the sacrifice is too big to be refused to God."

"The sacrifice is too big to be refused to God." Brave man of Christ! In his simplicity did he know that it was a tribute to his own bigness that God asked such a sacrifice? Petty little efforts could be asked by God of anyone, but the great big things that cost and therefore count are to be asked of a few, the chosen few, who really love Him more than life itself.

"Too big to be refused to God." What a fine way of putting it! There is many a time that thought ought to nerve us, as we tread the weary miles of the road of life. Here a helping hand can be reached to another, but its reaching will cost us much. We can lead the wayward soul back to God, but only at the expense of many an hour of our time and much of our comfort; and shall we hoard the time and treasure our comfort and refuse the big thing God asks?

It may be that false friends have slandered us and soiled our goodly name and spread much ill-report abroad against us and, yet, despite it all, the one clear thing to do is to forgive and forget the stabbing in the dark. It is a big forgiveness God asks of us, yes, quite too big to be denied Him.

Or it may be crude men with petty aims and shallow intelligences, who cannot see large issues in an adult way, block our path and spoil our plans that would have meant much upbuilding of men's souls. Something big to offer up to God? Ask those who have suffered and taken their pain like men. Again it may be love unrequited by those from whom we had expected much, because we had done so much for them. To be lonely and forsaken, to be cast aside and completely ignored, where the closest bonds of affectionate unity should exist, that is hard, quite too hard not to be given to God if He asks it of us.

Thus, now here, now there; not often—no, for that is the privilege of a very few—the crises of life come upon us and God asks of us that we give Him big pledges of our love, large earnests of our trust and confidence in Him.

Dear Jesus, I have told You often and now I tell You once again that I really love You. Long years back I pledged my love to You and promised to give You all I could, as the days and ways of life unfolded. I have been faithful at times, and then at other times have seemed to regret my promise and have denied You what You ask. But help me, dear Lord, to be more generous! When life's big sacrifices come, just let me say each time: "It is too big to be refused to God."

MONDAY WITHIN OCTAVE OF SACRED HEART

UNPOPULAR

I have watched, and have become as a sparrow, all alone on the house-top.

Psalm 101:8.

THE only unpopular person at that place was Jesus Christ," was the short, biting description given of a certain summer resort. Every other home was visited again and again, but across the threshold of Christ's door few feet strayed. In every other house there was the sound of music and of laughter far into the breaking hours of dawn, but where the Friend of mankind dwelt, there, and there alone, did night hold her wonted silence. In all that restless town there were no lonely ones thinking away the twilight hours, save One who long years back had trod the wine-press of Olivet alone and even yet must watch out many a day and night companionless. Often indeed might our Lord have repeated to Himself:

"Face on face in the city, and when will the faces end,
Face on face in the city, but never the face of a friend,
Till my heart grows sick with longing and dazed with
the din of the street,
As I listen to thronging thousands in a loneliness
complete."

Do we, do I, treat Christ our Lord, as did those giddy folk of that summer time? Christ is God and therefore happy beyond the touch of pilfering hands, but if His Manhood were not united to the Godhead, would it not be grieved, beyond the healing, at the unkindliness of men? Could He not say with a truthfulness not known to him who sang it: "A lonely man, oppressed with lonely ills, ... From all men's care, how miserably apart!" He, who came from Heaven for the one sole purpose of making all men happy, is the only one about whom we seem to care no jot or tittle how lonely He may be. That visit to this earth cost Him His mortal life and we will not return the call that sheer decency requires!

Oh! but it takes time and it would spoil our pleasant hours! Strange commentary on a friend's companionship! Will it cloud a summer's sky or heighten the winter's cold to stop and have a chat with the Lord and God of all? Will a few swift moments spent with Him, who is to be our joy "while ages course along," taint and tarnish our holidays or load an extra burden on our work-a-day life? Be it so, then the fault is not with Christ, but with ourselves or with the companions we are wont to meet or with the kind of holiday or work we have before us, and it were then a blessed bit of thoughtfulness, were He to spoil ahead of time what else would spoil our souls.

Jesus, a strange sort of friend am I, indeed, yet friend would I fain still be called and be! I hardly ever come to see You, and I pass Your door as though I knew not who resided there. But this must not be again and yet without Your grace it will be ever so. So give, dear Lord, and give again that grace that will make me know and love and visit You.

"Soul, from thy casement look, and thou shalt see
How He persists to call and wait for thee!
And, oh, often to that voice of sorrow,
'Tomorrow we shall enter,' I replied!
And when the morrow came I answered still
'Tomorrow.' "

TUESDAY WITHIN OCTAVE OF SACRED HEART

COMFORT TO FRIENDS

Let them that fear Thee turn to me, and they shall know Thy testimonies.

Psalm 118:79.

ONE of the sharpest spurs to renewed activity when we find our courage slowly but surely waning, is the realization that we shall be a "credit" to those who love us and expect a great deal from us. The mere thought of all the hopes that friends have held in their hearts these many years and the joy that will come to them, if we succeed in the allotted task makes the slackening will grow firm again and feeds new daring into a heart that would fain give up the fighting. Thus it was when we were growing children and later on at school, as we thought of the love that would gleam from mother's eyes and the words of commendation that would fall from father's lips. Thus it is now, for in our older years it is still the thought of friends that nerves us on anew.

Do we use like thoughts to urge us on to creditable activity in the spiritual life? When my life is overcast by shadows that grow alarmingly darker, and when my days are brightened by a sunlight that no clouds fleck, is it the thought of the hopes of our Lord and of His earthly friends concerning me that teaches me to read my sorrows and my gladness aright? It may be I am torn away from every task to which my heart has ever had a native attachment and I find it hard to make the sacrifice of the dreams of years. It may be again that while the lips of others move with laughter, my own are sharply closed with pain, that while other feet may go astraying where they will, my own are pinioned helplessly. Do we then bethink ourselves that we must prove a credit to our changeless Friend and give well-relished joy to His friends to see us tried and proven, to find us loyal followers of a thorn-crowned King, who count no costs where there is chance to follow Him more closely?

Again, when every shadow is gone and all life is full of such happiness as lies nearest to our desires, and our heart is rich in all best joys that earth can give, are we careful, very careful then, not to be mismanaged by these passing exaltations but to take them with a humility and with a lowly mien, that all Christ's friends may be quite gladdened that we have learned from Him to be meek and humble of heart? On dark days and on bright, in the morning and in the high-noon hours and in the evening of life, within my heart must ever echo those inspiring words: "They that fear Thee shall see me, and shall be glad, because I have greatly hoped in Thy words," hoped in the time of soul-silence and desolation, when the voice of my Friend seemed hushed; hoped amid the noise of strongest pleasure, when His voice was all but drowned by the noise of raucous creatures; yes, hoped, too, on through colorless days when existence itself was most drab.

Jesus, my God, am I now a disappointment to Your Sacred Heart? As I scan my life I feel I read the answer clearly written there, for despite the stout protesting of my love, my deeds lack much of that holiness You would find in them. I fear I do but little credit to Your service and can scarcely be numbered among Your holy folk. And so, dear Lord, it means You must be very lavish with Your grace that I may no longer bring discredit to Your Sacred Name.

WEDNESDAY WITHIN OCTAVE OF SACRED HEART

MAKING PEOPLE GRATEFUL

What is there that I ought to do more to My vineyard that I have not done to it?

Isaias 5:4.

IT takes an awful lot to make some people grateful," were the angry words which a high official spat out, when the people of a certain nation did not seem properly mindful of all the help that had been given them. Day after day aid had come and night after night huge stores were rushed to their relief. Neither men nor money had been spared and all the huge engines of modern commercial resourcefulness had been levied into service. Yet after all, scant gratitude—and very scant at that—seemed the only return.

"It takes an awful lot to make some people grateful." How often must these words be on the lips of our Lord as He looks out from His home in the tabernacle! Long years back, when He was yet visibly on this earth, He plotted and planned how best to help us. He saw our souls would be hungry for food that would make them strong and keep them pure, though the world was leagued against us and its filth was everywhere around. And so He gave Himself to be our food, Himself the strong "Lion of Juda" and the spotless "Lamb of God." He saw that our hearts would long for a friend who would understand them, who would look down beneath all the foibles, yes, beneath all the sins of our lives and see therein the deep craving for God that can be found tucked away somewhere in every human heart. And so He stayed with us as our changeless Friend and He abides with us by day and by night, that we may come to Him when we like and as we like, with no constraint placed on our coming or our going. His home is "just alongside ours" in a neighborly way that we may "run in" and tell Him all the joys and, much more, all the sorrows of our lives.

Long before He took up residence with us, He swung the lanterns of the heavens for our coming and laid the foundations of the world for us. Fold upon fold He stretched the earth's green carpet and cooled the air for us and watched carefully the admixture of its elements that it might support our frail breath of life. At His *fiat* vegetable and animal life sprang into being for our sustenance, pleasure, and amusement. Then when all was done, He brought us, His children, into the home of His own building and bade us know and love and serve Him there.

Such love! Yet as He gazes out upon us—or, if we cheat Him even of our visits, as He tarries waiting for a footfall that never breaks the silence—His Sacred Heart is lonely, lonely for His children's presence, and much more lonely for their gratitude. If He had not done so much, this isolating forgetfulness of His cherished loved ones would not so cut His sensitive Heart.

Dear Jesus, I, too, have been among those who have forgotten You. Indeed it does "take an awful lot to make some people grateful," and I am ashamed that, despite all You have done for me day after day, I have thanked You so very, very poorly. But, Jesus dear, this is the past, and for it I humbly beg Your pardon. I shall do my best, dear Lord, in the days to come to show You by my frequent visits that I really do appreciate all You have done for me, and I will be an ingrate no longer.

THURSDAY WITHIN OCTAVE OF SACRED HEART

CONFIDANTS

My Beloved to me, and I to Him, who feedeth among the lilies, till the day break and the shadows retire.
Canticles 2:16, 17.

MY friend's complete confidence is what I long for. He may give me other gifts that bespeak his love, but only let him grant me this, the knowledge of himself, then I am content that I have found full favor in his eyes. To know the projects that lie nearest his heart, to be asked to give my own untempered views on all his plans and aims and aspirations and to realize that whatsoever he holds best and dearest is felt to be in surest hands, if it rests in mine, that is the finest gift he can give me, the surest pledge of real affection.

So we would have it with Christ, our Friend. We know it is a bold desire, but who would not be bold in loving such a friend? Others have won it from Him. Mary Mother, of course, knew His inmost heart, and by her right as Mother. Then there was John, "whom Jesus loved," and lusty Peter, and the world-encompassing Paul. Again a Catharine and a Teresa, a Benedict, a Dominic, an Ignatius and even the boy Stanislaus—they were confidants of Christ. And why not we? But we are not Saints. Well, if the price be that we must cast off ourselves and put on the comely robes of sanctity, then we will pay the price, so be it we win our way to the inmost recesses of the Heart of Christ. All else is paltry, tawdry, worthless stuff, and we should be abashed to say that we had won such a priceless boon by the forfeit of such things. We want to know, as far as it is granted us, that He feels safe in trusting us with His work, that He feels free in speaking to us, as He did to His confidants of yore, of all He plans to do within us and within the souls of all. Yes, and we will pay the price, by check on eye and on ear and on tongue, that they may ever act as the eyes and ears and tongue of Christ did act; yes, and by ceaseless guard over the portals of our hearts that no intruder may enter there, "for He that would walk there would walk alone." Then, when He has entered in and we have made Him much at home, we shall find true of Himself the words He spoke by Solomon long ago: "Behold He standeth behind our wall, looking through the windows, looking through the lattices. Behold my Beloved speaketh to me: 'Arise, make haste my love'.... My Beloved to me and I to Him Who feedeth among the lilies, till the day break and the shadows retire."

Dear Jesus, I know as yet I cannot dare to ask that You treat me as Your confidant. So little of all my love has passed from word into fullness of work, that I feel a proper hesitancy in asking for this favor. Still this I will beseech of You, that I may so improve, so grow to be Your "second self," that in a nearing future I may, indeed, be one to whom You tell Your inmost secrets. Grant me this favor, dearest Lord, for it will mean that I shall love You more on this side of the grave, shall do Your work in better wise and then our meeting out beyond the stars will be a deeper joy for all eternity to both of us.

OCTAVE OF SACRED HEART

ONE WHO UNDERSTANDS

The Lord searcheth all hearts, and understandeth all the thoughts of minds.

1 Paralipomenon 28:9.

TO one who understands" read the card that came "from a grateful heart." Long had they chatted these many years and many a secret fear and hope had been told by the younger friend, always to find a deeper, truer, more helpful understanding. Now the danger was clear; at other times, vague, nameless dreads came on. Now new-sprung joys surged forth to the telling; and yet again fresh pains all but stilled the lips that would fain tell of a bruised and aching heart. At times it was hard to talk out, but "he always listened so that you felt like talking"; and so the story came and with it came understanding.

How our poor hearts crave for "one who understands"! Time and time again we hear the cry: "Oh, if you did but understand, my burden would be lighter." Indeed it would be, could not help but be, if we knew that the tangled puzzle of our life was read aright and sympathetically. Our sorrows must be understood and so, too, our joys; our moods and our fancies; our aspirations and our discouragements. One day, all creation smiles; another, there are clouds, but we can see the silver linings; and yet another, we find no sunlight anywhere. Strange things "of whim and wavering," changeling creatures "one day eager and brave, the next not caring to try," what will we not give to find a friend who can read our every effort and our every lack of effort, and read it all right?

It may be we can find among the multitude of men some one to help us much, but our souls are too deep to be sounded by any man, our hearts too infinitely wide to have them adequately scanned by any human eye. Are we then doomed to hopelessly unsatisfied cravings? No, we know we are not so doomed. There is One, human like ourselves, but God as well, and we come to Him and kneel before Him and know that there is no fold of character He does not know, no strangest craving He does not interpret, no ache or pain He does not want to soothe, no joy He does not want to bless. Sensitive to life's crosses more than we, bruised in body and in soul as we, there is no least thing in our lives He does not understand. To Him we may go when we please and as we please, and never need to stand upon the ceremony of our coming or frame the manner of our appeal.

O Jesus, changeless Friend, how can I thank You for Your friendship? I do need some one to read my life aright and solve therein all that puzzles me so sorely at times. There is none among men to do this, though they may try with gentlest kindliness to give me aid. And so, dear Lord, it is good, so very good, to know that I can come to You and tell You all—all the great things of life and all the little things, too—and best of all, to know that You will always "understand."

THIRD SATURDAY AFTER PENTECOST

UNDERSTOOD

The Lord searcheth all hearts, and understandeth all the thoughts of minds.

1 Paralipomenon 28:9.

I AM trying to pray but not in words. Don't you think He understands?" were the words that were penned by a soul that was sorely tried, but was doing much to win others to God. The night was very dark and the road was rough; and the numbed heart and the harassed brain left the lips dumb in prayer. But all through the day the little outcasts came to her and all through the day, forgetful of self, she eased their pains of mind and heart and body—and she did it all for God.

Would any one dare to say that He did not understand? Is it not the sign of truest friendship, when silence, long silence, can prevail and yet heart speaks to heart in language all their own? And if poor, misunderstanding men have wit enough to read dumb lips aright, surely our changeless Friend can match their skilfulness.

It were well to remember this, when all the friction of our days tells against us. It may be the leaden weight of sorrow pinions us so helplessly that not even a cry for help can escape our lips. But if we but look to Him, will not our Lord read the pleading in our eyes? It may be that the sharp stab of pain on pain holds our minds captive from all other thoughts, but surely to hold the crucifix mutely in our hands will tell our God nailed thereon more than our lips might tell in longest time. Again rude men or thoughtless comrades may have rasped our sensitiveness and our poor brains fairly burn beneath the smartings. Up, up the thoughts are boiling, fiercely, scorching our very souls, and only words of peevishness and hate find entrance to our lips. Yet if we but kneel before our Master who stood the huge revilings in Herod's court, surely He will take our kneeling as a prayer to gain self-mastery.

Dear Jesus, I really ought to know that You truly understand. I ought to talk to You and with You, and I do try at times. But there are other times when even with earthly friends, whom I can see and hear, I find it hard to talk. And so I find it hard with You. I will do my best, dear Lord, and not give way to laziness, but when I cannot, really cannot, talk, I know You will understand.

FOURTH SUNDAY AFTER PENTECOST

THROWN RIGHT UP AGAINST GOD

Cast thy care upon the Lord, and He shall sustain thee;
He shall not suffer the just to waver forever.

Psalm 54:23.

WELL, here I am thrown right up against God!" So shot the piercing thought through the mind of the young chap. Fierce difficulties had come upon him, but one true friend had stood near him, comforting and helping him. Many of the trials were gone but not all; and now? The friend must hasten away into a distant clime, and oh, the loneliness of it all! But quickly and tellingly the young man's faith cried out: "Well, here I am thrown right up against God!" And kneeling down he cried to God and begged for the grace to lean on Him alone.

"Thrown right up against God!" That is what commonly happens to most of us: with some rarely, with some most frequently. God may, indeed, grant us friends, tried and true, on whom we can lean and who can and do help us much in our times of stress and strain. For such friends we should thank God, and use them, as He would have us use them, as supports to bring us through all trials nearer and nearer to Him.

But such friends are not always near, and for some they are near very rarely. Then what? "Thrown right up against God!" Though all else be far away, He is always near; He can never be far away. He may *seem* far, far away from us, but that we know is only a temptation that we must thrust far from us. "Can a woman forget the child of her womb? And, even if she did forget, yet will I not forget Thee." Any thought of God's farness from us is only our vain, depressed imaginings.

And it is good, very good to be so "thrown right up against God." It makes us realize our own insufficiency and the utter futility of getting lasting help from fellow-men. They can aid us, yes, but only a little, and only for a time. The deeper, broader trials of life are too big for their puny helping.

And our own strength? It is in such hours of loneliness that we realize just what mites we are. Some days we seem quite big and brave and capable of solving all life's problems. But then the morrow comes and all our much prized valor is gone. Search our souls as we may, we can find no strength. Then it is we come to know with stark realization that only in God can we find the ever-present Friend we need, powerful to help and kindly to heal, buttressing our soul with His strong graces.

Dear Lord, I need You as only a creature can need God. For the friends that You have given me I thank You, and for my own strength, too. But these fail at times, yes, and must finally; for as Your handiwork I need *You*. But oh, it is so hard at times to come to You, to call upon You, to feel that You can and will help. So give me the grace always to have perfect confidence in You, above all then, when I am "thrown right up against God."

FOURTH MONDAY AFTER PENTECOST

MISPLACED CONFIDENCE

Work your work before the time, and He will give you your reward in His time.

Ecclesiasticus 51:38.

"NO, we are through with you. You cannot be trusted," and the accompanying gesture added finality to the words, as the employer dismissed the young man. The lad had given promise and had made those who knew him feel that much could be placed in his hands and that all would be well. He had entered that office highly recommended, and now after months of trial he leaves and there is no one to raise a voice to help him. They cannot. He was trusted much and many a responsibility was placed upon his shoulders. But the shoulders sagged and listlessly refused to grapple with given problems and so across his life is written large that no trust can be reposed in him.

When this happens to us in life in big or little things, we feel a deep chagrin and rightly so; for it means we are worthless, when men come to reckon with life's greater task. But what would it be, if God Himself were to tell us that we had proved recreant to our trust? Death has come and the last task of life is over and we stand for our testing before the judgment seat of God. Childhood and youth and maturing years are scanned and the years of full maturity are sifted for their evidence of work well done. All is weighed and all is tested. Far in the buried past we received our soul from God. It was a sacred trust, that carried with it an eternity of recompense of weal or woe. God Himself placed His highest confidence in us and now when life is over and His scrutiny of life is done, what horror to hear from Him who cannot deceive or be deceived those damning words:

"Fresh and clean and immortal you received your soul from Me, and now you bring it back a tawdry, smirched and stunted thing. I gave you a real work to do, but My confidence was misplaced in you. You have received your soul in vain."

Dear Jesus, by the love You have for me, never let me hear those awful words. You have placed a deal of trust in me and I must measure up to it. Yet at times I am very shiftless and the responsibility of caring for my immortal soul grows very irksome to me. Do save me from my laziness.

Grant me the grace to work my work before the time, to shoulder life's duties and to trace out its problems manfully that, when You come to judge the living and the dead, I shall not be found to have received my soul in vain.

FOURTH TUESDAY AFTER PENTECOST

KEEPING OUR EYES ON CHRIST

Remember the Lord afar off and let Jerusalem come into your mind.

Jeremias 51:50.

IT was to the captive Jews exiled in hated Babylon that Jeremias sent his warning note. "You that have escaped the sword, come away, stand not still; remember the Lord afar off and let Jerusalem come into your mind." He bade them turn their faces to the west and gaze beyond the rivers of Babylon, where they sat and wept, on beyond the sandy stretches of the desert, over the hills of Galaad, on, on to Sion, "great mountain of His holiness," until they knelt once more in spirit within the Temple walls. "Afar off" they were to think of God and His holy place, and to lift their eyes to the mountains, whence help should come to them, for "behold He shall neither slumber nor sleep that keepeth Israel." One and all they were to do as their fellow-exile Daniel, who "went into his house and opening the windows in his upper chamber toward Jerusalem, knelt down three times a day and adored and gave thanks before his God."

Twenty-five long centuries roll by, the scene shifts and other exiles hear those words that echoed first across Euphrates' waters. Exiles, we, too, must "remember the Lord afar off," and as we ply our daily tasks in simple daily ways in a land that is not our own we must think of home, we must "let Jerusalem come into our mind." Down in the hurried walks of business life, where greed for gain and lust for power cramp the soul of man and drag his heart away from the "land of the leal," the strong Catholic must "remember the Lord afar off," remember the prisoner-King, who while centuries rolled by has watched night and day amid the whirling cities of men to teach His own true knights that they were born for higher things, that the souls of men were not made to be dazzled by the glitter of purple or of gold. Hid away in her quiet home the tired mother, awearied with the work that is never done and wants of the children that ever seem endless, must "remember the Lord afar off," remember that the same good Jesus who is on our altar was once a little Child at Bethlehem, and needed His Blessed Mother's care; remember that it is unto His likeness that she must form her little ones and bring them to the fullness of His stature. When we are tempted to kick against the goad of colorless routine, when we are quick to hurl back the unkindly word, when prayer is quite distasteful and the higher life of the soul seems a barren, impassable desert, then we must "remember the Lord afar off." Afar off? No, not very far now, thank God; not over hills and valleys and widening streams, but, because of His mercy, only a bit of a way beyond our threshold, only down the street where Jesus Christ has made His home, a little apart from the crowded scenes of the busy world.

Jesus, my God, that I may remember You always; remember You in the early morning when a new day lies untarnished before me; remember You at the high noon, that You may pardon the lapses of the vanished hours and may speed the moments yet to come; remember You at the close of day, when the shadows fall, that You may guard our sleeping and wake us unto another day, be it the radiant day of Heaven or another twilight day in this valley of tears. Grant me, Lord Jesus, the grace to remember You when most I need You!

"We come to Thee, sweet Saviour,
And Thou wilt not ask us why;
We cannot live without Thee,
And still less without Thee die."

FOURTH WEDNESDAY AFTER PENTECOST

AM I CHRIST'S FRIEND?

You are My friends, if you do the things that I command you.

St. John 15:14.

WE are all very anxious to know whether we are the friends of our Lord. Sometimes we just wonder about it in a more or less idle way; at other times we grow nervously fretful about it; at still other times the sheer dread of not being His friends seizes upon us frighteningly. To be His friend is the most important thing in life, and to know that we are His friends is the most consoling consciousness that we could have. But can we know? And how?

Our Lord has been good enough to give us a test and, coming from Him, the test is infallibly true. He tells us plainly: "You are My friends, if you do the things I command you." No need of a revelation there. He tells us to read the language of facts, to look to our own deeds and if they square with what He wants, then we are His friends; if they do not, then even the strongest conviction that we are His friends is utter delusion.

So why idly speculate? Or why worry? Am I doing what our Lord wants? Look to my prayers. Do I say them, when He wants them said and as He wants them said? Do I speak to Him at least as politely as I do to a merely earthly friend?

Look to my eyes and my ears and my tongue. Do they see and hear and say only what pleases Him? Do they find Him in the highways and byways of life, blazoned in the glories of the setting sun, vocal in the music of the birds, told of by the praises that come from my lips?

At home? When I cherish those that are near and dear to me, and, in my love for them, try to bring them nearer to our Lord by word and much more by example; when the inevitable frictions of life are eased up, or, failing this, are borne without irritation, for Him; when all form a union in some slight way modeled on the Holy Family, then I need not ask whether I am a friend of our Lord, for "where there are two or three gathered together in My Name, there am I in the midst of them."

In the world of my work? When I yield loyal obedience to my superiors, and am square and impartial to my inferiors; when I am considerate of the weaknesses of others, but firm when principles are involved; when I deal with all with fairness and with courtesy—then, the answer is ready to hand to the question how I stand with our Lord.

It is so useless and such a waste of time for me to keep eternally mulling over the thought where I stand in the matter of Christ's love. He, the great Lover of souls, has in His goodness given me a test, easy to use, sure in its findings. Why not use it?

Dear Lord, there is no deeper wish in my life than to be Your friend, and to know that I am Your friend. I often wonder whether I am, and sometimes become quite fearful lest I may not be. But in Your kindliness You have given me a quick and certain test. So let me use it, Lord, but more than that, let me ever do what You command, so that when I use the test, the findings will always be that I am Your friend.

FOURTH THURSDAY AFTER PENTECOST

THE ONE WE'VE WAITED FOR

Lo! this is our God, we have waited for Him, and He will save us; this is the Lord, we have patiently waited for Him, we shall rejoice and be joyful in His salvation.

Isaias 25:9.

WE are kneeling in holy expectation at the altar-rail. God's minister with gentle warning tarries a moment on the altar-step before he brings God unto His people and stirs our hearts with the words of John of old, *"Ecce Agnus Dei, ecce qui tollit peccata munda,"* "Lo! the lamb of God. Lo! He who taketh away the sins of the world." How our hearts tremble within us for we are about to welcome our King! Lo! this is our God, we have waited for Him. Since yesterday morn when last we knelt here, we have counted the tardy hours that would bring again this moment of happy union. "This is the Lord, we have patiently waited for Him." All during the day when the battle of life pressed hard, when the call of duty seemed all too imperative for our weakling souls, when the warp and woof of life seemed textured with darkest colors, "we have patiently waited for Him." With that thought was our heart buoyed up to hold our heart's own citadel against our foes, with that star that gilds our morning hour, the darksome path of hidden labor was brightly lit, and now we kneel once more and wait till Jesus comes. "Lo! the bridegroom cometh." "He will save us... we shall rejoice and be joyful in His salvation." Life may have its sorrows that sting the shrinking heart, life may have its burdens that gall the wearied shoulders, but life has its King—and He is coming now.

Rabboni! Master mine, King and Master, God and Brother, You are to be mine as though no other soul possessed You. In the gray twilight of the morning, as of old You came to Magdalene, so now You come to me. You alone can win my heart. You alone can save my soul. Oh! what love to come to me to aid me in the warfare of this darkening world! Strengthen my arm, Lord Jesus, and make stout my heart, for the battle is hard and the way is long and my heart is weak. Lo! He is here—Jesus—my God and my All.

"Come to me, sweet Saviour,
Come to me and stay;
For I love Thee, Jesus,
More than I can say!"

FOURTH FRIDAY AFTER PENTECOST

DEEDS PROVE LOVE

If you love Me, keep My commandments.
St. John 14:15.

WHEN we were little children, and later when we became older, we often told Mother that we loved her. We really meant it, and Mother knew that we meant it. She took us at our word. But didn't she usually say: "Well, then always do what I tell you to do"? She asked of us a simple, easy proof of that love; yet it was the best proof we could offer that we really meant what we said.

We often tell God that we love Him. It is the first thing we tell Him in the morning; it is the last thing we tell Him at night before we fall asleep. When we visit Him in the Blessed Sacrament and when we receive Him in Holy Communion, we repeat our protestations of love to Him. And we mean what we say—of course we do. We may slip at times, we may offend Him occasionally, but we do want to love Him.

And what is His answer to our protestations of love? It is the same answer that Mother used to give us: "Well, then always do what I tell you to do." Even God can ask of us no greater proof of love. For "love is shown more in deeds than in words." It is easy to talk; it is much harder to do. And that is why the old adage, "Actions speak louder than words," is still true.

I show my love for God by praying when I should and as I should—with all the reverence that I can show, with all the attention I can give. I show my love for Him by my silence in church, where He is "really and truly and substantially present"; by my eagerness to assist at Mass; by frequently receiving Him in Holy Communion.

I show my love for Him by my obedience and helpfulness at home, by my thoughtfulness for others, by my kindness of thought and word and deed. At work or in school I again prove the sincerity of my profession of love by attending to my duties and fulfilling the tasks assigned me, by not skimping or slacking. If I am in a position of responsibility, I prove my love for God by being fair to all and by setting a good example.

I can best prove my love for Him during hours of recreation and pleasure, because it is at such times a bit harder for me to measure up to what He expects of me. He wants me to have fun and to enjoy pleasures; but He also wants me to be mannerly before Him at all times. Therefore, when I am dancing or playing tennis, motoring or swimming, when I am at a party or on the basketball court, He wants me to have a good time, but He wants me to conduct myself at all times in such a manner that He can set His approval on me. He is not a kill-joy; He asks only that we take our pleasures in such a manner as to win His approval.

Dear Jesus, when I tell You that I love You, I really mean what I say, and I am sure that You know that full well. I want to give You proof of my love at all times and in all places, whether I am alone or with others. Sometimes it is easy enough to do so, but there are times when it is a little difficult to do what You tell me to do. But I do want to try hard, and I promise, with Your grace, to measure up to what You expect of me.

FOURTH SATURDAY AFTER PENTECOST

HEART-WEARY

Come to Me all you that labor and are burdened and I will refresh you.

St. Matthew 11:28.

FAR into the evening they sat and chatted, the older priest and the young man who had long trodden the way of stern sacrifice. The twilight deepened and the shadows grew longer, and a felt peace came down upon the tired earth—and still they chatted on. The road of life had been rough for the young chap and his heart was more bruised even than his wasted body, and the years were re-lived in the quiet that came with the setting sun. "Chat it out, my boy; pour it all out; it will do you good, for I, too, have known like sorrows." And so they chatted on until utter darkness fell, and then, as they parted for the night, he said: "Good night, Father! That's the best talk I have had in a year."

"The best talk in a year!" Oh, what a weight of sorrow in those words! Summer had come and gone, and Autumn had burned itself away into the cold of the long Winter's days; Spring had come and unlocked the flowers, and now Summer was here again. But all the long while a struggling heart fought bleakly ahead, for no one took the time or had the thought to listen. No! No unkindness was meant, but just a broad lack of understanding that each one of us must talk it out; just a complete forgetfulness that pain must spell itself out in words or else it will not be eased; just a marked satisfaction that all was being done that should be done, when mere bodily wants were met. But the hungry heart had not been fed and the pent-up soul had not been freed, and the craving for sympathy, which is rooted deep, very deep, in every one of us, had not been seen nor had it been allayed. "The best talk I have had in a year."

How sad our lot in this valley of tears! We may be strong men and women and care no least whit for maudlin sentimentality or soft indulgence, but, strong though we be, we are men and women, and we crave and hunger for true sympathy that will take and understand our ills of body and far more our ills of mind and heart, and will ease them knowingly and well. There may be some great souls whose stark sanctity and sheer nearness to God rob them of the need of sympathy from their fellow men, but for most men the need is there and it is very deep and very real.

And so we must try to give this sympathy to others, to reach them a helping hand, when the way is dark and rough, to speak to them the cheering word that will lift up their heads again to the stars above and to God beyond the stars. And when we ourselves need the kindly word, we must not be ashamed to seek it. God has made us thus and we but fulfill His will, when in our weakness we ask another for a lift along the road of life.

But sometimes all human friends fail. It may be that we find ourselves far separate from any one who can read us aright, or, again, it may be that the sorrows have eaten too far within for any human eye to see the wounding to its depths. Then it is that we must go to that great human Friend, who is also God. We need Him always, but we need Him most then. He will never be far away from us: as God, He is always with us; as Man, He is down in the Tabernacle which is usually so near our homes. We can always turn to Him and there can be no hurt of mind or body which He does not understand, no heartache He cannot ease, no wound into the inmost depths of which He cannot see. To Him we must go and, if our hearts are strained unto the very breaking and our lips too taut to form a single prayer, He will see it all, He will understand it all. If we but stay and silently show Him our wounds, His healing will come swiftly and surely, and our hearts will grow strong again to battle on.

Dear Jesus, You made my heart as it is, and it needs sympathy and understanding. No, I do not want to be petted and coddled, for that were unworthy of one grown up; but I do crave the cheering word, the look of encouragement, the "Well done!" that comes from the heart. I can find this at times from human friends, but sometimes I cannot. But from You I can always find it and it means everything to know that You read me aright and understand and are near to help me and to encourage. Dear Jesus, just grant me the grace always to come to You, no matter how broken I may be on the wheel of life; for You will not break the bruised reed nor quench the smoking flax, but will always speak the helping word and reach the uplifting hand to those that labor and are heavy burdened.

FIFTH SUNDAY AFTER PENTECOST

WITHOUT CHRIST—A FAILURE

Simon answering said to Him: Master, we have labored all the night and have taken nothing.

St. Luke 5:5.

IT was early morning on the Galilean lake and the hills of Perea were still strongly flung against a new-born sky. All night long busy crafts had plied their harvesting of this inland sea, and weary men were guiding laden boats to the welcoming shore. But one rode high upon the waters and unfilled hands tugged listlessly at the oars. All through the hours with searching net they had swept the depths of the sea, but, strive and search as they would, their labors were in vain. "We have labored all the night and have taken nothing."

There is nothing men want more in life than success. Be it in the professions, or in the ways of the tradesman, or in the rougher walks of the journeyman, failure is the one thing dreaded, the one shadow that will darken each hour of life. To have labored as best as in us lay, to have played out our strength to the last notch of endurance, to have schemed and planned with our eye on yesterday and on tomorrow, and then to find that our life is strewn in ashes, spells the deepest discouragement that man can know. "I stand amid the dust o' the mounded years... my days have crackled and gone up in smoke, have puffed and burst as sun-starts on a stream," is a story that breaks the heart in the telling, and God grant that few of us will ever need the telling.

This of the passing efforts of our years, what then of the one supreme effort of life itself? What if that be failure? To go to the grave emptyhanded of the goods of this world may be a grievous lot, but to go beyond the grave with naught of the things of God to show, that means disaster for eternity. Here we are to labor and to traffic till He comes, here we are to use the fleeting hours to gain new riches that not time nor eternity can filch from us, that when the summons comes that Father wishes us, we may hasten unto Him with laden arms. Yet are we laboring thus? God grant there be no mortal sin upon our souls, for that would mean that we were poor indeed and quite void of all that tells for Heaven; but are we "jealous for the better gifts," are we ever alert to enrich our store of God's best gift of sanctifying grace? This search for the gold of eternity should begin with our waking moments, and sleep itself should be made to yield its measure of merit by being consecrated unto God. A little act of self-repression here, a passing deed that brings back a bit of joy to saddened hearts, the lifting of our own and other eyes to catch a clearer view of the farther shore, all these quite simple acts will leave us richer than we were. A hurried visit to our dearest Friend, a following of His footsteps when the steepness of the way would turn us back, or the quick, unyielding thrust that sends temptation far from us, these and their like will make us goodly traffickers in the ways of God.

Dear Lord, as I kneel and think upon my varied past, I find myself so poor in all that counts for Heaven. Strange child of passing whims, I am so eager to chase the tinted baubles of this world, so slack to labor for what You died to purchase back for me. Oh! let this be of the past alone and from this moment on, see, dear Lord, that I learn at length to cast aside my witlessness, learn at length to make my work, my play, my prayer, my every act bring me nearer home with hands filled full with the graces of Your kindly giving.

"Friend of my infinite dreams,
Little enough endures;
Little howe'er it seems,
It is Yours, all Yours."

FIFTH MONDAY AFTER PENTECOST

LOVE TO THE END

I am with you all days, even to the consummation of the world.

St. Matthew 28:20.

SWIFTER than the swiftest, eternity is moving on apace, soon to overtake each one of us. The sands of life are fast running out and the fall of a few more grains will bring most of us to the closing hour, when the Lord of all will come to visit us and take reckoning of our stewardship. That hour to wordlings is one of fears and forebodings, for they must then meet One who has stood in the midst of them and whom they have not known. They have not met our Lord before and then there will be no friendly introduction, only the sentence of the Judge.

But to us, as the years spin by, that hour grows sweeter and sweeter. We have loved the best Friend man has ever had, we have known "the beauty of His house and the place where His glory dwelleth." So when we sit and prayerfully ponder over the years that no voice can recall, we see to our comfort and our joy, the days and nights of the buried past gently darkened by the shadow of One, with whom it has been our joy to tarry in sunshine and in rain. Joy there was and the Friend of the bridegroom of Cana touched that joy and made it a sacred thing. The leaders weight of sorrow galled aching shoulders and the Man of sorrows laid bruised hands upon the crosses that no man can carry long alone and the yoke became sweet and the burden light indeed. We heard His cheering promise that He would be with us unto the consummation of the world and we have found Him so, true to His word. Other friends might come and go, other friends might show us love that would wax and wane like the fickle moon, but our constant, changeless Friend was with us all the time, ever the same in His kindness, ever the same in His love. Thus it has been, thus, we know, it will ever be. The shadows of the grave may fall thickeningly upon us, but there in the gloaming is the Friend of our hearts. Loving His own, He loves us to the end and, as the shadows fall, He clasps more strongly His children's trembling hands and leads us home through the dusk.

O Jesus, sweet Friend, it is hard to see my life running into ebb, hard to know my youth is gone and my maturer years fast numbered in the past. Hard, yes, Lord Jesus, very hard, unless I realize that each day that brings me nearer to the grave, brings me nearer home to You. Home to You! Oh, how that drives the shadows back that crowd around the grave! Home to You and Mary Mother and all Your Saints! O grave, where is thy victory? O death, where is thy sting, if the Lord of all, my Friend, is at my side to see me safely home? Dear Jesus, I trust You for my journey home. Oh, speed me in my coming!

Friend, while yet in mother's arms,
Friend, when youth's new hopes ran high,
Friend, as fade life's fairest dreams,
Be friendliest, Lord, when death draws nigh.

FIFTH TUESDAY AFTER PENTECOST

CHRIST STANDS GUARD

May the Body of our Lord Jesus Christ be sentinel over your soul unto life everlasting.

Priest's Prayer While Giving Communion.

SAVING Body of my King now really and truly dwelling within me, be sentinel over this wayward soul of mine unto life everlasting. My soul is all too unwary, all too prone to throw away its weapons of defense, to be able to fight the battle of life alone. Stand guard then, dear Jesus, over my heart and protect it from its enemies. When the smouldering fires of sensuality, of pride, of disobedience, of anger, begin to blaze anew and to show my crafty enemy where the weakness in my ramparts lies, call to my sleeping spirit and quicken it into action to stand and guard its own. When the lurking foe creeps upon me from without to crush me by the might of his embattled hosts, when he would tempt me to give up the hard conflict and join the rabble-rout of his doomed soldiery, stand guard then, Lord Jesus, and sound the alarm that will nerve my arms to do stout battle for the soul You died to save. Stand sentinel all during the busy morn of life when our spirits run high and we would fain like Peter and Thomas go with You to suffering and death, though we know not the pitiful weakness of our mortal frame. Stand sentinel when the glow and enthusiasm of the first call to Your service is but a faint echo amid the hills of memory and the dull routine of long campaigning, which has robbed the war of its zest, requires the strong, unflinching will of the veteran soldier. And oh! stand sentinel over us in "our failing years when our strength shall fade," when the call to battle will be the call to join the host of those who have "preceded us in the sign of faith and sleep in the sleep of peace." That will be our last stand; and may we die, Lord Jesus, beneath Your banner, fighting for the souls You have redeemed.

FIFTH WEDNESDAY AFTER PENTECOST

RESTLESS FOR GOD

Seek Him that maketh Arcturus, and Orion, and that turneth darkness into morning, and that changeth day into night; that calleth the waters of the sea, and poureth them out upon the face of the earth. The Lord is His name. Amos 5:8.

THERE is a restlessness about our hearts that is wont at times to puzzle us much. It is not merely the vagrant whims and moods of fickle worldlings, but a deeper, a quite fundamental unrest that has caused the wisest of men to knit their brows in thought. Why is it thus, when the world holds out so much that is good and beautiful and true? Why is it that the little heart of man knows no surcease from seeking, and that, too, in a world of which he is undoubtedly the proper tenant? No matter what we hold, we are ever clutching now blindly, now wittingly, for a good that will quiet this hunger of our souls. Riches are sought and mayhap are found, but peace comes not with them. Honor may be ours, but the ermine that fits our shoulders well, is but weight and irksomeness to our restive spirit. The fickle pleasures of sense, the sating of eye and ear and tongue, trail with them the inevitable rude awakening. Are we then merely the playthings of the lesser, viler creatures that surround us?

No, thank God! The light of reason and the light of faith both show us no. There is a goal to our staying desires, there is a term to our reaching hearts—but not where we are wont to place it, not this side the grave. Our hearts are small, quite small, but naught can fill them save Almighty God Himself. Our desires may be classed and numbered by learned men, but nothing can adequately stay them except the limitless goodness of an infinite Godhead. When we realize this, when we become intimately, completely conscious that the hitherto blind gropings of our hearts are instinctive strivings after God, what a chance we have of bringing down a magnificent unity into our lives! God for me, and I for God, everywhere, every time, always. That is the motive power of the saints.

How consolingly easy all this becomes for us Catholics! To give a speedier fulfilment to our hearts' deepest yearnings, to bring a quicker hush to their manifold unrest, Jesus Christ, Son of the living God and living God Himself, is with us always and will be with us, till He comes to judge the living and the dead. Generation after generation comes and goes, but to us as to our fathers and our fathers' fathers, our dear Lord is ever near, that those who seek may find, that the long quest of our hearts may have its goal.

Jesus, my God, my heart is so hard for me to understand. It seems "a strange, piteous, futile thing" and yet I know it was made for You, and none but You can satisfy its craving. Yet here it seeks rest and there it seeks comfort, where none that lasts can be had. Teach me the vanity of human wishes, teach me that "the great show of this world is passing by," teach me, and have me make the lesson live in my every act, that You and You alone are my heart's desire.

"Where the sun shines in the street,
  There are very weary feet
Seeking God, all unaware
That their hastening is a prayer.
Perhaps these feet would deem it odd
(Who think they are on business bent),
  If someone went
And told them, 'You are seeking God.' "

FIFTH THURSDAY AFTER PENTECOST

ME—A SAINT!

Soul of Christ, make a saint of me.

Anima Christi.

THE prayers of everyday life all but necessarily lose their native forcefulness and it is only at moments of special illumination that we are gripped once more by the strength of what we say. How bold these petitions—petitions that none but a God, almighty in love and all unlimited in power could fulfill! "Soul of Christ, make a saint of me!" Think of it—make a saint of me! We ask God to take this weakling will and to fiber it with the unyielding courage of the martyrs; to seize this sluggish heart and to quicken it with the terrific ambition of a Xavier. I ask Him to undo my pride that chafes hard at the slightest thwarting by instilling the sweet humility of a penitent Peter; to turn my harsh words and harsher thoughts into the gentle ways of the Apostle John. I ask Him to unravel the knotted skeins of a disordered life and to weave them into the pattern of His Sacred Heart. He is to take what is cold and sluggish and mean and low, what is earthly and debased, what is sensual and unchecked, and change it into the fiery, courageous, illimitably generous soul of a hero in His service. For this I must petition, not idly, not listlessly, not out of custom, but "with my whole heart and with my whole soul, with all my mind and with all my strength."

Can I ask anyone but God to undertake such a task? Can any but omnipotent love find a way to accomplish what seems so hopeless? To the soul of Christ then we must fly for help. It is from the Blessed Sacrament we must gain our strength. With Jesus in our hearts the dross of sinful ways will be burned away; with the sweet whisper of His voice will come our hearkening unto grace, and then we shall become like unto Him, for we shall grow "in age and grace and wisdom before God and man." "Soul of Christ," attempt what seems so hard, attempt to "make a saint of me." "My heart is ready, O God, my heart is ready!"

FIFTH FRIDAY AFTER PENTECOST

THE PLEASANTEST OF TASKS

Come and hear, all ye that fear God, and I will tell you what great things He hath done for my soul.

Psalm 65:16.

THE famous old Greek philosopher, Socrates, was dead, and his sorrowing disciples were again clustered together, talking of him who had been so vitally present in their lives. Each little trait, each slightest incident of his unwonted career was conned and reconned, that memory might lose nothing of all that precious lore. Often had they begged the favor of the story, but now again they turned to Phaedo, companion of Socrates' last hours, and asked that he tell them once more of the master's end. Quick was the reply: "Yes, I have the time and I shall try to tell you all. For indeed to recall Socrates, whether speaking himself or listening to another, is to me, at least, always the pleasantest of tasks."

Isn't this the story of all friends? Isn't it always "the pleasantest of tasks" to tell of a constant friend, who has been with us in sunshine and in rainy weather, on whom at times we have leaned heavily and then again have walked by his side with a song on our lips; a friend from whom we have hid nothing and who has opened all his secrets unto us? Look back over life, manifold with its passing joys, and we shall find that its hours went swiftest and our hearts beat fastest, when we spoke of dearest friends.

But, grievous though it be to say it, there seems to be a rude exception to this pleasing rule. There is one friend of whom many seem to hesitate to talk, one friend whose friendship some seem to want to hide. Strange fact it is that some of us are quite abashed to be found in love with Christ. We hide our prayers lest we should be caught chatting with Him. We steal into His church with questioning eyes, lest others might detect us. We while away the hours with earthly friends, yet His name is scarcely sounded, or, if so, with almost an apology. But why? Is there aught of fault or blemish in Christ, that we should hang shameful head, if known to have His friendship? Does it tarnish our honor to companion with the Man-God? Queer folk we are! Christ is God with all God's boundless perfections and He is Man, the highest, holiest, noblest man that has ever graced our world—and is it for this that we would keep concealed our love for Him? Men may know from the great facts of our lives that we hold Him for our King and God, but in the little ways of daily habit do we fear to let them see that we have a royal Lover to whom our lives are pledged in troth and whom we mean to please in all our ways? Men and women, be we young or old, be we of the larger walks of the world or of the cloistered paths of convent life, one and all of us have fallen in love with Christ and, we trust, desperately, too. Sweet, then, oh, sweet beyond the power of words ought it to be to us to tell all the well-loved ways of this our Friend, and let all men know that it is our one ambition to be like to Him in every thought and every word and every deed, for this is the mastering passion of our lives.

O Jesus, lover of my soul, You never were ashamed of having poor sinful me as the object of Your love. And yet at times, for fear of men's rude talk, I find myself almost abashed to be known to be in love with You. Jesus dear, I will not have it so. I love You as I love none other, I hold You dear as I hold none other, and men shall know my love.

FIFTH SATURDAY AFTER PENTECOST

LIMITS TO GOD'S GRACE?

I can do all things in Him who strengtheneth me.
Philippians 4:13.

THE Retreat was about to end and the young woman was chatting out her difficulties with the Retreat master. There had been definite occasions of sin and she was frankly fearful of the future. "But *you* put limits to God's grace," was the priest's answer. "Don't you see that?" "Well, I don't mean to put limits to His grace. Certainly not." "Then face the future, and lead the life of a normal, good Catholic girl determined to keep God's grace in your soul—and leave the rest to God. You do your part—God will bring victory."

How often when we face the future, and foresee the same old temptations, the same old difficulties, the same old annoyances, how often are we not like-minded with that retreatant? We want sincerely to serve God, but how we are going to do so seems quite impossible. It may even be that we feel, as did this young lady, that the only possible way to keep in God's grace will be to adopt an unusual way of living, apart from others, islanded off from all temptations. But that would be quite an unwise way out of our difficulties. We are in this world and most of us, by the sheer needs of our life's activities, must make frequent contact with the world. We don't solve problems by running away from them.

Difficulties and temptations there are in plenty; but more plenteous is the grace of God. And it is on that grace that we must rely. That grace will be given always, and with that grace I can overcome the sharpest of temptations, the most exasperating difficulties.

Husband and wife may have fought these many years, and home may have become a place of loathing; but if both will only let the dead past bury its dead and face the future with full confidence in God's strong grace, home will be once more a place of solace and of strength.

Youth may have found the sordid things of life all too alluring, and may have gone down ways where souls are soiled. Companions may have shown a sinful friendship, and the bonds may have grown until they seem to be unbreakable. But the future can be white again, and days of sinlessness will take the place of days that bring the blush—if only the will to mend be there, and full reliance be placed on God's grace.

It may be that my life should be passed hiddenly behind the cloister or within the sanctuary. And maybe it was for a time—but then the world came in, and its baubles caught my eye, and its music pleased my ears. And then—! Maybe the love of our Lord grew dim and His service grew irksome, and I came to follow Him only from afar and quite listlessly. But I see now my faithlessness—and I loathe it. But still the trinkets glint, and still the cadences appeal. What then? A will to be done with it all, but a stronger will to put my trust in Him who first won my love, that His grace can and will bring back my erring heart to Him.

No matter how far my wanderings, no matter how filthy my sins, no matter how vast my faithlessness in every department of life and along all the commands of God, I can conquer all—if only I put my trust in His grace. Through the prophet Isaias, He has told me: "Fear not, for I am with thee; turn not aside, for I am thy God; I have strengthened thee and have helped thee."

Dear Jesus, I get so discouraged at times, and I feel it is all so useless. The past with its sins is gone, yes, thanks to Your kind mercy. But the future lies ahead of me—and I see therein the same temptations, the same pitfalls, the same trials and difficulties. I am so weak! How can I ever conquer exactly there where I have fallen so often! But I must not forget Your ever ready help and on that help I trust. Then victory will be mine, for there are no limits to Your grace.

SIXTH SUNDAY AFTER PENTECOST

A LOVER'S WAY

I live, now not I, but Christ liveth in me.
Galatians 2:20.

A LONELY grave—and at the grave a lone man wept, as only men can weep. No weakling he, this gaunt, stark son of the forest but within the earth's unyielding hold lay the love of his young heart's choosing. "My heart is buried there," was his oft repeated cry and the requiem, that the rain beat out over her dreamless head, resounded wailfully in the emptied chambers of his heart.

So loved Abraham Lincoln. So love all true lovers. Love means the division of self, the sharing of our heart until it resides quite elsewhere than within our own small selves. That is what the pang of separation means, this pitiless plucking away and out of life of our other self.

Is Christ thus another self to us? We have been long years together and has He really grown to be, we say it all respectfully, "the other portion of our souls"? Yes, oh, yes, we trust He has. So real He is to us, so companionable on our way, that were all other friends to fail or die, He alone would make our pilgrim's progress a happy journey home. He was with us in the days of childhood's merry-making and, as youth swung strength within our grasp. He set our feet beside His own, lest they should go a-straying. Then, as the world and its maturing problems snatched, with rude definiteness, the heyday of younger years away, and we saw to our sorrowing that youth must be done with forever, He stood by our side and held fast to our hands that the unfolding riddles of life might not numb our timid hearts. To Him we turn in our joy, to Him we go when we are frightened even unto speechlessness. Our other self? We trust so—yes, and more. Our only self, for to us life means Christ and we would fain be utterly one with Him, even to the day "when the shadow-valley opens, unlighted and unknown." That will be our latest traveling—then He will welcome us to Father's home. Oh! if He were gone, quite gone forever from our lives, we should kneel before the emptied tabernacle, as Lincoln at the grave, as Magdalene at the tomb, and cry unto the fruitless easing of our hearts. Life would be blanked, the life of our life would be gone!

Jesus, the only Friend we need not fear to lose, save by gross, wilfull truancy to love, be more and more to me each day I travel homeward. Make me lose self and selfish aims and think quite always of You alone, for that is the way of lovers, and, poor as my heart may be, I long to be the best of all Your lovers. And yet a word, dear Jesus, more, for I must thank You from my deepest heart that You have pledged Your Sacred presence with me to the end of days—and You alone know what that means to frail and timid me.

"I could not do without Him,
Jesus is more to me
Than all the richest, fairest gifts
Of earth could ever be.
But the more I find Him precious
And the more I find Him true,
The more I long for you to find
What He can do for you."

SIXTH MONDAY AFTER PENTECOST

MAKING CHRIST KNOWN

The next day again John stood, and two of his disciples. And beholding Jesus walking, he saith: Behold the Lamb of God. And the two disciples heard him speak and they followed Jesus.

St. John 1:35-37.

TO make a friend better known is a distinct joy to us all. To have others realize how one stood by us when the shadows fell, how he nerved our hearts, when life's strain was hard, brings a ray of sunshine into our dullest day. Others must know my friend as I know him, and then they, too, will add their love to mine. This was the joy of John the Baptist that day he stood by the Jordan's bank and pointed out his Friend.

So, too, it ought to be and must be with us and that same Friend, Christ Jesus. When our lives were robbed of sunshine, no friend was ever so near as He. When sorrow gripped our soul and the darkness of lowering storms came swift upon us, there never was a time when we stretched forth our hands in the dark and found Him not at our side, nor listened for His voice and heard it not in its answering. Then when the day dawned bright again and the clouds were hurried away, who sweetened our joys as He, who hallowed our pleasures as He?

Sweet then it ought to be to tell of all His love in the days gone by, sweet to tell of His kindly help and of His cheering voice. Others may not know Him as He has deigned to let us know Him, others may not have enjoyed the closeness of intimacy that has been ours—and shall we let our best of Friends remain unknown? It may be in His hidden Providence He is waiting for me to introduce Him to other souls. Shall I keep the Lord of all waiting for the introduction? Oh, no! But rather I shall call the little ones around me and tell of the Friend that knows their little hearts and loves their tiny lives. I shall speak to older folk of the love that made a Bethlehem and then a Calvary, and made and still makes the God-Man find His home within the tabernacle. I shall tell of the burning flax He will not quench and the bruised reed He will not break, tell them one and all how weary hearts can gain their rest, where sunlit lives may find new joy. Even when my lips are still, even when my voice is hushed, shall I yet speak of Him by my self-restraint and by my thoughtfulness for others, which I have learned by keeping company with Him. But loudest shall this voiceless story be as I kneel in lowly adoration before Him and never once do aught that would be rude while visiting such a Friend.

Jesus, Friend where others fail, Friend where others cannot help, would I could tell all men the story of Your gentle ways, and bring them, one and all, to love You in return. But that alas, were an idle wish. Yet some there are with whom I live my shortening days, some whom I have with me at home and some whom I shall meet in the busy ways of life. These at least will I teach the gladness of Your friendship, these few at least will I bring to know Your priceless love and all Your blessed gifts. O Jesus, help me to make You friend to all my friends.

SIXTH TUESDAY AFTER PENTECOST

LET'S FOLLOW HIM

She answered: Be not against me to desire that I should leave thee and depart: for whithersoever thou shalt go, I will go: and where thou shalt dwell, I also will dwell. Thy people shall be my people and thy God my God.
Ruth 1:16.

Then Jesus said to the Twelve: Will you also go away?
St. John 6:68.

OFTEN have we stood with saddened Naomi in the far off fields of Bethlehem and heard her bid a last farewell to Ruth and speed her home again. We have seen her turn aside lest she might have to gaze on Ruth as she left, yet saw her turn and new joy light that darkened face. For scarcely had the parting words been hushed in the sorrow of that heart, when Ruth vowed fidelity strong and true to follow Naomi, whatever the hidden days might bring.

Thus have we stood in the fields of long ago and heard the pledge of a noble heart. Thus again we stand in that same old Eastern land not far from Ruth's ancient home and lo! Ruth's royal Child, our Lord and Master, is speaking to us, but not as Naomi. He would not have us leave Him, as foolish sheep that would stray from kindest shepherd. His is a question that searches our souls and sounds the depths of our hearts.

Following Christ is a strong, brave deed and calls for the unbending will of full-grown man. Sluggards and cowards and peevish souls are not those out of whom the followers of a thorn-crowned King are made. There are pleasant days in His service, yea rather, every day is "as a day in spring"; for deep down in the soul of everyone who "determinedly follows Christ," there is that peace which the world is as powerless to filch away as it is to give. But lusty battles there are to fight for our own souls, first of all, and then for the souls of others; sharp temptations to be swiftly overcome, or maybe the noiseless, galling rub of uneventful, hidden labor in His service. This is the work Christ tells us of, as we stand by His side on the Galilean plain. Are we brave enough to dare it, or, with a coward's heart within us, shall we too go away, as craven men and women before us? Are we brave to stem the tide of passion and check unruly eye and ear and tongue from all disorder? Are we strong to master our faultful hearts and their wayward ways? Shall we fight the fight of Christ for the souls of those who lean on us at home or at school or in our daily life and keep their souls free and pure amid the tainted ways of men? It is strong, fierce work this battle of the worlds of spirit and of sense and, when Christ calls, He makes no secret of the struggle. Frank He is to tell of all the hard campaigning of His soldiers, but quickly frank to add that His soldiers fight not single-handed and alone. He tells of His love that brightens weary hearts and of His grace that strengthens frail souls until unconquerable might is theirs to dare all things for Him, and one sweet day to die for Him. He tells it all—and pauses. Shall we, too, go away?

Jesus, my King, one only answer can there be to all that You have said. I am weak but You are strong, I am fearful but You are brave, and You are ever near to aid me. I know the fight is hard and the war is long, but "my heart is ready, O God, my heart is ready." As Ruth to Naomi of old, so now to You, my changeless Friend, I pledge myself. Lead on, dear Jesus, lead on to where the battle rages fiercest, for I have short time to be Your soldier in this vale of tears.

"Send me men girt for the combat,
Men who are grit to the core. . . .
Send me the best of your breeding,
Lend me your chosen ones;
Them will I clasp to my bosom,
Them will I call my sons. . . .
And I will not be won by weaklings,
Subtile, suave and mild,
But by men with the hearts of Vikings,
And the simple faith of child."

SIXTH WEDNESDAY AFTER PENTECOST

GIFTS TO GOD

But every one shall offer according to what he hath, according to the blessing of the Lord his God, which He shall give him.

Deuteronomy 16:17.

IT is the "Hill of Martyrs" in Japan and another doomed troop of Christians stands to, that they may hear the "taps" of their service-day in Christ's army. A woman of Japan is there with baby Ignatius high in arms, clad in festive dress, and across the space that holds them separate, she calls to Blessed Spinola:

"See, Father, here's my boy, and glad he is to die with me. My cherished best, my child and myself, I give to God with joy."

"Look, darling, upon him who made thee a child of God and gave thee life far better than the life I gave thee, which is now hastening to its close. Kneel, dearest, and ask his blessing."

Down knelt the lad, then hurriedly the moments flew, and the axman did his work and mother and boy, and Spinola, too, stood before the throne of God.

"A man's heart in a woman's breast" surely, and one, which knew and dared to give to God until it hurt! Elizabeth had caught aright the value of the things of time and had weighed them well against the things for which God shows a care. Herself she gave to God unflinchingly and her boy, the music of her heart and the brightness of her eyes, she held not back from her Maker. Yet a few months ago Elizabeth had not heard of Christ nor His love for her, for the night of the pagan world was then cast around about her soul.

As we stand on Nagasaki's hill and see the head of mother and of child roll in the reddened dust, are not our coward hearts accusing us? What of Catholic parents who refuse a boy or a girl to the service of God! It may be He deigns to call for their best, to ask for the one who has been twined most closely around their hearts. Yet they would seem to want, if God insists, to have Him choose the ones less dear, would seem not to hold that "God must have my best." Must God choose the leavings of men, and have in His cloistered courts but the dross of mankind? What again of the man and woman, who follow the ways of the world in all its pitiable frivolity, yet know in their hearts that a Christian life cannot be led with pagan folk for comrades? Are they brothers and sisters to Elizabeth the martyr?

What, too, of each and all of us, even when we try to be true to the blood of martyrs within us? Do we give always our best and give it with a smile? The big things of life we gladly give or would gladly give to God were He to ask; but are we quite ready always for the little sacrifice? Please God, we are, or at least we shall lustily strive to be, for we would never have it said that the new-born Christians of old had found a greater love for our Lord within their hearts when but a few short months had sped, than we, His petted children, find after the lapse of many a year, teeming with gifts from His hands.

Jesus, you know that I have told You time and time again that I love You and would love You daily more and more. I mean it all, dear Lord, yes, every word, and like Your stalwart lovers of Nagasaki's hill, I, too, will give You just whatever You may ask, be it little or be it great, be it myself or what I call my own. Only give me Your nerving grace, that when the hour of sacrificing comes, my courage and my love may not grow frail and spoil the work I promised.

SIXTH THURSDAY AFTER PENTECOST

THE UNKNOWN GOD

I found an altar also on which was written: To the unknown God.

Acts 17:23.

AH! dear Lord Jesus, how truly these words may be applied to our own altars! These altars of our vast and glorious cathedrals, these altars of our numerous stately churches, these altars around which cluster the scanty cottages of the straggling village, are they not all built to "the unknown God"? You are not known, my Jesus; else how explain the ways of men?

Your justice is unknown, else man would not sin. Your mercy is unknown, else the despondent sinner would not tarry in his guilt. Your patience, Your kindness is not known, for if it were, would we play into the hands of the enemy by discouragement and irritation at our all too slight progress in perfection? Oh, we do not know You. You have been long with us, have tarried often in our hearts, and yet You are unknown. Your infinite love for us, Your infinite sympathy for us in all our trials is unknown, it so far surpasses all we can imagine. "Lord Jesus, make me know You," know the great desires of Your Sacred Heart, know the inspiring secrets of Your life, that I may follow You unto perfection. Make me know You in Your Blessed Sacrament so that my love for You may be a living, real love for a living, real person. Be not nineteen hundred years away from me, but be vividly, intimately, feelingly present for me behind the tabernacle door. And when You come into my heart at the hour of Holy Communion, be not unknown to me. Take away the incognito of Your sacramental Presence. Remove for my inward sense the veil that hides You from my earthly eyes and in the sweet lineaments of Your sacred Humanity speak unto me "as a friend would speak unto a friend." Then, Lord Jesus, I'll learn to make Your house my home, learn to come to You when the friction of mortal life wears deepest, learn to come to You and in Your sacred presence to enjoy a slight foretaste of the long bright day of eternity when I shall be safe at home with You.

For those "who find Thy saying hard"
And who this wondrous Gift discard,
Lord! let my faith atone!

But there's one soul whose want of love
Should most of all Thy pity move,—
My own.

SIXTH FRIDAY AFTER PENTECOST

TUCKING TROUBLES AWAY

Be not as a lion in thy house, terrifying them of thy household, and oppressing them that are under thee.
Ecclesiasticus 4:35.

NO, don't go near him now, he is in a bad humor." This was whispered all about the office and then again, when the day was done, throughout the home. A snappy word, a bit of chiding and a deal of fault-finding, and at best an evident incivility was all that could be expected of the man today. And so, servant and clerks, friends, wife and children all avoided him and left him in the isolation of his churlish ways. Unschooled in self-control, the man was wont to make his distemper of soul or body a veritable cross on all about him, and happiness was scarce when his moods came on.

Can I find aught of likeness to myself herein? Were my friends to hear these words, would they bethink themselves at once of me? If so, it would be prudent and very Christlike to read my life aright and mend my ways that others, already bearing their own crosses, might not be forced to bear mine too. A headache comes and temples throb and eyes are burning with pain, but is it right, because my nerves are all distraught, that I should set my neighbor's nerves a-tingling? Sickness lays its felling hand upon me, and I am quite unable to help myself in aught, but should I then make life a drudgery for all who have to deal with me? My own life would be far sweeter and joy would rest more insistently upon the lives of those around me, were I to take my cross and kiss it lovingly and then hide it away in my heart. At work, or in the office, or in the classroom, it is the weak, the immature, the uncontrolled who make their attitude of mind, their views, their decisions, and their approachableness depend upon a passing pain or trifling disappointment.

But it is hard to get an iron grip upon yourself! Of course it is. Whoever said otherwise, knew not of what he spoke. "But can you smile with darkened mind, and pain of heart, and nerves stretched wide in agony?" Of course you can, but only then, when you have sought the Man of Sorrow and kept His company long, and breathed in His broadened views of life, and caught the contagion of His massive will.

Jesus dear, I fear that I do not bear aright my crosses. Long years ago I should have learned to wreathe a smile about my lips when pain would tighten them, to speak a kindly word when ill-temper clamors for expression, to be quite affable when rudeness seems the proper way to ease my nerves. And yet I find these traits so absent from my life! Oh, for the sake of my dignity as man, and much more for the sake of my higher calling to be another Christ, grant me plentiful grace to carry all my crosses hidden away within myself, and all my troubles tucked away from sight.

SIXTH SATURDAY AFTER PENTECOST

"THE CEASING OF EXQUISITE MUSIC"

The memory of Josias is like the composition of a sweet smell made by the art of a perfumer: his remembrance shall be sweet as honey in every mouth, and as music at a banquet of wine.

Ecclesiasticus 49:1, 2.

THERE is a line in Longfellow's "Evangeline" which pictures vividly the effect holiness and purity of life have upon others, even passing bystanders. Of a Saturday afternoon, Evangeline is coming home from Confession. Down the road home she walks, passing now this group, now that. Not a word is spoken; she merely passes by. But all know her for the pure, thoroughly good young woman that she is; and Longfellow sums up her journey home in a line unexcelled in literature: "When she had passed, it seemed like the ceasing of exquisite music."

What a bit of imagery! We know how exquisite music affects us. It lifts us up out of our commonplace world, high, high above into the realms of clearer vision and purer ideals, and when it has ceased we drift back slowly to earth, but so changed, so refreshed, so tingling with purified emotion.

That is what Longfellow meant to tell us of Evangeline, and that is what the Sacred Writer thousands of years ago meant to tell us of the holy king Josias: "The memory of Josias is like the composition of a sweet smell made by the art of a perfumer: his remembrance shall be sweet as honey in every mouth, and as music at a banquet of wine."

That is the effect my life should have on all I meet, at home or abroad, at work or at play. Yet is it? When I leave the folks at home for a short spell or for a long while or for just the daily comings and goings, does it seem to each of my loved ones "like the ceasing of exquisite music"? Or do they rather heave a sigh of relief that I am gone? When I leave school or work, am I really missed and do I leave a void? Or again does a knowing glance go the rounds that indicates a sense of security that an irritant has been removed?

It is so easy to be selfish and avoid the harder tasks and shirk the heavier burdens. It is simple to say the nasty word and to grow peevish and sullen when extra work is asked. None of that requires self-restraint, none of that demands a decent regard for others.

But to be pleasant and agreeable at all times, especially "when things go wrong"; to be generous enough not merely to take the harder work or the longer hours when such burdens are imposed but even to volunteer for them; to deal with difficult characters kindly; to turn an angry remark away with a gentle answer; to actually live what is right and true and pure—all that requires a firm hand on ourselves and a vigilance that never tires.

But the result! Home becomes the heaven it is meant to be, and the blessed tarrying place where loved ones dwell in happy unison. School and office become a larger home, when all join together happily in the hours of toil. And when the hours come wherein we refresh our souls and bodies with the lighter things of life, those times will leave no sordid marks but only the sweetest memories, "like the composition of a sweet smell made by the art of a perfumer."

Would I leave, like Josias, a "remembrance . . . sweet as honey in every mouth" if I were to die right now? Would the ending of my life seem "like the ceasing of exquisite music"? I wonder!

Dear Jesus, for Your sake I want to do all the good I can, and I want to make all as happy as I can, and I want to lead all nearer to You. I am afraid I have not done so and I can scarcely believe that if death came now that my life would be as a "remembrance . . . sweet as honey in every mouth." But, honestly I want to leave just such a memory—for Your sake. So please help me so to act and so to live at all times, in all places, that when I have passed, for the time being or for good, it will seem "like the ceasing of exquisite music."

SEVENTH SUNDAY AFTER PENTECOST

MOMENTS WITH HIM

I rejoiced at the things that were said to me: we shall go into the house of the Lord.

Psalm 121:1.

MANY a year the captive Jews had served their cruel taskmasters and day after day had sat by the waters of Babylon and started the echoes with their plaints for the land they loved so far away. Deep had the lash bitten, low had the labor bent the exiles' shoulders, and sad were their hearts in that foreign land. But at last a day dawned bright for them and the hiss of the scourge was hushed and the burdens were laid aside to be lifted no more. Exile was over. They were going back to Sion, Sion that was the one cause of joy. Not the thought of home, not the thought of the fields and the mountains where their younger steps had strayed; no, but just one word came ever to their lips, "We shall go into the house of the Lord." Just one spot in all the Chosen Land from Judea to Galilee came up ever before their famished eyes, and that was Sion, "great mountain of His holiness." That was home, that alone meant peace and happiness, and once again would their voices tremble with a song that would be sung in a land that was not strange.

Is it so with us? Is there a thrill in our exile-hearts when we are called to the house of the Lord, not the ruined temple where God had dwelt in sign and symbol only, but the house of the living God, the home of "the man, Christ Jesus"? It may be the call is the voice of His Church beckoning us to her official prayer; it may be the gentle whisper of our Guardian Angels, urging us to visit their God and ours; it may be a thoughtful friend, mindful alike of us he loves and of Him who loves us both. Come as it may, that call does come, and thanks be to God, for many of us very often. And are we glad? Do we feel real pleasure when we hear the news that another visit to our Friend is soon to be our own, another chance to talk with one we love so deeply?

It is always good to talk our soul out to a friend, to lay all our joys and all our sorrows at the door of his own brave heart—and what braver, truer, more loyal heart than that of "the man, Christ Jesus"? Other visits we may pay to faithful earthly friends, but no visit can compare with the moments spent with Jesus. That invitation must find us ever ready, and, like the exiles of old, we shall ever draw near to the home of our best of friends with a "song as in the night of the sanctified solemnity, and joy of heart, as when one goeth with a pipe, to come into the mountain of the Lord, to the Mighty One of Israel."

O Jesus, no sweeter moments have ever been mine than when I knelt and spoke with You, my God! Exile that I am, my poor heart finds its rest in the silent sanctity of Your earthly home. There all sorrows are forgotten, there all joys are sanctified, with never the fear of wearying Your Sacred Heart. Call me often, Jesus, to Your sweet company, call me and bid me come to You, because, Lord Jesus, I am happy when I am with You.

" 'Tis my trysting place with the Divine,
And I fall at the feet of the Holy,
And above me a voice said: 'Be mine.'
And there rose from the depth of my spirit
An echo—'My heart shall be thine.' "

SEVENTH MONDAY AFTER PENTECOST

GOD'S MARCHING MEN

After this I saw a great multitude, which no man could number, of all nations, and tribes, and peoples, and tongues. . . . And they cried with a loud voice, saying: Salvation to our God, who sitteth upon the throne, and to the Lamb.
Apocalypse 7: 9, 10.

OUT from the solid rock which rears its mountainous mass upon Georgia's soil march with unending tread Robert E. Lee and Stonewall Jackson and the numbered hosts of less known, but none the less noble, men who fought in the uniform of gray, when civil strife tore our country in twain. There they march, these men of stone, whose names are loud on every Southerner's lips and whose deeds are cherished in every Southern home. Silent is their tread, but it thunders in every heart over the wide world. Men they were who had hearts as tender and as true as any other men, but hearts, too, big and brave and daring to do great deeds that won for many of them only a nameless soldier's grave out in the fields where warring brothers fell. Heroes they were and out from earth's own citadel they call to younger generations to emulate their deeds.

The South does well to carve into unyielding stone the story of her valiant sons that each new youthful folk may mold their lives to highest actions. Yet there is a greater troop of men who go marching down the centuries and their tread has thundered wherever man dwells. The great host of God's Saints advance and readvance upon us from New Year's Day to New Year's Day. Greece and Rome and western Europe send forth their hosts of victorious warriors; Asia and Africa and far-flung Oceanica summon their hero folk to God, and latest-born America marshalls the forces of her saintdom. These are not stolid figures of stone, fit indeed to awaken memory's fruitful store, yet cold and unresponsive to every call, but men and women living and lithe and quick in God's final home in Heaven, and day after day they march from out the Missal and the record book of Saints we call the Martyrology, beckoning us on to do and dare as they. Our hero ancestry of martyrs calls to us to stand our ground and not to yield when pain is the price we must pay for godliness, for they are arrayed as kings in garments of their own blood's dyeing. Virgins tell of souls kept white when men knew naught but filth and all the world was madly rushing after pleasure. Confessors unfold their ordinary lives lived in just an extraordinary way, which was the way of doing all quite seriously for God. An Aquinas learned in all the lore of his day assures us we can be scholarly and yet very near to God. Xavier, "who had the world for cell," would have us find God everywhere, yet find Him most at the altar on whose steps he slept his fitful sleep. Men and women of the world and of the cloister; men and women joined in sainted wedlock and other some living virginal lives; men and women learned and many, many unversed in the studies of men; on they come and the silent ring of their unearthly marching strikes well upon the ears of each true Catholic and we fain would be off and march with them, keeping the eternal "night-watches of the Saints."

Jesus, strong leader of God's army, a hero ancestry beckons me on. Noble folk they were, and their deeds stand emblazoned wherever man has found a home. Would I were as they! Yet my heart grows weak and my spirit numb when I face the little trials of life I have. I have the blood of martyrs in my veins and yet I quail and tremble before the scorn of men. Confessor sires brought me forth and my robe is soiled and tainted by my faithlessnesses. Yet what are my struggles and my difficulties to theirs! Strong leader, make my right arm valiant and nerve my heart to lead my life aright for You and not to shame my sainted ancestry.

SEVENTH TUESDAY AFTER PENTECOST

THE PRICE OF NEARNESS TO GOD

And I will have mercy on the house of Juda, and I will save them by the Lord, their God; and I will not save them by bow, nor by sword, nor by battle, nor by horses, nor by horsemen.

Osee 1:7.

OUR Lord always demands trust in Him, but sometimes He is quite definite that our trust must be in Him *alone*. His designs are usually hard to fathom, but at times His relentless pursuit of some souls is startling in the extreme, especially to the souls themselves.

To some, as they journey through life, He leaves friends, and health of body, and joy of mind, and at least a competency of this world's goods.

To some He grants a meed of success and public approval that nerves on quite rightly to further efforts.

But from other some He takes now this, now that, until with the poet the soul cries out: "My harness, piece by piece Thou hast hewn from me, and smitten me to my knee; I am defenseless utterly." "Hewn" is, indeed, the right word, for only strong blows from an omnipotent God can break our clutching hold on the things we love. It may be that my health is gone, and with it all my capacity to do any work for others; and everything I craved to do and on which my heart was set has been swept beyond regaining. And friends, too, fail to read me aright, and my heart grows numb at times in the growing isolation wherein I find myself. And then, inevitably, and full naturally the cry reverberates loud within my soul: "Why?"

Why? Because our Lord wants my love undividedly. Of every soul He is a jealous lover; but in some He shows no least tolerance of the slightest affection for earthly things. They are to be His and His alone. Why does He do this? No man can answer. But answer can be made that it is a privilege priceless beyond the telling to be so singled out by God; a privilege, yes, a searing privilege, but a wondrous one, a gift the accepting of which means much pain, nay, rather self-annihilation, that God and God alone may live within me.

Thus was won the stark grandeur of many a saint. Rising up in sheer loftiness among their fellow men, they have paid their price for eminence. And the price of eminence? Loss of self in nearness to God. They won it, even as Juda did of old, not "by bow, nor by sword, nor by battle, nor by horses, nor by horsemen," but "by the Lord, their God," who snatched them out of themselves and hewed away from them the cramping harness of earthly things and left them His own—utterly and completely and irrevocably His own.

Is God asking this of me? Then, cost what it may, it were wise to yield to this "tremendous Lover"; for "who hath resisted Him and hath had peace?"

Dear Lord, You have made the things of time and sense very appealing, and it was Your purpose that men should find joy therein. But out from all mankind in every age and in every clime You have mysteriously given the command to many a soul: "Go forth out of thy country, and from thy kindred, and out of thy father's house." And, even as to the Levites of old, so to them You "gave no possessions, because the Lord the God of Israel Himself is their possession." Will You ask that of me? That would be a privilege beyond my best hopes. But remember, Lord, if You do ask it of me, give me much grace to clasp the painful gift right mannerly.

SEVENTH WEDNESDAY AFTER PENTECOST

BORROWING FUN

I will greatly rejoice in the Lord and my soul shall be joyful in God.

Isaias 61:10.

THERE is not much fun in it, unless you do it for God" was the brief characterization by Ven. Philippine Duchesne of her nine weeks' travel across the ocean. The nineteenth century was yet young and the boats which crossed the ocean were sorry things, when this woman of God set out to turn the hearts of the Indians toward Heaven. Now a calm held them still upon a sea of glass and now a storm tossed them across a mountain of billows. Again the sinister pirates of the sea gave chase, while within the ship's narrow hold sick men breathed death into an atmosphere already heavy with unendurable heat. Yet to Mother Duchesne and her valiant followers there was fun in it, because they were doing it for God.

All of us complain at times that life is colorless. With hearts attuned to high romance and minds a-straying through castles of the air, we find it hard to see existence through aright and to catch the smile hidden in the open places of the day. Yet catch it we must. But how? By bringing God right down into our lives and playing the hard, gruelling game of life with Him and for His sake. Then there will be lots of fun in it, for we would be seeing it through with Him, who is our infinitely happy God. Mother at home "will start an Angel's wing" when she calls her little ones at dawn, sends them off to school and gathers them by her side as they kneel and say "good-night" to God. The men and women who must thread their daily way amid the crowded fastnesses of business life, will catch the smiles of Guardian Angels, as they record deeds well done and temptations spurned indignantly. Teachers, too, will smile, as their Teacher-Master did these centuries now gone, when children crowded round Him, though the task be hard at times to mold young hearts to know and cling to Him with all the love their growing lives can find. No matter where we are, no matter what our work may be, the richness of God's smile will bring a merriment into our life that will set our hearts throbbing and will put fun there where only monotony reigned before.

Jesus dear, there is a lot of fun in life when You are present and I am conscious of Your presence. But when I forget You and try to play the game of life according to my own ways and rules, how blank and dull it becomes! My heart soon tires of it all and keeps calling for a change and newness of work and the quittance of old scenes. Oh, stay with me always and let me catch Your smile when You are pleased with me! Let me look within the shell of things and be conscious always of the deep abiding realities of my life and what a happy, joyous thing it is to see it through for You! Just teach me the fun of doing things for God!

SEVENTH THURSDAY AFTER PENTECOST

A FRIEND IN NEED

And I say to you: Ask, and it shall be given to you: seek and you shall find: knock and it shall be opened to you. For every one that asketh, receiveth; and he that seeketh, findeth: and to him that knocketh, it shall be opened.

St. Luke 11:9, 10.

IN our hours of sorrow and darkness, there is nothing we dread so much as a rebuff or any faintest manifestation of inconsiderateness. Our souls, sensitive beyond their wont, swiftly recoil before the slightest touch of harshness, fearful of another bruise, dreading another weighted cross. That is why, when joy's sunlight is hurried from our lives and the lengthening shadows fall athwart our paths, we turn our groping steps away from those that know us least and love us little, turn them away to search out one who understands us well and who will lay none but gentlest hands on our seared and quivering hearts. We seek a friend who knows our strength and our weakness too, knows our faults of character and whatever virtues may offset them, and thus knows how to shift the burden so that we may bear it best. But if there be no shifting of the full, dead weight, then with friend's true skill he will recall in vivid freshness the motives that quicken us best and spur us most instantly into action, and we shall rise again and find our burden lighter because our hearts are brave, as they were of old, and young with a youth we had thought forever lost.

It is a blessed thing to find such friends and we should grapple them to us with hooks of steel. Yet there are men and women in this great, seething world of ours, whose solitude of sorrow is never broken by a cheering word, who listen to the feet that hurry by and sickeningly know that none will ever turn aside to seek them out. Other some there are, whose friends are kind for the hours when laughter's peal is still unhushed, but miserly scant of even a word of pity, when the smile is quenched and gone. Other some there are, and maybe God has seen fit at times to have us numbered with them, whose hearts are so sorely harassed and whose shoulders are so galled by the frictioning of mortals' cares, that no human touch, however kind and gentle, can bring them surcease of their woe.

Oh the deep, strong consolation in these lonely hours to come to the "Man, Christ Jesus," to come to Him in His hiding behind the sacramental veils! To Him we may tell the tale He knows so well, but which He will never tire of hearing from us, so be it our hearts are eased thereby. His house is the house of prayer, the home of all supplication, the trysting-place where the sick and the halt and the blind of soul and of body come when the shadows fall, to meet their Divine Friend who never once has crushed the bruised reed nor quenched the burning flax. There the most poignant of human woes, there the most secret sorrows of human life may be whispered and ever will fresh hope and stouter strength arise new-born within us, as Jesus, the Man of Sorrows, who trod the wine-press alone, cheers and consoles us in our faintness. There is no boon we can plead for, that He cannot give, no gift we can ask for, that He will not bestow if only it be for our good. Give, He always does, whether it be the object of our own poor prayers or a grace He sees more fitted to our needs. Then when we kneel in our parting genuflection, courage is in our souls "to strive, to seek, to find and not to yield."

Jesus, friend of the weary and faint of heart, who can tell what You are to us in hours of loneliness and grief? Life has its joys and we thank You from our hearts for these sweets, brief foretastes as they are of eternal bliss. But life has its sorrows, too, sorrows so often unsharable and unshared. To You then, we come and lay before You the wounds wherewith we are wounded in the struggles of this vale of tears. Jesus, You will help us bear them, You will listen to our oft-told tale, will You not, dear Lord? If You do, dear Saviour, will not the joy be Yours, as well as ours, when we, Your blessed saved, meet You on the farther shore?

SEVENTH FRIDAY AFTER PENTECOST

IN LOVE

O God, my God, to Thee do I watch at break of day. For Thee my soul hath thirsted; for Thee my flesh, oh, how many ways.

Psalm 62:1, 2.

OUR thoughts are telltales on our hearts. There is no surer way to find out just how large a share our friends have of our love than to examine how frequently they are present in our thoughts. If they be but seldom before us, then our love is scarce and scant; but if at early morn and then again in the bustle of the high noon and yet again in the quieted hours of the evening we find their faces ever present to us, their wishes ever guiding us, their ideals ever beckoning us on, we know our love has been won most fully and our hearts are no longer our own.

We claim to be in love with Christ, and, please God, we really are. Some there are whose young love is still, in childlike artlessness, clinging to Him whom sainted father and mother taught them to love well. Some again have plighted at His altar love for another human heart and promised the God of sacred wedlock that their union is to be hallowed with a higher, deeper love for Him. Other some again have found the insistence of His love so compelling that they have bound themselves to Him with the bonding of those triple vows that make them plighted liegemen and spouses of their King. Yes, all this is true, and yet it were well from time to time to test out our love that we may never have it grow the least bit less. No need of lengthy searchings. Just this one simple question: "How much is our Lord in my thoughts?" As the day goes by from the moment when our awakened hands first sign us with the saving cross until the closing hour when tired fingers thread our Mother's beads, let us watch our thoughts. Ever and anon are our thoughts filled with Him, the lover of our souls? Ever and anon do our hearts go reaching after Him for whom they are a-hungering? Do we bethink ourselves of all His kindly ways and yearn and really try to duplicate His life a bit in ours? Do we dream of all that He holds dear and then resolve to secure Him what He desires within our own souls? That is the way with earthly lovers. Is the King of hearts, is the Lord "who loveth souls" to be the only loved one who does not claim a share in every thought and every heart's desire of the lover?

O Jesus, dearest Lord, I love You with my whole heart and with my whole soul, and with my whole mind and with my whole strength and I would love You more. And yet at times You do not share my thoughts as a loved one ought, nor do You steal into every pulse of my searching heart. Oh, no! I have not yet learned to love You as I ought, You are not yet the silent companion of my every moment, whose image buoys my every step. But, Jesus dear, just grant that it may soon be so!

SEVENTH SATURDAY AFTER PENTECOST

WHEN I'M THROUGH, I'M THROUGH

Forgive us our trespasses, as we forgive those who trespass against us.

St. Matthew 6:12.

SHE sat there, a petulant, wilfull young lady. She had just had a falling-out with her best friend and the right was but slightly on her own side. Motive after motive was put up to her but the stubborn head kept waving "no" and from the stubborn mouth came the refrain: "When I'm through, I'm through." "Well, all right," said her friend, in a last desperate attempt to bring her to a semblance of reason, "suppose God said that to you? You've offended Him—what if He said: 'When I'm through, I'm through'?"

Our Lord knew human nature and how hard we find it to forgive. He knew how hearts rankle and how brooding over offenses makes them worse and heightens them beyond all recognition. And so it was that into the one prayer He taught us He put those words that cut right into the heart of common human fault: "Forgive us our trespasses as we forgive those who trespass against us." He makes us ask that the measure of God's forgiveness to us will be exactly the measure of our forgiveness to others. To put it crudely, He "makes us take our own medicine."

There may, of course, be times when I might legitimately deny, not forgiveness—no, never—but a renewal of close intimacy. No one can claim my friendship anew when he or she has seriously sundered it. My friendship is something I may give or withhold and none can exact it of me. Christ Himself was not a "friend" to each and every man He met; He was a "friend" to His chosen Disciples. He certainly was no "friend" of the Pharisees and Sadducees.

But forgiveness is another thing; and Christ has told us that we must forgive not seven times but seventy times seven times. And how many of us are ever offended even in the longest life that often by any one friend?

"Forgive and forget" is a wise piece of advice and it makes life much happier if we follow it. What a silly thing it is to "hold in" some trifling offense against another! Do I like it if some one "holds in" against me some picayune slip that I never meant? And even when I meant it and am sorry afterwards, don't I expect them "to be reasonable" and forgive? And is there not a very old saying: "Do as you would be done by"? Life is hard at best, without making it harder for all concerned by silly unforgivenesses. And is it not generally best to mend even a friendship when it has been strained? Isn't every one happier thereby?

Dear Jesus, You touched the sore spot of our human littleness when You taught us to pray as You did. You know how petty and mean and small we are, and how prone we are to "hold things in." It is a mean trait and we hate to have others act so to us. I say the prayer You taught me often each day and I cannot say it honestly unless I forgive and forget. And I do want to say it honestly.

EIGHTH SUNDAY AFTER PENTECOST

ONE WITH GOD, A MAJORITY

If God be for us, who is against us?
Romans 8:31.

FOUR ducats and Teresa are nothing, but four ducats, Teresa and God are more than is necessary." So spake St. Teresa centuries ago, when men challenged her with folly for daring the impossible. She would found a house of Carmel and many balked her plans and none would aid. Only four ducats she had and no place for her nuns and herself to live and no food to eat, but Teresa had long since learned that "one with God is a majority." The plans of men might not fit in with hers, but hers were of God and why should she be afraid that God could not manage to see His own plans through? And so she watched and prayed and was firmly but gently insistent, as holy folk are wont to be when they know they are inspired of God. And thus long months passed and men's hearts grew changed—and God's plans won.

Many of us grow worried at times and seem to forget the enduring fact back of St. Teresa's words. My resources may indeed be small, and men may be leagued against me; but what of that, if I call God in and have Him on my side! Parents look upon their growing boy or girl, against whose soul the forces of the world are battling, as in every age, and they grow afraid. What can they do, so frail in strength, so circumscribed in efforts, so unused to each modern deceit, what can they do to save their child! What can they do? Plan and plot, of course, and be vigilantly watchful, but finally down on their knees they must fall, calling on God to shield their little one—and His. Out in the business world crafty men are scheming to crush me to the wall and steal from my purse, by tricky ways of trade, all the wealth I have. The future looms dark indeed and wife and children are pictured in want and of course I lie awake at nights, scheming against the coming of thieves. It seems I cannot win; no, not alone, but take God into partnership and then fight lustily.

Many of us too have plans on larger or smaller scale, by which we think to do much good for ourselves and for other men. We try hard and would play the game straight, but the dice seem loaded against us. And so at home, or in the classroom, in our smaller societies and in our greater organizations we find our best laid plans doomed to failure. What then? Are we to fear "the loaded dice" or are we to ask God to take a hand and play the game for us? Of course we shall call Him in and then we shall win the game, for no dice can be loaded against Him.

It may indeed be that even in the end no external victory seems ours. It may well happen that, before the eyes of men and in our own eyes, we have lost the game. But that is only to the seeming. God is with us, and while the surface game of today or of tomorrow may go against us according to our short-sighted way of sizing things up, the one great game of life is won—the game of playing straight and true and valiantly for the things of God. That must be so, for God and I are unbeatable.

Dear Jesus, there is so much opposition to good in this world that often all of us feel like giving up. You know how hard I try at times to serve You and to keep others in Your service or to win still others to Your love. Yet so often, very often, I have every reason to believe that my efforts are doomed to failure. And so, dear Lord, whatever I plan to do, and whatever I undertake for good, just let me remember to call You in, to take You into partnership. Let me not be worried over the outcome, let me not grow anxious when the dice of life are loaded, but let my confidence be firm; for one with You, my God, is a majority, and we are bound to win.

EIGHTH MONDAY AFTER PENTECOST

"WHEN GOD NEEDS US"

But if any man shall ask you: Why do you loose him? you shall say this unto him: Because the Lord hath need of his service.

St. Luke 19:31.

WE count it a privilege to help persons of high station in this world. Whether it be that need forces them to come to us in unaccustomed suppliance or whether a gracious condescension on their part moves them to solicit our co-operation, our wonted pride makes us conscious of great pleasure, since we are asked to give of what we have to one so much above us. Children show this visibly when asked to lend a helping hand to work usually reserved to their elders, and older folk smile pleasedly when called upon to aid in tasks beyond the sphere of daily labors wherein their lives are cast.

Yes, so it is we act with those who hold a little higher place among the pigmies of this world and yet the shame of it all, that when God asks for our aid we often find the heart to say Him nay. God, almighty and eternal, who needed not to bring a single creature out of its native nothingness, and, after having drawn it out of non-existence, needs it not, God self-sufficing in the rich amplitude of His being, at times, yes, all the time deigns to need my aid. Down from His infinite self-sufficiency He seems to descend and to need the pittance of co-operation I can give Him. Not only the sense of what is requisite for our own soul's safety and peace, but far more the consciousness of the unequaled honor of being so asked should make me quick to hearken to His call. Yet at times I refuse quite absolutely. He needs the act of my own free will that His grace may bear fruit in my life and what of the times when I will have none of that grace, because I want to do "my own sweet will"? He wants a bit of self-restraint here and a bit more of prayer there and the checking of an unruly passion elsewhere, and I find His request most inopportune! He asks of parents that they guide and mold the lives of their little ones and how many there are who put but listless hands to a work that God holds greatest? They are given the chance to help people Heaven with saints and they find it is too much trouble! Others are asked within their sphere to say a word or two to lift men's hearts above the things of time and to pour therein a bit of sunshine from another world, that sunshine which comes flooding into every heart that is gifted with the true faith, and they are afraid to say the word, ashamed to be thought "pious"!

A sad and humiliating confession surely, but is it not too sadly true? I run after the petty potentates of time and slave for them and grow weary in my work for them and count it a privilege to be thus fatigued, for it means that I shall have my name spoken along with theirs. Only when it comes to God, "King of Kings and Lord of Lords," to "serve whom is to reign," do I find such opportunities ill-timed and too exacting.

Jesus, how is it You have such patience with me? What I ordinarily grant to others, I withhold from You, and dare I make comparison? I readily yield my best to fellowman and when You ask, oh, You know but too well just what I do. You deign to need my help for my own soul and the souls of other men, and now, despite my faithless past, I thank You for this privilege. Let not my past occur again but in the future, by Your good grace, may I be ever ready, yes, and ever most eager to give You anything You ask! Let me count it highest privilege to grow weary in serving You!

EIGHTH TUESDAY AFTER PENTECOST

I WISH I HAD NEVER MET YOU

After this many of His disciples went back; and walked no more with Him. Then Jesus said to the Twelve: Will you also go away?

St. John 6:67, 68.

I WISH I had never met you!" were the words of a soul, stricken hard on the road of life. God had given a high vocation to serve Him in ways wherein most folk are wont not to walk, and His call had come and been heard and hearkened to awhile, but then poor human nature found the way hard and the darkness great, and it would fain faint and fall beside the way. But God in His mercy had sent a friend to shore up that sinking soul and to lend a guiding hand. All went well, but soon the old struggle was on and now today a pitiable, beaten form cried out: "I wish I had never met you. The ideal is too high, and the road is too rough. It is all too hard."

How often in the life of souls this happens and they almost regret they had met our Lord in a way more unusual than that of other men. To be called by Him to higher and holier living, whether out in the great reaches of the world or sheltered within the cloister, is to be honored above the sons and daughters of men. We knew that, when we heard the call. We knew, too—dimly perhaps but none the less truly—that, like every other special call, it meant more service, more self-sacrifice. But we really loved our Lord and we gladly pledged Him our love.

At the altar-step years back two young hearts pledged undying love each to each "for better or for worse . . . until death do us part," and that God-blessed love lighted the road for many a day. But then the "worse" came and the pitiful, yet seemingly inevitable, misunderstandings of life. If these grew unchecked, the day dawned when that cry burst forth, "I wish I had never known our Lord, for then I would do as worldlings do and break the marriage-bond."

In the business world they play a plunging, cruel game and there is often small reverence for the laws of God or man, provided wealth can be gained. It is hard to see other coffers being filled and to know our own could bulk as large, if only we would play a "trifle shady" game. Yet we know the right, and we know the wrong must not be done. But "it is all so hard," yes, so hard, that we must down the desire that we might be as other men, ignorant of God's true ways.

In youth we had been trained to reverence all that is pure and holy, and to feel it were an utter degradation to soil our souls in the gutters of the world. Yet, as day after day "the concupiscence of the flesh and the concupiscence of the eyes and the pride of life" beat in upon us, maybe we begin to wonder whether we are veriest fools to be so much afraid, and to think unholy what men madly seek. Maybe then we almost wish we had not known our Lord and all the purity of our Mother Mary.

Dear Jesus, I blush to say it, but sometimes I almost wish I had not met You. Deep down in my heart I am very glad and I thank You now, as I have before, that You have deigned to call me thus. But "it is all so hard" at times, so hard to hold my will firm to what You want, so hard to realize that what really counts are the things You value. The world's appeal is strong and I am but a frail human being. So help me, Lord, and never, never let me say those words: "I wish I had never met You."

EIGHTH WEDNESDAY AFTER PENTECOST

WANTING TO BE NOTICED

Lord remember me, when Thou shalt come into Thy kingdom!

St. Luke 23:42.

"YOU know the whole secret is she needs to be noticed," was the very wise diagnosis of the older woman. Blithe and lively and chipper, generous to a fault, the girl simply demanded that some one take notice of her. She did not work for that; she did not consciously hunger after it. But, there was a deep-seated craving for it in her nature. She would work, and did work without it, but with what sufferings! A quiet "Well done!" would thrill her to new, fresh efforts; omit it, and the pain of not being noticed would smart her buoyancy almost into inactivity. And the older woman in her wisdom tried always to say the word that brought the comfort that was well-deserved.

"She needs to be noticed!" How true of all of us! Some, it is true, need less than others, but every child of Adam, old or young, needs some notice, and all are the better for a bit of it. It is hard to work diligently ahead day after day, and never have a single word said to me that shows that my work is appreciated. It is discouraging to give the best that is in me and never once be told that it is at least tolerably good.

And one of the tragedies of life is that we get so little of this notice. Yet, when all is said and done, it is best for us that we do not. Some of it we ought to get, yes, and give too, for it smooths life's road out a bit. But to get too much of it would sap our energies and we might then begin to work for it, making it the test of success.

But is there not any notice we can crave and seek unstintingly, without the fear of harming ourselves? Yes, and we all know the answer. It is to be noticed by our Lord. The prime purpose of our lives is to have a final notice of approval from Him, when life is over and we stand before Him to have that life noticed and checked up in every detail. Yet we may and must want Him to notice us now too, that, when we do well, He may give us more of His grace to do even better, and that, when we act awry, His help may come to stay our wanderings from Him. His approval is what we must seek by the sheer instinct of our nature and His displeasure is the one thing we must fear.

So when men fail to notice us, as they inevitably will, and even when they notice us, it will be very wise to count only on His notice. After all, that alone is worth while.

Dear Lord, I do crave to be noticed. It is an instinct rooted deep within me. At times men notice what I do, yet very often they do not. And even if they do, their approbation is not always helpful. So I must learn to look to You, and You alone, to take lasting notice of all I do. There will be no danger then; for, when I am noticed by You, my soul is safe, and Your noticing will mean new grace. "Lord, remember me!"

EIGHTH THURSDAY AFTER PENTECOST

LEAVING HIM ALONE

Go your way, my children, go your way: for I am left alone.

Baruch 4:19.

SOLITARY confinement is the worst punishment known to man. Sorrow may tread upon the heel of sorrow, but, be there one lone friend beside us, our backs are to the wall, and we face each new antagonist to fight the victor's fight. The best of joys may come but it is all a tainted sweet, if we must taste of its cup alone. To be isolated from our fellow men, sundered from them in body, or maybe held apart from them by the deeper cleavage of differing aims and diverging views, is to carry a cross that has made strong men and women totter to their fall.

As we, so too our Lord "hates to be alone." Prisoner by choice, He never wanted to be cheated of the company of His friends, never meant to be kept in solitary confinement. Locked behind the tabernacle door, lest the careless elements or sinful man should work the sacred species harm, from earliest morn until the hours when goodly folk gather home to rest, He waits with church doors open wide, and His is a patience only God could have. Some come often, and some come now and then, and other some, as far as it touches them, leave Him most completely alone. If they were the only ones who passed along the way that leads to Him, long, long ago that path would have been overrun with grass and vagrant weeds. Of other friends they have a care, should sickness or sorrow come to hold them apart from the wonted walks of men, for then they are quick to hasten to their sides to help the creeping hours pass pleasantly along. Gifts they send, as tokens of their love, and little sweetmeats, too, and many a word of sympathy and inquiring concern. But of Christ our Lord alone they think not. The world is calling and they must hasten and must hearken, and Christ can wait and wait and wait—until they quite forget there is a hidden Friend awaiting them.

Again there are other some who come to visit our Lord, but He finds but little companionship in their presence. Their minds are far apart from His, their views so dissonant and in such harsh and utter contrast with His, their hearts so twined about with things of time, that there can be no happy interchange of what lies nearest to His Heart and theirs —and Christ is lonely in their company, and we can almost hear Him say to them: "Go your way, my children, go your way: for I am left alone." "I am become like to a pelican of the wilderness: I have watched and am become as a sparrow all alone on the housetop."

Jesus, Prisoner by Your own choosing, oh! never let me leave You so entirely alone. I am privileged to know Your love far better than most men. I know the secret yearnings of Your Sacred Heart. And shall I then be less mindful of You than I am of merely human friends? No, Jesus, no, but I shall come to see You often, come to chat with You, and in friendly wise shall while away my moments with my God. Thus, dear Lord, Your own great human Heart will have its own delight—and I my own.

EIGHTH FRIDAY AFTER PENTECOST

BLIND EYES

Father, forgive them, for they know not what they do.
St. Luke 23:34.

I AM sick and tired of the whole thing and I can't stand it any longer. One would have to be a saint to get along with him." Thus spoke an angered, fretful man, and he was but repeating words we hear very often. Nothing in life so taints and sours it as unlikeness of character. Nothing so spoils the sweetness of life as the necessity of dealing with men and women who rasp our very soul. It is indeed a difficult thing "to get on" with everybody and this is doubly, triply hard when the one who grates on us enters into the daily warp and woof of our lives, and must be met each morning, noon and night.

Of course the fault is frequently divided. I am perhaps sensitive and given to moods, and just a bit inclined to pride and prone to challenge any suspected invasion of my rights. Perhaps, indeed, I brood where a smile would chase the words away. And yet again, no slightest fault may be mine. The wrong may be wholly on one side. It may be that the one I have to deal with is nervous and fretful and quick to utter carping words, when things go ever so slightly wrong; or he may be fickle and hard to learn and thus quite hard to please, since no one can know what next he may chance to do. It may be that he is partial and favors noticeably those he likes, and holds all others to a very strict accounting for every single fault. If this be so, then it is hard, quite hard, to see life through smilingly and with the calm of Christ throughout our days.

A sense of humor should make me laugh to see the way a poor mortal can utterly spread confusion, yet at times the tragedy looms too darkly for me to wear a smile throughout, and the constant irksomeness of unpleasing ways becomes too galling for me to catch the funny side of things. Then it is that I must go out beyond the western gate of Jerusalem, and up the slope of Calvary, and kneel down beside the Cross whereon is hanging my Leader and Friend. Scarcely have I knelt and put my thoughts in prayer, when out over the sun-robbed hillside rings a prayer: "Father, forgive them, for they know not what they do!" A prayer for Judas who betrayed Him, for Peter who denied Him, for all His friends who fled and left Him alone! Do I catch His words aright? Forgive Annas who insulted Him and Caiaphas who blasphemed Him, and Herod who poked fun at Him, and Pilate who gave the order for His death! Forgive the men who are walking in front of His Cross and taunting Him, and casting up into His face that His claims are false pretenses? Forgive them! Can I kneel there and hear that prayer and then look up to my dying Lord and tell Him I cannot forgive?

Jesus, gentle, forgiving Saviour, how very, very much unlike You I am. I fret and grow moody when those about me give me annoyance. I yield to spiteful thoughts, and con and re-con the faults and failures and unlikable traits of those who grate on me, and yet You prayed for those who insulted You, and railed at You, and murdered You! Dear Jesus, give me just a bit of sense and let me learn from You patience and forgiveness. Give me blind eyes, when I would fain see faults.

EIGHTH SATURDAY AFTER PENTECOST

GOD WILL HAVE LAST SAY

Therefore, my beloved brethren, be ye steadfast and unmovable; always abounding in the work of the Lord, knowing that your labor is not in vain in the Lord.
1 Corinthians 15:58.

HE had worked hard and faithfully, and entirely for God, in a work which meant much for souls. Yet, as usually happens, jealousies had sprung up and a deal of spying and undercutting and double-crossing. Those who should have supported him, failed him and turned against him unwarrantedly. Fight ahead he did, bravely, painfully, with suffering of head and heart and body. He would not give up the fight. But the day came when the order of removal was issued—and out he went—"kicked out," as many a good man and woman before him. His heart bled much, and to assuage its bleeding, God's priest reminded him that God knew the "inside" story, that He knew the splendid work that had been done; and best of all, that God would have the "last say."

What an invigorating, steadying thought! "God will have the 'last say.'" Men may misunderstand me; they may thwart me; they may block my work; they may have me sent elsewhere, and thus ruin my efforts completely. No one may know of the cruel game played against me. To all the world my removal may be "just another change." But God knows—and He is to have the "last say."

Oftentimes within the little family circle father is quite misunderstood. He loves his own and tries in his own way to help them all he can. But everything he does is misconstrued, and a wicked meaning put upon it. Or it may be that mother slaves the entire day and plans how each moment may be used for those she loves. Yet, maybe she finds a growing isolation that seals her away from her own flesh and blood—and there is no way to clear up the difficulty.

Between friends, difficulties arise because motives are misread and deeds are misinterpreted. Explanations are not welcome, and are not accepted. The guiltless one has no redress—except to wait until God's "last say" is heard.

St. Paul knew what it meant to be thwarted and misunderstood, and to be fought against unjustly. He was lied about and misjudged by the very ones to whom he had made Christ known. His life was one long battle. No wonder that he himself could sum up one particular case (at Ephesus) so well: "For a great door and evident is opened unto me and many adversaries"—plenty of opportunity for good, plenty of good to be done, but plenty of adversaries, too. That is God's unchanging law—and we must abide by it—and suffer. Yet, we remember always that God will have the "last say."

Dear Jesus, life is a bitter potion at times. To try to do what is right and then be misunderstood; to try to further Your Kingdom on earth in souls, and then be blocked by the very ones who should be most helpful—that tries my soul beyond measure. Yet, that is what You have willed, and by that law I must abide. Yet, it is hard, dear Lord, and I do rebel at times, for it seems so utterly unjust and futile. But You know best. And so, when men thwart me and misunderstand me, I shall try to preserve my soul in peace, remembering that You know things aright, and that You will have the "last say."

NINTH SUNDAY AFTER PENTECOST

A FRIEND'S MEANNESS

For even my familiar friend, in whom I trusted, who did eat my bread, has lifted up his heel against me.

Psalm 40:10.

EVEN in the closest of human friendships, there is a point of tension beyond which there is sharp cleavage. The unwarrantable repetition of the same offense, or the wilfull accumulation of varied insults and injuries at last costs us the love of our friend, and rightly so. The least that is expected from friends is some little return of love, and so when all show of affection has ceased and in its stead ungrateful discourtesies abound, then a parting comes, and re-union is denied forever.

This we know well of purely human friendship and is that not often why we are prudently thoughtful not to try our friend too keenly? For though his love be deep, it is at best a limited love of a created being. This wholesome restraint seems not to be present in our relations with our Lord. I know it is a grievous thing to offend the God who made me, the Saviour who died for me, and the Friend who is ever present on the altar to be the food and life of my soul. I know it is traitorous to forswear my changeless Friend in any least way, and yet what of my life? Am I really as careful to avoid what displeases Him, as I am to leave undone that which would irritate an earthly friend? When I chat with Him in prayer, do I not often, very often, rudely break the conversation off and pay no least attention to my Guest? Again I have an appointment with Him every morning and evening, to greet Him as the day breaks, and when it wanes, and again each Sunday morning to come to His home to be with Him, when He once more offers Himself in sacrifice for the sins of man. Do I, with proper politeness, keep the said appointment and come with becoming promptness?

I have a pressing, very urgent, invitation from the same dear Lord to come and break my fast with Him each day and feed my soul on His nourishing Flesh and Blood. Yet time and time again I have spurned this invitation and yet other times I came and acted quite rudely, with straying mind and wandering heart, while yet my heavenly Guest was with me. Yes, at times I so far tired of His company, that I shortened the time of entertaining Him and rudely lessened the precious moments of thanksgiving after Communion. Then in all the other ways of word and work, do I show a decent respect for my Friend's feeling? Can it really be that just because I know His patience will never give, I find myself emboldened to be unwontedly discourteous? Is the very goodness of my Friend to be cruelly used as a means to injure His sensitiveness? For, indeed, our Lord is very sensitive and feels our slights and petty meannesses more than any earthly friend could ever feel them.

Jesus, was ever anyone as rude and boorish as I? The story of our friendship is a story that would make a decent man hang shameful head and yet I seem to lack all shame. I prate so loudly of my love for You and yet I do not hesitate to cause You pain, whenever and wherever I so choose. I tell all men You are my best Friend and then when we are alone, nay sometimes even before others, I start again to play my insulting part. Oh, Jesus dear, it looks all too black and yet You must forgive me. It is all a shameful lack of courtesy, sheer impudence, that earthly friend would never tolerate. But have mercy on me now, and forgive me all, and I shall strive to act more decently hereafter.

"We who can love awhile, then hate and sever,
  We who dare boast our iron wills that fail,
What can we hope from Thee, who changest never,
  Before whose steadfast light the sun grows pale?

Take Thou my iron will, change and subdue it!
  Thy will be done, not mine! Thou hast sufficed.
O meek and humble changeless God, renew it;
  Let it be dead, and rise, in Thee, O Christ!"

NINTH MONDAY AFTER PENTECOST

SEEING BUT NOT ENTERING IN

Thou shalt see the land before thee, which I will give to the children of Israel, but thou shalt not enter into it.
Deuteronomy 32:52.

THERE you are, Father, and what is the use of trying hard and playing square" were the fiercely bitten-off words of the man whom his fellows had "double-crossed." "I worked hard, yes, far into the night. I took no thought of self. I quite lost sight of personal aims and ambitions that the work assigned might go well—and look at it all! Kicked out of the firm! On the street! This grand fiasco of playing straight—Bah!" The little room was fairly vibrant with the tense energy of the thwarted man and the priest of God knew he was face to face with one of life's starkest tragedies—a man cheated of his well-earned reward, a man who had played straight in the game but found the dice were loaded; and he knew that quivering, embittered soul must be handled gently, lest the hurt mar utterly.

Life, indeed, has many disappointments and trials and it is hard to measure one against the other, for they all hurt so much and hurt variedly. Yet surely that is a searching trial which shakes strong men when, at the peak of success or as long-laid plans are just maturing and ripening unto fruitage, one is severed rudely and definitely from one's work. It may be the chance give-and-take of life, or maybe, harder still, misunderstanding, or, hardest yet, jealousy which has thrown the switch that caused the wreckage. Hard it is then to see others come and reap the harvest that has been sown and nurtured carefully with untold weariness. They stand before the world and win its praise—and the other? No man ever thinks of him, who did the work, or pays smallest tribute to his labors.

To all of us such trial may come, and it were well to steady our soul, when it does come. It may be parents have slaved, as parents do, many a year and stinted themselves in many things that their child might profit more of this world's goods than they. Then the child grows up and oftentimes mother and father are forgotten, or worse still, snubbed. The child reaps now, where it has not sown.

A teacher toils in school, and after school does much with the little ones to push back the borders of ignorance and to bring healthy discipline into romping lives; and then another, more assertive or more ingratiating, gets the credit of it all, and the one who did the drudgery is passed by. Is that an easy dose to take? Does it not need a full-grown will to stand by silently and show no lack of manners then?

So too in the world of business; so too in the ways of public service and private helpfulness. It is not an easy task of self-control to have played straight and given much of self and yet see another reap the glory of it all.

Such is life, time and time again. The trial is a hard one, but it means everything in those hours of trial to be fully conscious that we have done all for God. If, in all truthfulness, I can say that the one thing I sought was to do God's will and further His glory, then, indeed, will my cross be lightened, then, indeed, shall I reap where none can steal from me. I did it all for God and He knows it. Why, then, bother with the praise of men, a praise which has been so well described as "a dying echo from a falling wall?" Anything more unsubstantial than that? And if so unsubstantial, is it worth being hankered after?

Dear Jesus, I find it very hard when others get the meed of praise that is by every right my own. I know it is supremely foolish for me to care what men may think, but that is the way we creatures of Your handiwork are made. You know my weakness in this line and You must pity me for letting my immortal soul crave so incontinently for such a fitful, unsubstantial thing. But the stark fact is—I do. So help me, Lord, to be less foolish and to care only for the praise that comes from You.

NINTH TUESDAY AFTER PENTECOST

GOD SEES THROUGH AND THROUGH

For man seeth those things that appear, but the Lord beholdeth the heart.

1 Kings 16:7.

"AND you look so well—never better in years and years"—that was the greeting she met with everywhere. To the eyes of all, the young woman enjoyed perfect health and perfect happiness—but to herself there was a daily, hourly stabbing of internal agony, a lethargy that required a massed strength of will to overcome, a bleeding heart that had been cut and torn until each shred seemed to vibrate pain.

How often in life is that tragedy repeated! For man "seeth those things that appear," but only "the Lord beholdeth the heart." The more visible crosses of life which men see, bring from them ready and well-meant sympathy. Yet, it is those precise crosses that we may find it easier to bear. The other hidden crosses none can help us to carry, for none see or know them. Yet, they are the very ones that cut most deeply, for they are so imbedded in our souls.

Here it is a devoted husband and father, who all think has an ideal home. Yet, the horrid curse of drink has fallen upon the wife, and life behind closed doors is a veritable hell.

Here a mother who really loves her children and is truly devoted to them finds her love misconstrued, her every action misinterpreted—her every wish and command thwarted and disobeyed. Friends and relatives may know naught of the bickerings that are hourly occurrences when no others are around to hear them.

A young man or woman wears a brave smile, and seemingly dances through life most merrily. Yet, if one were to know, that laugh is but the forced echo of pain and the tripping feet are leaden-soled. Back in the home the problems are many and dark, and few have any inkling that they exist.

Our worst troubles are not, and cannot be, "worn on our sleeves." We must bear them alone. Yes, quite absolutely alone so far as other human beings go. But not alone, if we but turn to God.

There is no sorrow that is too concealed for His all-searching eye to detect; there is no heartache He cannot find; there is no cross which can be carried unseen by Him. To Him we can go at any time and in any place, and our coming cannot be ill-timed. To Him we may speak about any trial and cross, and He will know whereof we speak without further question. We can go to Him in any mood, sad or joyous, patient or peevish, and He will understand. With that consoling conviction we shall find little difficulty in taking up our crosses and following Him.

Dear Jesus, thank You for the invitation to take up my cross and follow You. To bear my cross alone is intolerable, and yet I can never show my heaviest cross and cruelest trial to human eyes. The hurt is too deep for human touch. It is so good, then, to know that You read me through and through, and that there can be nothing in my life hidden from You. That makes me brave; and with Your grace, I will try to follow You no matter how rough life's road may be—for You understand.

NINTH WEDNESDAY AFTER PENTECOST

GOD IS LOOKING

Thy Father, who seeth in secret, will repay thee.
St. Matthew 6:18.

AND you know our Lord could not possibly be thinking of you more if no one else existed than He is thinking of you now. And yet, you sit there and say that He does not care!" The poor woman winced a bit, and hung her head. Then quietly, shamedly, but very definitely she murmured: "I'm sorry, Father, but I forgot all this. But God knows it's gone hard with me." Yes, it had gone hard, very hard, and all her life seemed to be tumbling down about her. Yet, it did help her to know that God was watching it tumble, and had His own good reasons for letting it so tumble.

Certainly life has brought many a cross to each of us, and doubtless has many more hidden from us in the future. The dead weight of it all nearly crushes us at times; and even the lesser ones chafe and nag us almost beyond endurance.

All men suffer thus: pagan and Jew and Protestant and Catholic alike. It is part of man's warfare, which we call life. Am I to expect to be different from others just because Christ our Lord has called me to His Church? Has He promised me Heaven now, or only as a reward, when I have "fought the good fight" according to the rules He has laid down?

Of course it is hard. I would not be human if I did not feel the hurt. And therein precisely lies my merit—that it does all hurt, and I take it and "offer it all up." Just to "grit my teeth and see it through" does not help very much. But it does spur me on to know that here and now, when all is dark and my trials gall me almost to rebellion, God is looking at me, and has such special care of me that He could not have more if I alone existed. It does nerve my heart to "keep on going" though the cross almost pins me to the ground, to realize that each moment God sees me, and each moment sends me grace, and each moment counts another victory to my credit. Infinite in knowledge, He is not distracted from me and from what is happening to me, even though unnumbered myriads claim the same attention from Him. He simply could not be more attentive of me and of my wants, if He and I alone existed.

Dear Jesus, what a thought to feed new courage into my soul, to know that always and everywhere Your whole attention is centered on me! The way of life is hard at times, so hard that I want to quit and lie down and "let things slide." But I cannot act thus if I know You are watching me and caring for me and noting my every effort. Dear Jesus, thanks for Your watchfulness—and please, never let me forget it.

NINTH THURSDAY AFTER PENTECOST

LIFE'S UPS AND DOWNS

And the Lord will create, upon every place of Mount Sion and where He is called upon, a cloud by day and a smoke and brightness of flaming fire in the night: for over all the glory shall be a protection. And there shall be a tabernacle for a shade in the daytime from the heat, and for a security and covert from the whirlwind and from rain.
Isaias 4:5, 6.

NO man's life runs smoothly and unbrokenly. To us all in God's good time comes the constant interchange of light and shade, that perfects so well the great masterpiece we call our life. Sorrow comes and joy rides close behind in the shadows. Today we sit about our fireside and no darkness reigns in our little home, tomorrow the vacant chair tells once again its world-old story. Life is a hard reality, at times a very hard reality, so hard that our poor hearts are affrighted at the gaunt vision of our own cheated dreams. Childhood days pictured a fairyland where "grown-ups" moved and were wondrously happy, envied masters of themselves. But childhood days have faded into the misty past and with them their fairyland, and time has made life tell its own true changing story. Grief has long since burdened our faltering hearts: grief for those that are with us no more; grief for the living whose wayward lives make it hard to check the ever-rising prayer that God had deigned long since to call them to Himself; grief for our own sad mistakes that maybe line all too closely our waning days. But then as day drives back then night, joy, too, has come: the joy of well-merited success and the fullness of heart as we told our loved ones the long story of efforts crowned at last; the joy of father and mother as they watch their little ones growing into maturity, safe-shielded from the world's dark shafts; the joy of holy men and women who have prevented the sun with their cloistered rising to praise their God and labor all day in the classroom or at the bedside of the sick, teaching souls to love the God who made them.

Life has its sorrows and life has its joys, too, but its sorrows will be all too heavy and its joys will be tainted and unsanctified unless we bring them one and all to the foot of the altar. There is the "tabernacle for a shade in the daytime from the heat," the daytime of pleasure when all is well with us and we are prone to forget our God, and "for a security and covert from the whirlwind and from rain," and the darkness of trial and overburdening grief. To us the Prophet Balaam speaks in ways beyond his knowing: "How beautiful are thy tabernacles, O Jacob, and thy tents, O Israel"—the tabernacles where Emmanuel dwells, the tents where the Son of Man lingers yet a while—"as woody valleys, as watered gardens near the rivers, as tabernacles which the Lord hath pitched, as cedars by the waterside!" There is our good Master, Rabboni, waiting for us in the dawnlight as He waited of old for Magdalene; listening for our footfall at eventide, even as He listened for the knocking of the sick and the halt at His humble home in Galilee. He will be to us "a cloud by day and a smoke and brightness of flaming fire in the night," ever guiding, ever leading us on unswervingly to our home beyond the grave.

Jesus, gentle Saviour, God of wondrous forethought for those You love, life is all too strange a problem for me to face alone. I need You for my guide, that I fail not in the dark and wander not in the noonday of my powers. Be close to me, then, good Jesus, and leave me not alone. I know You do not, but what I mean is, make me know, make me remember that You are with me always. When the sun of life shines full, make me mindful of You, the Man of Sorrows, "who having joy set before Him endured the Cross, despising the shame," and when the night of grief steals from us the light we love so much, let me remember that "this everyone is sure of that worshippeth Thee, that his life, if it be under trial, shall be crowned: and if it be under tribulation, it shall be delivered: and if it be under correction, it shall be allowed to come to mercy. For Thou art not delighted in our being lost: because after a storm Thou makest a calm and after tears and weeping Thou pourest in joyfulness."

"When all the world is comfortless,
  And wrapped in gloom as black as night,
Remind me, Lord, in my distress
  One spot on earth is always bright—
    The Tabernacle."

NINTH FRIDAY AFTER PENTECOST

IT IS GOD'S BATTLE

The battle is not yours, but God's.
2 Paralipomenon 20:15.

JOSAPHAT, the king of Juda, "stood in the midst of the assembly of Juda and Jerusalem, in the house of the Lord, before the new court." Their enemies, "the children of Ammon, and of Moab, and Mount Seir," were warring against them to cast them out of the Promised Land, given to them generations back by God. Hope there was none from human hands; and so, before God's altar, king and people prayed:

"As for us we have not strength enough to be able to resist this multitude, which cometh violently upon us. But as we know not what to do, we can only turn our eyes to Thee."

And God's answer was:

"The battle is not yours, but God's.... It shall not be you that shall fight; but only stand with confidence and you shall see the help of the Lord over you."

And God did help, and the children of Ammon and of Moab and of Mount Seir destroyed each other; for "the Lord turned their ambushments upon themselves."

The battle is not yours, but God's! What a wealth of hope and of trust is hidden in those words! And they are as applicable to each of us today as they were to Josaphat over two thousand years ago.

Of course, some of our petty schemes for ourselves, some of our self-willed plans are not God's; and, when matters go awry, we cannot in any least honesty put them up to God as His.

But the really big things of life, the issues that touch my soul, these are God's. When reverses come and our souls are rocked to their very foundations, and our faith grows weak and hope dims utterly, and "we know not what to do" to make firm again the very foundations of life, then it is that the battle is surely not ours, but God's.

And in the decision of our state of life, when we stand at the crossroads and know not what path to follow, there again the struggle is not ours, but God's.

And the lesser trials and temptations of life, wherein our souls are formed, these, too, are God's concern; for our victory or defeat will be carried out through all eternity.

But do we realize this quite clearly? If we do, then we go often before God's altar and cry out, as Josaphat did:

"But as we know not what to do, we can only turn our eyes to Thee."

But do we go? Or, rather, do we have recourse to human aid, or sit in isolation, bemoaning our hopeless lot? And all the while God wants, with our aid, to win *His* battle!

Dear Jesus, what unbounded confidence I should have in You and Your all-powerful help! The battles of life are hard at times and I get very much discouraged. But should I grow so disheartened, if I clearly realized that my battles, my struggles were not so much mine as Yours? Give me much grace, then, to come to You, and to plead with You to win Your own battles!

NINTH SATURDAY AFTER PENTECOST

DEAD DREAMS IN THEIR EYES

After this many of His disciples went back, and walked no more with Him.

St. John 6:67.

THERE she sat—not insolent, not aggressive—just there. "No, Father, I don't even want to be helped. It's not that I intend to do wrong. I have done wrong, and if he recovers, probably will do wrong again. I don't know. But I just don't care either way any longer."

And as the priest sat and looked into her eyes, dead dreams looked out. There before him was a corpse. Not the corpse of a body, but the more terrifying soul-corpse from which life had fled. And the dead dreams in her eyes laid icy hands upon him.

That woman had had her fair dreams of womanly virtue. She had long held to them, from girlhood into maturity and on through the years. But reading had done much to tarnish her ideals, and companions had struck again and again at them, and professors in the classroom had sneered at them—and slowly but surely the vision faded, and life was now a dread, drab, dull thing which held out nothing.

Dead dreams in her eyes! And as the priest pondered how he might re-light those dreams, his thoughts swept over the world and peered deep into the throngs of men.

Here were young folk who were being trained in Godless schools, and from their souls were daily snatched the dreams that are childhood's rightful heritage. "There was no God, there is no God, there can be no God" rang out of the classrooms of Russia and Mexico. "There are no Ten Commandments" sounded across the teacher's desk in almost every non-sectarian university in the world. And the dreams had not even a chance to die!

Men and women of older years had learned of God and His manifold goodness. But flippant philosophers and near-thinkers had turned their thin minds from such deeper thoughts, and had taught them to fill their souls with the husks of the things of time. And lean, hungry eyes met his own, and God's priest knew that once again the age-old famine was upon the land.

But sadder sights swept before him. Within Catholic homes, and beyond cloistered walls, and even within the sanctuary rail, gazed out eyes dimmed with fading and faded dreams. Christ had won their younger hearts, Christ had heard them pledge their love to Him—undividedly as priest or nun, or shared with human love in holy wedlock—and Christ had blessed that love and sealed it as His own. And then the years swung slowly by, and the friction of life rasped hard, and the baubles of time took on fresh allurements—and Christ seemed not so lovable, and his wishes not so worth while—and the vision began to dim. Dead dreams of Christ in Catholic eyes!

Dear Jesus, You have been good enough to teach me much of Your love and to win my love in return. I know You are worthy of the best that is in me, and that, try as I may, I can never be worthy of Your love or measure up to Your ideals. But the world is loud in its clamors, and the things of the world beckon very appealingly, and at times it is quite a task to hold my vagrant heart from truancy. But I do want to keep the vision bright, and I do want to love and serve You always—and so, please never let there be in my eyes dead dreams of You!

TENTH SUNDAY AFTER PENTECOST

SHORT-SIGHTED CHILDREN

Are not two sparrows sold for a farthing? And not one of them shall fall on the ground without your Father. But the very hairs of your head are all numbered. Fear not therefore: better are you than many sparrows.

St. Matthew 10:29-31.

I CAN picture you busy with important work, writings, vital questions, and important people. Then I can see you stop, and answer, and grant a request from one so small as I." Thus he read and the great man smiled almost wistfully as he handed me the note. "Father, doesn't that make you feel like a two-cent piece?" He was a busy man, yes, with affairs of state and public functions and all that goes with high office. And he was a great man too, because he was truly humble, and could forget all the "big stuff" and lay it all aside to listen to the lowliest. Then as I sat, I thought of One greater than he, who had important things to do, who ruled the universe and poised the stars in their places and traced the way of the planets; who made the sun to shine by day and the moon by night. Yet He pays strictest heed to each and every one of His creatures. None so small that it can escape His notice; none so unimportant that He fails to mark its every move.

Yet how often in our foolishness or in our discouragement we tell ourselves that God is not listening to us, that He does not hear our prayers, and is not interested in our problems. And for proof of this we cite His failure to answer our prayer the way we want, and the continuance of the anxieties wherein we find ourselves.

And yet if my faith means anything at all, it means that God has a very personal, intimate interest in me as an individual. I stand out from the crowd, isolated and unique, before God. Christ Himself has told me this in no unmistakable words: "Art not two sparrows sold for a farthing? And not one of them shall fall to the ground without your Father. But the very hairs of your head are all numbered. Fear not, therefore: better are you than many sparrows" (St. Matthew 10:29-31). If the very hairs of our head are counted by God—and they are of such trivial importance—can we evince the least doubt that all else is known and noted by Him?

He is busy, yes, as only God can be busy; busy with infinite details, yet that does not tax His omnipotence or distract one iota of His attention from the briefest happening to His smallest creature. And if He does know all and does note all, is it then at all sensible to complain when He does not answer my prayer just the way I want Him to, or does not lift my burdens and crosses every time I ask Him? May He not have larger views than I and see things better than I? And may not I and my worries and trials fit into a bigger plan that He Himself has fashioned? Children rebel at class and at the efforts of parent and of teacher to train them. But parent and teacher have a larger view of life and look beyond the present moment to the later days when the child must work out life's problems maturely and alone. And may we not be just as short-sighted as unruly children?

Dear Jesus, I grow restive at times and become quite impatient with You when You do not answer my prayer just the way I want. In my calmer moments I realize that this is very unmannerly and shows that I am too much wrapped up in my own little self and my own small plans. I ought to be bigger and ought to see life in a bigger way, the way You see it from the watch-towers of eternity. I am sorry for my petulance in the past and promise, with Your grace, never again to act like a short-sighted child.

TENTH MONDAY AFTER PENTECOST

KEEPING THE PAST IN MIND

Thou shalt not molest a stranger, nor afflict him: for yourselves also were strangers in the land of Egypt.

Exodus 22:21.

THE Jews had fled from Egypt, had crossed the sea dry-shod and were now camped in the great plain of er-Rahah at the foot of Sinai, "the mountain of God." There for eleven long months they were taught by God through Moses, and today they are listening to solemn words that chide them unto justice and all fair dealing. They are told to be mindful of their own hard past, of the days and the weeks and the months and the years of their own exiled labor and slavery in the land of the Pharaos, that when strangers would come to them, and ask harborage and succor from their hands, they might be merciful and hearken to their prayers.

To remember our own sad and sinful past is to bring a steadying and maturing force into our lives. Not that we must see only the dark spots that fleck our outswept years, for that would be unfair to self and hardly decent to the generosity of our Lord. Yet we must keep our failures well in sight and with healthy introspection view and review the times and manners of our falls, that we may not "molest a stranger, nor afflict him," since we ourselves "also were strangers in the land of Egypt."

If we recall the days, when angry words escaped us and we quite lost that poise of character that befits even pagan men and women, we shall have a bit of patience when another acts with the same childish lack of control wherewith we have so often acted. When others rasp our very souls and unthinkingly ride rough-shod over our high-strung nerves, would it not be very helpful to go back into the past and recall how often we have unwittingly, wholly unintentionally made other hearts bleed? Yes, and even if the pain be deliberately and wilfully inflicted on us, may there not be at least a few occasions in the bygone days, when we, too, mercilessly found it within ourselves to cut and wound and take gloating pleasure in making another exiled heart go aching? Again we find others following low, or maybe lowered, ideals, and our foolish hearts are wroth within us, and we would play the harsh censor; but not if we remember the days when we, too, gave up the quest of higher things and slackened in our one-time zeal for the ways of sanctity. Prayers neglected or apparently ill-said will make us think of many a morning and evening when we were scant in our politeness to God. Petty deceits will bring up the picture of actions on our part that we would not have scrutinized too closely, and ways quite selfish and self-centered will make us blush because of their striking likeness to the many, many acts wherein the "I" was all that could be seen.

Jesus, dearest Lord, remember that years and years ago to that same strange, olden folk You said: "I am the Lord, thy healer." Oh, heal me then and cleanse me clean of all that is displeasing in Your sight. I learn so little from my past, I profit so scantily from experience. I know my own pitiable frailty, and yet when I see a fellow-struggler fall, I am so prone to lift an accusing finger, so quick to raise a chiding voice. Give me grace, then, I beg of You, plentiful grace that I may always keep fresh the memory that I, too, have been "a stranger in Egypt."

TENTH TUESDAY AFTER PENTECOST

REVERENT OF GOD

And I have been with thee wheresoever thou hast walked.
2 Kings 7:9.

THERE is always a sense of reverence, of subduedness in a holy person. About them we catch that atmosphere of restraint that is present in every decent man and woman when they stand in the presence of properly constituted authority. There is poise, of course, and an adult graciousness of manner and yet no least cowardice in us when we find ourselves before those who rightly rule their fellow men, but at the same time we demean our ways and we guard our movements out of reverence for the power that is laid upon them.

So too with holy folk. Wherever they be, within the walls of cloister or of private home, in the classroom or out lecturing, at work or in the hours of recreation, their every word and act, however trivial they be, bespeak the presence of Another, whom they reverence as their superior. God is unmistakably present with them and they are quite noticeably in His presence, and yet they may say no single word of Him. He is there —that is all—and out, full tangibly, on their lives is stamped their humility before their present King.

Does aught of this high sense of proper conduct in the abiding presence of God find itself in my life? There is no use of trying to put it there deliberately, for it cannot be plastered on from the outside. It must be a gentle, quiet growth that has its hidden roots in the very inner consciousness of God's seeing eye and His unlimited presence. And does my mind thus unbrokenly tell itself that here is God, and there is God, and everywhere is God? Out to mid-ocean I go and God was and is there before me. Up to the mountain-top I climb, and ever as I climb God is with me. I stay at home and He is there; I go abroad and I leave Him not behind. Into the market-place I go and I find Him amid the barterings of men, and thence I go to seek an hour of lawful pleasure and I know He is with me in theater and in the dance-hall, in the drawing-room and down upon the beach, and out upon the motor-trail.

God everywhere, in every place, and God, too, there at every moment! Day breaks the East and finds God with the earth and the folk He has made. Noon comes and God watches men rest from their labors even as

He rested when the seventh day came. The shadows of night close in on a tired world and, even as kindly mother sees her little ones to rest, so God closes "tired eyelids upon tired eyes" and watches while His children sleep.

Surely no man can think thereon and not be reverent. Ever before the King of kings and Lord of lords, I cannot bring myself to do aught that would offend His majesty or show myself untutored in the manners of His court. And so I shun all sin, and more than that, I try to take on knightly ways before Him and to become a saint; for saintliness is mere politeness in His presence.

Dear Lord, I have often wondered what it was in Your holy folk that made me feel uplifted when I met them. I know the answer now; it is their reverence for You, their King, in whose presence they conduct themselves as courtiers. I, too, would be as they, and so I pray that You grant me an unbroken consciousness of Your presence in the evening and when the morning breaks and all through the hours of the day. Wherever I may be, whatever I may do, give me the grace to realize abidingly that You, my God, are looking on. Then I, too, shall be reverent of God.

TENTH WEDNESDAY AFTER PENTECOST

KNOWING MY FRIEND

Grace to you and peace be accomplished in the knowledge of God and of Christ Jesus, our Lord.

2 Peter 2:2.

ONE of the keenest pleasures of friendship is the study of my friend. To sit long hours through, and to look deeper and deeper into a soul whose aims are lofty and noble, to sound a heart that ever responds to highest appeal, that is my privileged pleasure when I am with my friend. Each time I come, new folds are laid back and hitherto hidden recesses of his character give up their treasure to me. Then, when I bid him a lingering farewell, my mind is full of crowded thoughts and my heart leaps eagerly to respond to the call that has come from out his soul to mine, urging me on to the highest heights of virtue.

So, too, it ought to be and is with Christ our Lord. My keenest pleasure ought to be to con and recon the lessons of His holy life, to read between the lines of His sacred Word and find therein new meaning, as the days of our friendship lengthen. My greatest joy should be to meditate again and yet again each slightest trait, each smallest deed of my best of friends. I look upon Him before the world began, hidden in the bosom of His Father, the inner spoken Word of God, yet speechless with the thunderous silence of Divinity. I see Him leap the bounds of space and time and tarry nine long months in Mary's womb and I begin to realize what lowliness of mind can mean. Poverty I learn and complete dependence, too, on those God places in authority, as I study that Sacred Heart at Bethlehem, in Egypt and at Nazareth. Then, when the years have brought the age of manhood, the carpenter of the Galilean village will teach me lessons of hidden toil and enduring prayer, love for His own and care for their sanctification. In after days, along the Jordan and in Perea and up where the sea washes the shores of Tyre and Sidon, in Jerusalem and in Capharnaum He will show forth a consuming zeal, a royal eagerness for souls. Then, when men have had their way and hunted Him to death, the lessons of pain and utter ignominy are read in that Heart where alone they can be read aright. Oh, "the unsearchable riches of Christ!" I read His Heart and then again I read, thinking to know it well, only to find, each time I return to the pleasant task, my own shortsightedness. The richest of human characters is there and the inexhaustible, limitless nature of God is also there. Sound to the right or fathom to the left, reach up or delve down and still we find new treasure-trove. And are we happy in our quest and jubilant at our findings? The answer comes, when we answer another question: "Is Christ my friend?"

Jesus, dearest Lord, how pleasant a privilege meditation shows itself to be. It is all a study of Your own dear self, a seeking to know You better, that I may love You more and follow You more closely. From earliest years I have been taught the lessons of Your life and yet I have a deal, a great, great deal to learn about Your own dear self. So teach me to love my prayers and, when I pray, let me learn more and more each time, until that day when You come to call me home. Then I shall see You face to face to know You well throughout eternity. Then, indeed, shall grace and peace be accomplished abidingly within my heart.

TENTH THURSDAY AFTER PENTECOST

GOD MADE ME PURPOSELY

Thou hast ordered all things in measure, and number, and weight.

Wisdom 11:21.

ONE of the major things to realize in life is that God had a set purpose in mind when He made *me,* that He had a very definite idea what He wanted *me* to be and what He wanted *me* to do. That puts a special stamp on my life and gives a determination and a precision to my whole outlook.

I am not here by chance, a by-product of an evolution that is headed nowhere, but just happens to be putting out new products of its own unending changefulness. I come definitely from somewhere—from God. I am headed definitely toward somewhere—toward God. In the meanwhile I have something quite definite to do—something set by God.

My origin, my purpose, my work in life, is precisely what we mean by a vocation in life. Vocation means "calling," something to which God is calling, is inviting me. It may be that I have not yet been able to decide just what it is to which God is beckoning me. Then I must pray that I may hear His call clearly and hearken to it readily.

It may be that He calls me to a married life, when I shall pledge my love and loyalty and receive in return a like pledged love and loyalty. Then will God want us both to seal that love within His love and guide our blended lives according to His law. Hand in hand He would have us walk Heavenward and make the way thither a holy and happy one.

Or He may be calling me to give Him my undivided love and to serve Him alone within the sanctuary of cloistered walls. He will be a jealous lover and will want my all of love. And in return? He will give me lavishly of His love and fill my soul with grace and give me a peace that the world does not know and cannot take away. Will my way be a lonely one? Yes, if one can be lonely with God.

Or again He might be asking me, through circumstances over which I have no control, to forego the happiness of marriage and yet to live outside the cloister. Those at home demand my time and care and support. Or sickness forbids to me those other ways of living. Then God is calling me definitely to serve Him. The sacrifice may be a very great one; but if I make it cheerfully and for Him and because He wants it, then I can reach great sanctity, because I am co-operating with God's plans for me.

Dear Jesus, I want to make of my life, just what You want it to be. I want to serve You at all times, cheerfully and willingly and generously. In every place and under all circumstances I want to carry out Your plans. You made me purposely, and I want to fulfill that purpose no matter what it is.

TENTH FRIDAY AFTER PENTECOST

FALL IN LOVE WITH GOD

But you, my beloved, building yourselves upon your most holy faith, praying in the Holy Ghost, keep yourselves in the love of God, waiting for the mercy of our Lord Jesus Christ, unto life everlasting.

St. Jude 1:20, 21.

WELL, the rooms are rather small, and I am not over-pleased with the neighborhood, but– Well, Mary wants it–and I guess it's all right."

"Mary wants it"–that solved the problem and made quite satisfactory things which would otherwise have been distasteful. For as St. Augustine said many hundred years ago: "Where there is love, there is no toil; or if there is toil, the toil is loved." So Bill was willing to overlook the things he did not like, because Mary wanted them–for Bill and Mary were in love and were planning their first home.

Love makes all things easy. That is why we would be very wise to fall desperately in love with God. Life has many joys and happinesses, but life has many a shadow, too, and many a cross. None of us finds it hard to accept life's joys, but we need help to manage life's trials aright. And they will be managed aright when we know God and see His guiding hand in everything and love Him above everything.

Differences inevitably arise between husband and wife. Sooner or later the surface thrill of newly won love wears off, and straight and colorless years lie ahead. And when the gilt is worn off, it is so easy for them to let things get "messed up" if they think only of themselves and their petty selfishness. But it is so easy, too, to take the jolts of life with a smile and to shoulder the crosses as they come if God's love has remained lighted in their hearts.

Between friend and friend old joy wanes and sharp clashes break in upon comradeship. This seems to be almost unavoidable. Yet if both still love God, the "spat" is soon forgotten, and the friendship is resumed.

The same holds true in my own individual life. If life brings weakened health and pain of body, I shall withal be mannerly; none will see me straining at the leash; for there will be little straining when once I realize that God has sent me these crosses. If my pet plans go awry and my castles in the air dissolve, the fact that God has allowed these things to happen makes me accept the frustrations readily. For He knows best; and I am in love with God.

If only we would really fall in love with God! What a changed thing life would be! There are times when His law seems so hard; His law seems to cheat me of so much that I want, so much to which I seem to have a right. That law binds me here and checks me there; so often it cramps my style. Yes. It binds and checks me, unless I love God and love Him with my whole heart and soul. Half-love has never yet made anything easy. But true love can make of a squalid neighborhood a garden. And if love between man and woman can and does do that, what will not the love between man and God do?

Dear Jesus, even from a selfish standpoint I ought to love You. But selfishness is quite an unworthy motive. I want to love You for Your own sake and because of all You are and all that You have given me. Then, whether sun shines or clouds gather, life will be filled with peace, that peace of Yours which the world cannot give and cannot take away. Dear Lord, grant that I may fall in love with You.

TENTH SATURDAY AFTER PENTECOST

SOLE SOURCE OF KNOWLEDGE

Pride is hateful before God and men.
Ecclesiasticus 10:7.

THE office was in quite a state of hushed excitement. Clerk winked at clerk, and the "higher-ups" walked about with a knowing look stamped upon their faces. It was Monday morning and the District Superintendent's door was open and her chair was vacant—she had gone. Resigned? No, she had been fired. Yes, fired by order of headquarters and every one knew why. "You just could not tell her anything. She knew it all!"

One of the saddest states into which a human being can fall is that of omniscience. For a man to consider that he is the sole depositary of all knowledge and wisdom; to deem that he has always and everywhere the one and only correct solution; to judge it sheer imprudence and impudence for anyone to initiate any program without previous consultation with him is sheer madness.

Such mad insolence afflicts few of us because most of us have sense enough to realize that we have some limitations. But may we not be guilty in part of such know-it-all-ness? It is so easy for me to get into the habit of thinking that my opinion is really worth having, at least along certain lines; and that I really should be consulted when certain plans and programs are under discussion. I may quite readily admit that I know little about gold-mining or sheep-raising, but—

And how can I tell whether I do consider myself an oracle? How? Just by watching my own mind and its reactions when I am not consulted. I do not wince when my opinion is not asked on astral physics, but do I wince when I am not permitted to express my views on running a home? I do not chafe if I am not called into conference on how to build a pig-pen; but do I when there is question of how to teach class?

That little wince, that slight sense of hurt, that almost undetectible feeling of chagrin—those are the infallible signs that I do consider myself a "somebody" along those lines. Of course, I need not consider myself a nitwit or an ignoramus. My common sense tells me I do know some things well and can do some things well. But it is a bit of pride when I consider that I know and do them so well that I and my opinions must be brought into the picture all the time.

Dear Jesus, give me just ordinary common sense. It is so silly for me to preen my feathers and to strut about; and it must be so distressing to You; for You have told me: "Learn of Me because I am meek and humble of heart." I have some talents, of course; and I certainly do not fumble everything I take up. But even though that be true, how false I am to You and to my own better self to let my pride grow over it! So help me please to keep my balance and my common sense as well. I just cannot know it all, even along one line.

ELEVENTH SUNDAY AFTER PENTECOST

ANYHOW—I DID IT ALL FOR GOD!

For the Lord searcheth all hearts and understandeth all the thoughts of minds.

1 Paralipomenon 28:9.

LONG had she worked and hard, as year after year was told off. Not a child in the school missed her kindly vigilant eye; not a penny had been spent foolishly; not one teacher had a single complaint against her. Then suddenly, swiftly, devastatingly, she was torn from her work, and her successor started right in to change everything overnight, to condemn all that was done, completely ruining the morale of teachers and pupils alike. There she sat—almost broken, quite stunned. Then slowly, painfully, lifting her bowed head, she said softly but firmly and with a confidence born of another world: "Anyhow, Father, I did it all for God."

The tragedy of that woman's life is repeated in the lives of so many. But how many can speak as confidently of their motives as she? What matters it if every bit of the work I have done is scattered to the winds if "I did it all for God"? After all, no human work lasts long, and all will perish at least when the Day of Judgment comes. Of course it is hard to see the well-worked-out schemes of years tossed into the waste-paper basket. Of course it hurts to see real good undone by a witless "know-it-all." But what of it—provided we did it all for God? It is smashed to pieces in time; but the reward of it all will last throughout eternity. A man or woman or a group of them condemns what I have done as worthless; God, whose judgment alone counts in the long run, places His seal of approval thereon, and that approval will never be reversed by Him or by anyone else.

So that must be our motive throughout life, in everything we do: the big things and the little things; the flashy things and the hidden things: the serious things and the playful things. Whatever we do, we do for God—at least ultimately. We eat to keep our health and because we like it, but we "offer it up." We study because it is our duty to prepare ourselves for our adult life, and we "offer it up." We dance and go to the movies because it is right for us to have a deal of pleasure in life, but we "offer it up," too, so that all pleasures are sanctified. We go to Mass and we receive Holy Communion that our souls may be more holy, and we go, too, to please Almighty God.

"Doing it for God" does not mean that we must of necessity do extraordinary things. Few of us have the chance to do "big" things. But it does mean that I do each and every job in life the way I ought, and take every pleasure in life the way I ought; and when and as and while I do it, I ask God to bless it and I tell Him that I am doing it for Him. That will make the hard things less hard and the pleasant things more pleasant. It would be easier to study if our Lord were with me, would it not? And would not the ice-cream soda taste better if He sat beside me—as He did at the wedding feast of Cana?

"Doing it for God" will mean success in life, unending, unlosable success. My plans may go astray, my work may be thwarted, my pleasures may be spoiled—in my own eyes and before the eyes of men. But from God they will win approval. And when all is said and done, is not His approval the one that is worth most?

Dear Jesus, life at best is a hard game and many lose badly, even when they play well and hard. Of course I want to succeed even in a worldly sense. But success before men and in this world is very unimportant after all. To be a success in Your eyes and for eternity is what I want most; and I know I can be that if I do everything for You. So please give me much grace at all times and in all places to offer up the hard things and the pleasant things to You and to "do it all for God."

ELEVENTH MONDAY AFTER PENTECOST

AN EPIC OUT OF TWO GRUNTS

These things I command you, that you love one another.
St. John 15:17.

IT was a movie "location" and the filming of the picture was being held up because of a thumping fight between two actors as to which one would grunt the two grunts called for in that scene. Suddenly the "boss" appeared, sized up the situation, and then roared like a bull:

"Jumping Piltdown elephants! Don't make an epic out of two grunts!"

It sounds very comic—doesn't it?—and very stupid too. But what occurred then, goes on unfortunately a thousand times a day in human lives: at home, at school, in the office, in social affairs; and the squabble over "two grunts" can bring much unhappiness and offset great good.

Some little thing goes wrong at home, and, instead of overlooking it, father "flies off the handle." A child is troublesome at just the wrong time and mother gets into a rage that is quite uncalled for. A son or daughter asks for some small permission that is denied and, forgetful of obedience, "stages a scene." All could have been forgotten in a moment; but instead, the peace and harmony of home is lost for many a long hour.

In the office, a clerk makes some trifling "fool mistake" and, instead of remembering that such mistakes are almost bound to happen, the poor clerk is "put on the carpet" and thoroughly "hauled over the coals." It was a mistake, yes—but was it any bigger than "the two grunts" of the movie scene? Or maybe the boss is out of sorts and snaps out an order quite rudely, and the clerks will get into tantrums and stage a "slow-down" in the work, whereas they could best handle the situation by a shrug of the shoulders and an "Oh, let's forget the old man's grouch!"

Maybe a committee is formed and I wanted to be chairman, and some one else is appointed for that so-called "position." Or a teacher is named for a higher class which I had hoped to get. Or a play is to be staged at school or in the parish or by my club, and I am not chosen for the part upon which I had set my heart. It is easy then—and quite natural, though equally quite unseemly—to pout and to get bitter. Any child can do that, just as the "ham" actors could over the two grunts.

But is all this sensible? Will it make one iota of difference one hundred years from now? Will it make the slightest eddy in the whirlpool of history? Will "generations yet unborn" read tearfully of the gross injustice done me?

And is it what our Lord would wish? Honestly, if He were present on the scene, am I certain that He would approve my way of acting? Hardly. "My peace I leave you; My peace I give you"; "A new commandment I give unto you: that you love one another as I have loved you, that you also love one another"; "These things I command you, that you love one another"; "But I say to you, love your enemies: do good to them that hate you: and pray for them that persecute and calumniate you: that you may be the children of your Father who is in Heaven." His command was love, repeated, insisted upon, and made the test of being His disciple. Surely He could never approve of making "an epic out of two grunts."

Dear Jesus, give me a bit of common sense, and, more than that, give me a bit of Your own poise. There are many things in life that bring irritation and friction. Others *are* thoughtless and inconsiderate at times, and even unjust. But I would be more of a grown-up and more of a Christian if I handled the upsets in a seemly, self-controlled way. It's all very clear to me now in the quiet of prayer, but it is not so clear at the moment when things snap wrong. And so I beg You now to give me then, and always, grace enough not to make "an epic out of two grunts."

ELEVENTH TUESDAY AFTER PENTECOST

LIVING OUR LESSONS

But you have not so learned Christ.
Ephesians 4:20.

ST. PAUL is speaking to the Ephesians, and warning them not to return to their former evil ways from which their conversion to Christ had won them. They are to "put off the old man," which meant all the evil ways of acting which they had learned as pagans: impurity, disobedience, hatred, quarreling, self-seeking, and a complete surrender to a mad attempt to have all the pleasures of this world without any restraint. They had become Christians now, and had "learned Christ"—learned what He thought, what He desired, what He wanted them to do, and what He wanted them to avoid. Living in a city that was notorious for its vice and thorough rottenness, wherein temptation was ever present, St. Paul warned them to be on their guard, for they "had not so learned Christ."

That warning is sound for us all today. Ephesus was filthy, and the world today is following Ephesus closely. Today we have the lewd dance, the vile show in theater or restaurant, the sex-drenched novel, the cult of nakedness at the beaches. In unmarried life there is openly approved freedom between the sexes. In married life, a sinful birth-control is practised, divorce is quite the ordinary thing. In the business world, men of the old standards of decency are rare; and politics and public office is rife with graft and scandal.

But we Catholics "have not so learned Christ." We know His law and His counsels: purity and modesty; honesty and truthfulness; self-restraint and self-control. All that is highest in life He stands for; all that is noblest, all that is truest. He is no "kill-joy," no thwarter of our happiness. But He must insist that we be true to the basic demands of our nature. And, while not obliging us thereto, He does hold out to us the higher reaches of sanctity, to which the Saints have climbed and to which He calls each willing soul.

Thus have we learned Christ, and thus should we show forth to the world the lessons we have learned.

Dear Jesus, I have not been a very apt scholar. I know well enough what You want me to do, and how You want me to behave myself. I have learned the lessons of the head well enough; but not the lessons of the heart, which bring my life in line with what I know. I have followed the call of the world in many things when I know You would not approve, for I "had not so learned" You. I am sorry for these failures, and with Your grace I shall carry Your lessons out in my life better hereafter than before.

ELEVENTH WEDNESDAY AFTER PENTECOST

MY FRIEND'S FRIENDS

Amen, I say to you, as long as you did it to one of these, My least brethren, you did it to Me.

St. Matthew 25:40.

CRITICISM always shows lack of maturity. To sit in superior judgment on others, to define offhandedly the method of procedure in cases that have taxed (though we may not think so) many an older mind, to parade abroad the defects and sins of others is to show that we know human nature, neither in general, nor our own in particular—and that is an adequate immaturity. But when the criticism is of my friend or of my friend's friends, then it is a bit of childishness, deeply tainted with the unseemliest of faults, untrueness to my friend.

It were well we thought of this often. To criticize my fellowman, whoever he be, stamps me as yet in my youth, and, more, brands me as unfaithful to friendship's finest trait, for all men are the friends of my own best friend, Christ Jesus. He has loved them all unto His dying on the tree of shame, and loves them yet. Some there are sin-stained and smirched with blackest crimes, but He loves them so, that He still reaches out His precious Blood for them. And other some there are who love Him fitfully and in changeful mood, though all the while, despite their fickleness, His love for them is changeless still. And still other some there are who love Him with undying, eager love and serve Him well and these are, too, His friends. No man alive but is Christ's friend, and is it not an act of sheer impoliteness for me to talk about my Friend's friends and that in His presence, too, since He is everywhere? Oh! there may be faults, yes, grossest crimes upon their lives; but shall I speak of these? Is it not enough for my Friend to know that many that He loves are quite spoiling His handiwork, without my blazoning that fact abroad? Then, too, if His dearest friends, the saintly men and women about us, fail at times in little ways and measure not fully up to the stature of Christ shall I further pain my Friend by pointing the noting finger at their lack of love? All have their faults, as I have my many own, and yet Christ, who knows them all and all their wonted frailties, still holds them as His friends. Friends they are of His and as His friends I must learn to think of them and speak of them, and find no pleasure in the conning and the telling of their waywardnesses.

Again, dear Jesus, with You alone do I fail in friendship's least demands. Of those whom my earthly friends hold dear I never speak unkindly, yet of the souls You love I fain would tell the slightest faults, forgetful of Your sacred presence and the pain I cause You. Oh! let this never be again. Your friends must be my friends and, if they have their faults, I shall try to keep them hid, yes, and if I can, lend helping hand to make them grow more like unto You.

ELEVENTH THURSDAY AFTER PENTECOST

OUR GUARDSMAN

May the Body of our Lord, Jesus Christ, stand guard over your soul unto eternal life.

Priest's Prayer while giving Holy Communion.

THE worth of a thing is known by the care with which its guard is chosen. What we care little for or what can be easily replaced, we lay here and there thoughtlesswise; for it matters naught, if it be gone when we come back to look for it. But what is worth a deal to us by reason of the love with which it came freighted to us or by reason of the labor we were forced to spend in gaining it, that we watch and guard and place away behind huge doors which none save the trustiest men may open. Thus it is with gold and precious stones and treasures of our family which come to us heavy with memories of other days and of loved ones gone before. We guard them with massive locks and stalwart men keep watch.

So it is with that which is priceless beyond all else we have. Wealth is good and the credit of a great name, too, and health and strength of body, yes, and life itself is very good, but beyond all these in worth and utter pricelessness is our own immortal soul, and so we choose to guard it Him who alone can be trusted absolutely. Mere man may guard the treasures that rust and moths may steal away from us, but only One—and He, our God,—can ease our anxiety lest our souls be lost. Thus it is that, as the priest feeds us with our daily Bread at the silent altar-rails, he prays as Mother Church has prayed these many hundred years: "May the Body of Christ stand guard over your soul unto eternal life!" Time will run its course and be no more, the trinkets of time will scatter and be lost, the frail bodies of time will at last be gathered to the dust from which they came, yet far beyond and unendingly will endure our souls, and it is these that we ask our Lord to guard. We are weak but He is strong and no one stronger can be found to wrest our souls from Him. We are dreadfully unwise and oftentimes become the dupes of cleverer men who steal from us our earthly wares, but He is wise with knowledge none can equal and no man can trick the least of things away from Him. We are so imprudent and walk so constantly into danger, but He "reaches from end to end mightily" and sees all things and none can take Him unawares. How good it is to know that our undying souls are safe with Him! How restful it is to realize that our improvidence and spendthriftness and carelessness will be offset by Him provided only we ourselves take not our souls away from His loving care! Little wonder, then, that, as we come back from breakfasting with God each day, we feel a bravery unknown to other men and a strength to face the fateful facts of life with an assurance only they can have who have on guard about them Jesus Christ, to whom "all power is given in Heaven and on earth," before whom angels bow in lowliest adoration, at whose Name every knee doth "bow of those that are in heaven, on earth and in hell," from whose hand none may snatch away.

Jesus, strong guardian of my soul, oh, keep Your watch most faithfully. It were a dreadful thing for me to lose my soul. Yet there is manifold danger lest my careless ways bring it to ruin. Just keep me safe by You. Offset my stupidity by Your wisdom, my unwariness by Your providence, my weakness by Your omnipotence. When thieves would come and steal away from me that which alone must count, stand sentinel and warn me of the need of care. You have kept Your guard these many years and I thank You for Your watchfulness. Just a few more years, dear Jesus, is all You have to stand on duty, and then, in Heaven, I shall be safe forever.

ELEVENTH FRIDAY AFTER PENTECOST

HE WANTS SINNERS

For I came not to call the just, but sinners.
St. Mark 2:17.

NO, don't call the doctor. I am too sick." The friend rubbed his eyes. "My dear Jack! Are you crazy? Too sick to call the doctor?" "Yes, too sick. Doctors don't want to see really sick people. And I am really sick."

Doubtless we should all think Jack crazy. Doctors are doctors precisely for the sake of the sick, and most so for the sickest of the sick. Jack's viewpoint seems ridiculous, but before I condemn him I might ask myself whether I have ever acted thus with God.

I hold it as an article of Faith that Our Lord came to redeem me, that He actually died for me a most horrible death. I admit all that and am quite convinced, when only the ordinary sense of sin is upon me, that it is fully right to ask His pardon and to expect His forgiveness.

But when things "go all wrong," when the very bottom drops out of existence, then, somehow or other, I find that my confidence in His forthcoming relief wanes rapidly. And if gross sins be mine, and I have seriously spurned His love, I almost doubt His willingness, even His ability to help me.

Quite as foolish as Jack, am I not? Too snarled up in life's meshes for God to untangle, yet He came down from Heaven precisely for this! Too rottenly sinful to be redeemed, yet He died to save me, as though no one else existed!

I do not mean it, but I do put limits to God's omnipotent love, forgetful of His words: "For I came not to call the just, but sinners." There is a bit of sneaking pride in me, that, after all, when I am really good or only middling careless, God does find me somewhat worthy of His love. And so when I have wandered far from Him and badly soiled my soul, I judge that I have placed myself beyond His reach.

Foolish! Foolish beyond words, and most unfair to Him. The sicker I am the more I need His healing, and the fouler I am the more I need His cleansing touch. And never—as long as I live—can I be so foul that He will not be longing to touch and cleanse and heal the soul He bought with His own blood.

Dear Jesus, how I wrong You when I doubt Your love and Your willingness to help me. In brighter hours it is not so hard. But when life is all a wreck, I do find it difficult to trust it all to You. And hardest it is to rely on Your love when I have outraged it by grievous sin. But Jesus, dear, that is not fair to You. So never let me wrong you again by doubting thus, but let me always remember that You came and died, precisely, not for Saints but for sinners.

ELEVENTH SATURDAY AFTER PENTECOST

GOD IS ALWAYS POLITE

And Mary said: Behold the handmaid of the Lord; be it done to me according to Thy word.

St. Luke 1:38.

GOD has many plans for the universe and for each one of us in particular. Where creatures are concerned that have no free will, He works these plans out Himself. But once He has given the high gift of freedom to Angel or to man, He respects it, and the unfolding of His plans and the observance even of His rigid Commandments, binding under eternal penalties, then depend on the consent of the creature itself.

We see what happened at Nazareth when God wanted to become Man of a virgin mother. The whole plan of Redemption lay before Him: the birth, upbringing, death, and resurrection of Christ, and the founding of the Church thereafter. Just think of those stupendous facts and of the omnipotence of God that they required. Yet He sent the Angel Gabriel, Heaven's high messenger, to the lowly virgin Mary, told her of His plans and of the part He would like her to play in them—and then, with a Divine politeness, awaited her consent. Never did suitor await more expectantly for a pledge of returned love than God awaited Mary's answer. She had the proffer of Divine spouseship and motherhood; she could have refused. God politely waited.

So it was when, having created the Angels, He wanted to give them Heaven. So it was when He placed sanctifying grace in the souls of Adam and Eve but awaited their consent to have it remain there by their exercising their free will and obeying His command. So it is in the life of each and everyone of us in matters small as well as great. He has many things that He wants each of us to do; He asks us through His grace to do them—and, having asked, awaits the answer.

It may be that God wants you to pledge your love to another for life at the foot of His altar and to bring new lives into existence to people His Church here and Heaven hereafter. But it rests with your own free will to take the marriage vow and thereafter to assume its responsibilities along with its pleasures. It may be that He wants your love all to himself, unshared by any other, that you may make many another know and love and serve Him better. But to take the three-fold vow and to give Him your all of love rests entirely with you.

Then, too, married or vowed to God, God wants you to become a saint, since highest sanctity is within the reach of each of us. But again, highest holiness within the home or within the cloister will not be forced on you; it is for you to seek it or to refuse to be interested in it.

The big and little things, too, of every day are also matters of choice: a goodly care of the home or slovenliness; diligent or sloppy work in the office; stimulating or lack-a-daisical teaching; a proper or an unrestrained behavior in times of merry-making; consideration for others or petty meannesses. All these—and many more—which go to make up the warp and woof of life, lie wholly within the freedom of our wills, even when God's Commandments and our eternal happiness are at stake. God always asks us by His grace to do the seemly thing. He asks—and then awaits our answer.

Dear Jesus, how wonderfully considerate You are and—I say it with all reverence—how polite! You are omnipotent and could have Your way in everything. But You don't. Instead, You tell me what You want me to do, and then leave the answer to me. In the past I have often done just what You wanted me not to do. I am sorry for that now. At least I, the creature, should be as polite as You, my Creator, are. Please help me to be so hereafter.

TWELFTH SUNDAY AFTER PENTECOST

WASTED LIVES

Thou shalt love the Lord thy God with thy whole heart, and with thy whole soul, and with all thy strength, and with all thy mind.

St. Luke 10:27.

ONE of the bleakest comments that we can pass as we stand at the grave of a man is to say: "His was a wasted life." Poor fellow, he may have striven hard and worked with brawn and with brain, but he did it all misguidedly. Now this quest, now that, and then again another led him on and he has gone the way of all flesh, leaving sad wreckage behind him.

Sad this is when said of one's natural life, but sad unto tears, bitter tears, if the Angels of God must say it of the soul. There lies in death an old, bent father, whose days had been spent in endless searchings for riches and the goods that may be bought therewith, yet rarely did he think to kneel at God's altar and ask for the wealth of Heaven for himself and those he loved. Around mother's silent form her children gather, but, as they look back over the past, few are the nights she called them to her side to speed their evening prayers to God, fewer still the days wherein she taught the folly of the world and the breakableness of all its flashy baubles. And others lie in death, men and women, who though they did love God and tried to serve Him quite decently, forgot the words: "Thou shalt love the Lord thy God with thy whole heart and thy whole soul, and with all thy strength and all thy mind." To some the love of the ringing praises of men made strong appeal and they forgot that the silence of death hushes all but the voice of God. Other some the love of bodily ease set a-hungering for the delicacies of this world and sapped their stalwartness in the service of their King. Yet others again have let the love of a fellow-creature steal in upon a heart that should have had a single Lover and Him upon the altar-throne. So they all let other and mean loves come into their lives and cheat their God of an undivided heart.

Oh, if such our lives have been and are, as we look towards death, do not our minds keep saying: "And after that—the dark"? But, if with God's help we have learned that "the end of the commandment is love," that all the fulfilment of our lives lies in "knowing and loving and serving Him in this life," then as the grave comes nearer and nearer to us, we know—"and after that—the light"—the light of the eternal love of God and of Mary Mother's face and the welcoming smiles of those that have gone before and sleep the sleep of peace.

Jesus, save me from my own heart's truancy. I know it well that You must be the only object of my love and in my thankful moments I would have it always so—but then! Away I go, back to the tinseled, loud-mouthed world, and many, many a time my heart is weaned from You, at least in little things. Teach me, dearest Master, teach this backward child that Yours is the only love worth having, that You and Heaven are the only goals worth striving for.

TWELFTH MONDAY AFTER PENTECOST

BUM SPORTS

The Lord gave, and the Lord hath taken away. As it hath pleased the Lord, so is it done. Blessed be the name of the Lord.

Job 1:21.

THERE is a phrase drawn from athletics which is very expressive: a "bum sport." A bum sport is a man who always wants to win and "crabs" or "jumps the umpire" or "quits" when the decision goes against him. He is a poor loser, and whether he plays cards or chess, baseball or football, polo or tennis, his side must come out on top—or there is trouble. Of course his outlook is warped; and of course nobody likes him.

Life, too, is a game, and in that game each of us sometimes wins and each of us sometimes loses. It is true of every man's life, and there are no exceptions. We all like to win—there is no denying that. We would not be human if winning were not to our liking. But in life, as in every other game, we must be ready to lose and to be "game" losers too. It is hard to take a loss, and hardest when we lose just where we wanted most to win.

A man and a woman at the altar pledge inseparable love. Rightfully they look down the vista of the oncoming years with joy in their hearts. That joy rings loud and clear for many a day; then the discords come, and life's frictions begin to appear. The man and the woman took the bright days smilingly. Will they whine when the clouds begin to gather?

A man has set his heart, not on wealth, but on a competency of this world's goods. For a while all goes well and the road of life seems to have no down-grades. But then come the days when business ventures fail—and all his hoardings go. Will he "grouch"? Or will he be as brave as Job and say: "The Lord gave, and the Lord hath taken away. . . . Blessed be the name of the Lord"?

Another lays plans for study and research; hours are spent in thinking and planning ways toward success in a definite work. All goes well, until one day the tide of life ebbs; shattered health and broken nerves bring enforced inactivity. Will he praise God and show Him the same love now that he did in the days of toil?

It is easy to serve God when all is well, just as it is easy to play through a winning game. It is easy to be smilingly holy while we take the lawful joys of life. Will we be just as gracious when we must forego a forbidden pleasure? We can take "in stride" pleasures that God blesses; will we walk away "in stride" from pleasures that His laws forbid?

Anybody can play a winning game; but only a "real sport" can put his every ounce of strength into a losing game right up to the time when the whistle is blown.

Dear Jesus, I want to play the game of life as You would have me play it—as You Yourself played it. You took the unpleasant things as well as the pleasant things. You took Calvary as you did Tabor—may I say it?—"in stride." I do not want to play well only when life goes well. I want to play a hard, clean game in life all the time. Please do not let me ever again prove myself a "bum sport" in the game of life.

TWELFTH TUESDAY AFTER PENTECOST

A BAD BET

Then came Peter unto Him and said: Lord, how often shall my brother offend against me and I forgive him? Till seven times? Jesus saith to him: I say not to thee till seven times: but till seventy times seven times.

St. Matthew 18:21, 22.

THAT lad's a bad bet, Father," were the words the learned mental specialist said to the priest, as they spoke of an inmate in the great city hospital. Indeed, if ever there seemed to be a "bad bet," it was this. Long years of sin and much of drink and then the crash came, but with the crash new friends who held out helping hands and high ideals and much encouragement. Then new resolves to be up and doing, but then another slip and again a rise, and yet again a further slip. No wonder that those words were said, "A bad bet, Father." Yes, bad, very bad and much disheartening but, despite it all, much help was given to the poor, weak lad to try and try again.

Do we ever think of how our Angel Guardians must look on us at times and then turn to our Lord and say, "A bad bet, dear Lord." There is every reason for their saying so, as we ourselves realize from time to time. Just unroll the scroll of time and re-read the story of our lives. Through other lips at Baptism we pledged ourselves to God and swore that we renounced the devil and all his works and all his pomps. As years came on and passed into eternity, fuller reason came and a more self-governable will, and then the world called quite appealingly to us. A small world then it was, but there was much room for wilfulness and we soon learned to stamp our feet and follow our "own sweet ways." Again and again we knelt at the feet of God's priest and pledged our Sacramental word that we would hold our wills in check. Try we did, but maybe as the years were added on and our world threw out its margins farther and farther, the lure of pleasant things bewitched us much and we fell from the high commands of God. Yet again and again we knelt and asked forgiveness because we really meant to be good again. "Bad bets"? Rather —if the reckoning of men were the reckoning of God—to be down and up and down again.

But more than that. Morning after morning we knelt at the banquet-rail of God and partook of "the corn of the elect and the wine that bringeth forth virgins." Day after day we became the tabernacles of God and housed Him within our poor bodies. We begged Him to keep us very near Him and told Him we would have it so, but as the long day waned and on our knees we checked back over the hours, what did we find of all our fine resolves? What stains upon those souls that should have been immaculate for having harbored God Himself! "Bad bets"? Rather, if Infinite Purity kept our souls cleansed so shortly.

Dear Jesus, sometimes Your infinite patience dawns upon me and the tangled wilfulness of all my waywardness stands before me, and then I wonder—how can You stand it all? So many protestations of love, so many, oft-repeated acts of sorrow and of resolve—and then? The same old slips, the same old faults. Much thanks, dear Lord, for all Your patience! Only You could be so patient. I really want to try, and so please be patient always, even though I am a "bad bet."

TWELFTH WEDNESDAY AFTER PENTECOST

NOT YOURS, BUT YOU!

For I seek not the things that are yours, but you.
2 Corinthians 12:14.

IF we want to have influence over others unto their good and to have their souls brought nearer and nearer to God by reason of our dealings with them, the surest way to secure this is by an utter oneness of purpose, which shines out smitingly from our every word and deed. It must be clearer than the noonday sun that we seek not theirs, but them; that we have no least hankering to filch from them, even under the guise of freest gift most freely given, aught of all they have. What we want is their good, their upbuilding, their sanctity. What we want is themselves, that they may be Christ's. Then, and only then, can we really bring them to Christ.

That is the unwritten, but inviolable, law of influence. Parent must abide by it, teacher, too, and friend. "Not yours—but you!" When, not from words but from every least deed, the child, with that swiftest intuition which is his, realizes that father and mother have only his good in mind, then that little heart will turn unerringly to them. It will run to them in every hurt; it will lisp its every joy to them. As the years come on, it will lean all the more heavily on them for that advice, which the growing years will demand increasingly. Youth with its unknown stirrings and broadening horizons will find in father and in mother surest guides; for it will realize that they, more than and beyond all others, seek what is best for the one they love.

In the classroom, too, where only too often the restive children seem bent on challenging every effort, victory over those turbulent souls will be won when somehow or other teacher has transferred to their minds a strong conviction that she wants to help them and be their friend. They may not be able to tell you why, but they will like the teacher who loves them and dislike the one who loves herself. Children are shrewd, and to try to deceive them is as vain as to walk abroad in the full light of day and expect not to be seen. "Not yours, but you!" That must come to them at every turn of the textbook page, at every stroke of the crayon on the board, at every moment of the recreation hour.

So, too, with friends, if I am to mold their loves aright. They will soon know if I seek their friendship because of the gifts they may bestow on me or the position in life they may secure for me or the goodly things I may enjoy with them. Yes, they will even sense the difference, if they come to realize that I seek their company for any joy I may find therein and not solely for the good I may do them.

"Not yours, but you!" Thus cried St. Paul to the Corinthians, lest they might think him greedy of their support or expectant of their gifts. Poor he was, and a sufferer, too, but what he needed he would work for, lest he might be burdensome to them. By every right he could claim support of them but no—"Not yours, but you!"

Dear Jesus, I do want to bring men and women nearer to You and to teach them to love You more. But I cannot do this, if I am selfish and self-seeking and anxious to have them share with me what is theirs. I cannot win them to You, if they see that I want to win them to myself. So give me much strength and courage, Lord, to have but a single purpose in all my dealings with those whom I must help. Let my every word and deed, yes, and my life itself cry out aloud to all—"Not yours, but you!"

TWELFTH THURSDAY AFTER PENTECOST

IMPOLITE

The son honoreth the father and the servant his master. If then I be a father, where is My Honor? And if I be a master, where is My fear? saith the Lord of Hosts.
Malachias 1:6.

SUBSERVIENCE to legitimate authority is characteristic of every correctly trained child and every right-thinking man. Father or mother speaks, and is heard with reverent deference and forthwith the child will endeavor to fulfill the spoken wish and gratify each manifested desire. In the menial tasks of the home, in the bustle of business hours, and in ways of the professions, those in authority are listened to and their views respected, for men know instinctively that there is no bond so strong between men as that whereby the lowest is ruled by the intermediate and the intermediate is ruled by the highest.

Of this God reminded the Jews through His prophet Isaias and then put to them a question which it would be well for us to answer too: "If I then be a father, where is My honor? And if I be a master, where is My fear?" With my lips I acknowledge God as the "Creator of Heaven and earth," and I greet Him as my "Father in Heaven," and yet, do my actions square with my words? God is my master, master of my body and my soul, master of my mind and of my will, master of my eyes, and my ears, and my tongue, master of them all in the early morning, at high noon, and when the night comes on, master of them all in my youth and in my maturing years and in the years when "my strength shall fail." Yet, may He not rightly ask of me, "If I be a master, where is My fear?" Where is the fear of God which would keep that body and that soul, which are His, from violations of His law? Where is the wholesome dread that would make sin a thing unknown to mind, and will, and eye, and ear, and tongue? Then, too, God is my Father and has loved me from eternity. How do I show Him honor? Is it by prayers ill said and frequently omitted? Is it by rarely thinking of Him as the long day draws to its close, or when pleasures following pleasures snatch irrecoverable time away from me? Is it by the fewness of my visits to my sacramental Lord who has waited these nineteen hundred years for the pleasure of the visits I might pay Him during my brief stay here on earth? In all honesty, can I give any solid, candid reason for the way of acting with my changeless Friend that would not be tolerated between man and man?

Dear Jesus, patient, very patient God, how shabbily have I treated You in the days gone by! Sheer politeness, not to speak of the demands of justice and gratitude, should have made me act differently. Yet the fact is, that I have been rude and wilfull, and scant in my respect. I failed to pay You the homage due a master, I kept from You the love I owed You as my father. But that is past. Just let the future bring a change of ways.

TWELFTH FRIDAY AFTER PENTECOST

BEARING THE CROSS GRACEFULLY

But if I go to the East, He appeareth not; if to the West, I shall not understand Him. If to the left hand, what shall I do? I shall not take hold on Him; if I turn myself to the right hand, I shall not see Him. But He knoweth my way, and has tried me as gold that passeth through the fire.
Job 23:8-10.

JOB has been tried hard by his physical suffering, and harder still by the friends who came to comfort him but scolded him instead. He defends his innocence, but admits that he cannot reason out the ways of God, least of all in the miseries which have come upon him. God is everywhere, even though one cannot see Him or find Him. And God knows all things, and so Job is content to leave his cause in God's hands: "If I go to the East, He appeareth not; if to the West, I shall not understand Him. If to the left hand, what shall I do? I shall not take hold on Him; if I turn myself to the right hand, I shall not see Him. But He knoweth my way, and has tried me as gold that passeth through the fire." God may try him and lay heaviest crosses upon him, but "my foot hath followed His steps, I have kept His way . . . and the words of His mouth I have hid in my bosom."

Job was afflicted as few of us will ever be afflicted. All his children and all his wealth had been taken from him, and he was struck "with a very grievous ulcer, from the sole of the foot even to the top of the head," and he who had been so wealthy and so powerful "took a potsherd and scraped the corrupt matter, sitting on a dunghill." Yet his cry is:

"The Lord gave, and the Lord hath taken away; as it hath pleased the Lord, so is it done; blessed be the name of the Lord!"

What faith! And that in a man who lived long centuries before Bethlehem and Nazareth and Calvary. He was of the Old Testament times, when God showed His justice more than His mercy; when God was far away, it seemed, and hid in the inaccessibility of His invisible nearness.

And does Job's spirit of faith make me blush for mine? I have knelt at Bethlehem's crib and seen Him in visible form. I have gone to Nazareth and found the Child playing with His companions. I have walked the banks of Jordan with the Son of Man, as He heralded tidings of God's new mercy. I have stood beneath the Cross, and seen Him die a shameful death. And I have known that it was all for *me,* that it was all done that *I* might learn to take up my Cross and follow Him.

Yet, when those crosses do come, and when sorrows crowd out the joys of life, what do I do? Complain, and grumble, and wonder why God has forsaken me. Others are happy—why can't I be? Others succeed—why can't I? Others have health—why haven't I? And I *have* tried to be good—and here is what I get.

Job . . . and I!

Dear Lord, I am quite ashamed of myself for the way I have acted in the past. I have grumbled and grown surly when trials came my way. I have felt that You were really mean to send me such crosses and such disappointments, sometimes just then when I was trying to serve You best. Of course it's hard, dear Lord, to take up one's cross gracefully. But Job did it—and You did it—and I'll try to do it, too.

TWELFTH SATURDAY AFTER PENTECOST

LEARNING TO WAIT

The learning of a man is known by patience.
Proverbs 19:11.

IMPATIENCE is always the outcome of a narrow view. God alone knows best how to wait. Reaching "from end to end mightily," without beginning and without a term to His existence, He sees all things aright and measures them wisely and well. There is no hurry in His works, there is no haste in His action. From the heights of eternity He looks down upon this teeming world and what is now a tangled skein to lesser eyes, He sees unraveled in the distant future. What seems amiss to-day, need not be hurriedly jolted into place, for there is a morrow and then again a morrow's morrow. He "ordereth all things sweetly" and abides the outcome with a patience that is infinite.

Would that I might learn this lesson! Seeing only a bit of all this wide world's activity and having to play but a lesser *rôle* therein, how impatient I am if my own little part seems not to go quite smoothly! I grow restive under any restraint that is placed on me or at any even seeming tardiness in others who do not hearken at once to my requests. I must push on at once or else the whole is lost!

Isn't that the way with me many and many a time? I just cannot wait. I must get things straightened out at once and woe betide any one who tries to slow me up or block my path.

Mary, my mother, was not like that. She had learned to bide her time and to await the solution on another day. When motherhood came to her miraculously, she let God take His time to make Joseph aware of her privilege. When shepherds and Magi came and went again, she "kept all the words, pondering them in her heart." Simeon spoke of the sword of sorrows, and the Child when found in the Temple spoke strange words, and once again "his mother kept all these words in her heart." She saw all things in the light of eternity—and so she could be patient and await time's unfolding.

I can never be as wise as Mother Mary; no, but may I not try to grow more like her patient self? It is hard to wait, to stand quietly by and let things move on; but often that is the wisest way of all. Husband and wife can avoid many a quarrel if each will only wait a while when things go wrong. Father and mother keep the love of child longer if they ponder a bit and do not correct too hastily. Teacher in school or boss in shop or manager in store will soon find that it pays to sit silently, watchfully waiting until the real hidden reasons for petty upsets and disturbances become clear.

Anyone can get excited. Anyone can get impatient. Anyone can lose his temper. No self-control is needed for that. But it does require a check on our will and it does demand a guard on our tongue to be able to do nothing and to wait until things calm down. And so "the learning of a man is shown by his patience" for real learning brings much poise of character, much self-control, and increasing likeness to God who in all His eternity has never once been impatient.

Dear Jesus, one of the hardest things for me to do is to be patient. I want to do things and "have them over with." It is not easy for me to bide my time and to wait until tomorrow. It always seems so absolutely necessary for me to do things *now*. Is that because I am not sure of tomorrow? Perhaps, dear Lord, for life is filled with so many uncertainties. But all the same, whether tomorrow is to come or not, give me the grace to learn to take today and its problems patiently.

THIRTEENTH SUNDAY AFTER PENTECOST

SAYING THANK YOU

Were not ten made clean? Where are the nine?
St. Luke 17:17.

TO say "Thank you" is the minimum of politeness expected and required of all. To snatch a gift from the hands of the giver and to hasten away without even a hurried expression of thanks, stamps one as a selfish ingrate and such a one finds himself, sooner or later, shunned by all. We must be gentlemen and ladies, if we wish to make and keep friends.

Tested by this, how many of us would be found to be gentlemen and ladies with our Lord? He would have all be polite with Him, but more especially those who lay special claim to His dear friendship. Yet, if the recording Angel laid out before us the Book of Life, how many would be the pages of petition and how scant and poorly filled the pages of thanksgiving! Sad commentary on the choicest of friendships!

In the dark hour of trial we come with hurried steps to our Lord and entreat and beg and plead with Him for all His love and call upon Him in tenderest terms to free us from a chalice that is too bitter for our tasting —and He hearkens to our cry. The bloom of health comes back to wan, dear cheeks and frail limbs grow strong again, yet do we think to go with the one that was cured before the divine Physician and thank Him for His kindly healing? The lightsome life of God's grace has been shed anew into a soul long robbed of it and the shackles of sin have fallen off at the Master's voice, but we fail to kneel in grateful prayer for His leading captivity captive to His love. Perhaps in the night of our soul we cry for light as we stumble along a stony, narrow path; but when the light is given and we run merrily along the way of perfection, we forget to be thankful for the brightness of the way and the music of our hearts. We forget—but suppose our Friend had forgotten to hear our cry!

What, too, of gratitude for the daily gifts of nature and of grace; for life and the wonderful powers of soul and body, the love of parents and of children and of friends; for the still more precious gifts of faith and sanctifying grace, of the communion of Saints and of the Sacraments of the Church, and in special wise His consoling presence on our altars? Never a hearty "Thank you, Lord," for all of these?

Dear Lord, why is it I forget the niceties of friendship only with You? To all other friends I am grateful, but when You give a gift, I snatch it with the swift eagerness of childhood and hurry away with no thought of the kindly Giver. But, Jesus dear, You know I am grateful, if it be with the gratitude of only a thoughtless, loving child. So pardon all my impoliteness and trust me, dearest Lord, for a better, more thankful future.

THIRTEENTH MONDAY AFTER PENTECOST

CHANGING GODS

Pass over to the isles of Cethim, and see; and send into Cedar, and consider diligently; and see if there hath been done anything like this. If a nation hath changed their gods, and indeed they are not gods; but My people have changed their glory into an idol.

Jeremias 2:10, 11.

JEREMIAS has been sent by God to plead with the Jews to win them back to His love and service. They have forsaken Him, not He them, for God has told Jeremias: "Go, and cry in the ears of Jerusalem, saying: Thus saith the Lord: I have remembered thee, pitying thy youth, and the love of thy espousals, when thou followedst Me in the desert, in a land that is not sown. Israel is holy to the Lord, the first-fruits of His increase." God will not let them have their wilful way in running after false gods. By Jeremias He will awaken their old love for Him. He will shame them into loving Him again by making them realize how strange is their sin, even when matched up with all the strange sins of the wicked nations round about them. "Pass over to the isles of Cethim and see; and send into Cedar and consider diligently; and see if there hath been done anything like this." Other nations sinned and lived in grossest immorality, but see "if a nation hath changed their gods, and indeed they are not gods; but My people have changed their glory into an idol."

Foolish people, we are inclined to cry, so forgetful of all that God had done for them in Egypt, at Sinai, in the desert, and after they had come into the Promised Land. But before we blame them, it were well to turn our eyes inward upon ourselves.

We have known God and known Him well, thanks to all His gracious kindness to us. As He espoused the Jewish people, so has He espoused our souls in a special way, from the day when the waters of Baptism first brought grace into our souls. Yet what is our own life-story? Just that of the Jewish people. Thanks be to His grace we have never left Him entirely, but we have countless times set Him aside and let creatures take His place in our lives.

The pleasures of life can be enjoyed, and holily, too, and God meant them to be so enjoyed. Yet we may have misused them and may have acted as did the pagans "whose god was their belly," and we may have let the lowest pleasures of life demand our whole-hearted service. That was, indeed, to change our glory into an idol.

The honors of life can be rightly sought and justly attained, and God is pleased if we so seek and hold them. But base ambition may have spurred us on unworthily, and we may have used means that would not bear the scrutiny of honest men. Or we may have coveted pride of place when our station in life demanded of us a large humility. And so our hearts were weaned from God and with our whole heart and our whole soul, with all our mind and all our strength, we sought after the high places among men.

Wealth, too, is good and a certain competency is most to be desired that we and our loved ones may be protected against lean days. But the lure of gold may have caught our souls and we may have become fretful in our pursuit of it. Instead of trusting God for the morrow, we have trusted in wealth; and maybe in the days of our soul's own need, that could never be touched by all the wealth of the world, we heard God's word resounding in our hearts: "Where are the gods, whom thou hast made thee? Let them arise and deliver thee in the time of thy affliction."

So, after all, before we censure the witless Jews, we might turn our purging anger against ourselves.

Dear Jesus, You have been very good to me, and have shown Your love in countless ways. To no one have You been more gracious than to me, and yet—! What a contrast my past makes when matched up against all Your goodness! You wanted to have my undivided love, but I would not have it so, and gave much of it to creatures, setting them up as idols in my heart. But let the past be, dear Lord, and give me much grace to give You my love—all, and whole, and irrevocably.

THIRTEENTH TUESDAY AFTER PENTECOST

CHANGE THE SIGN

Whosoever doth not carry his cross and come after Me, cannot be My disciple.

St. Luke 14:27.

DID you ever study algebra, my dear fellow?" "Why, yes, Father; but I don't see how that's going to help me in this trouble." "Well, maybe you don't, but here—this figure is 2. It can be +2 or −2. If it is 'plus 2,' it is a help; if it is 'minus 2,' it is a liability." "But again, Father, what in the world has that got to do with my trouble?" "Well, Jack, it has this much to do. God has sent you this cross of ill health, which cheats you of your ambitions and irks you much. That state of ill health will be a liability to you, if you grow peevish and get out of sorts and murmur and complain. But it will be a real asset to you, something worth while, a positive help, if only you accept it gracefully from God's hands. That means carrying your cross—not letting it knock you down."

"Change the sign: plus 2 or minus 2." Isn't that the story of life? It is all in the "sign," all in the way that we take the troubles that come upon us.

Ill health comes—and no one likes ill health. I can balk at it and chafe under it, becoming a burden to myself and a source of endless irritation to others. Or I can take it with a smile, and bear my pain without a whimper, and be a real consolation to all those about me.

My best laid plans go awry, and all my hopes are laid in ashes. If this defeat overpowers me, then I get discouraged and do not want to try again, and act quite like a spoiled child that cannot have its own way. But if I master that disappointment and remain in control of the situation, then I am stronger and holier by very reason of the defeat.

"Change the sign." There is nothing that happens to me in life, that cannot be turned into asset or liability. Success can make me become proud and "lose my head"—or it can make me humble. Happiness can make me forget God—or it can bring words of thanksgiving to my lips. Good health can make me too self-reliant, or it can spur my efforts to be very close to God and to help as many others as I can.

Dear Jesus, help me to learn to "change the sign." Each and every thing that happens to me will either help or hinder me—and it is I who make the difference. At times it is really hard to make each cross or trial—yes, and harder at times to make each success or happiness—bring me nearer to You, because I am so weak and fickle. But Lord, by Your own example You have shown me how to carry my cross aright; and You always give me grace to handle the situation well—so I will try always to "change the sign."

THIRTEENTH WEDNESDAY AFTER PENTECOST

UNMANNERLY TO GOD

And Jesus answering, said: Were not ten made clean? And where are the nine?

St. Luke 17:17.

NO, I hardly expect to hear from him. Everything is straightened out now, and he is contented. Yes, I managed it all for him; but he is just forgetful. No, not ungrateful. Just forgetful." So spoke the older chap, who had teased out a nastily snarled condition for the younger man. It took a deal of time and thought, and a bit of patience, too. The young fellow had been worried lest it would not be solved; had pleaded his case well, and had won the unstinted help of the older friend. But he got what he wanted—and then did not even write a line of thanks!

No, it was not ingratitude; it was just forgetfulness; just a dropping away of the cares and anxieties that had brought him in search of aid; just an absorption in the newly-won happiness.

As between man and man, so too between man and God. To God we come in our hour of need of soul or body. With Him we plead; before Him we kneel and beg imploringly that He will hear our prayer and grant surcease of our pain and trial. Our prayer is long and most insistent, and most pleading. Then God hears us—and as the pain is dulled and the cross lifted, we at once forget.

Thus did the nine lepers long ago when Christ had cured them. They did not mean to be impolite; and in their hearts they were truly grateful. But the newly-won joys of life so distracted them that only one retraced his steps to say the expected "Thank You."

But can't we who know His love be a bit more mannerly? Shouldn't the finer courtesies of life find ample room in our relations with Him? They should. We owe Him all we have in soul and body, in the way of friends, in the substance of this world's goods. There may be some slight excuse for being forgetful of the gifts that are ours in common with all other men. Their very usualness may give some color to our not remembering that, though every-day gifts, they are gifts still.

But when our hearts have been set on some special prize in life, and we have begged and prayed for it, and importuned God almost petulantly for it, is there any least excuse for snatching the gift and never saying even a hasty "Thank You"? A sense of sheer decency should prompt us to make quick acknowledgment of our gratefulness. That were elemental politeness.

Dear Jesus, I certainly cannot be proud of my politeness towards You. For my whole life and each and everything in it I should be grateful, and I should tell You so frequently. But I don't. Yet, that is not the worst. When I do ask something special from You and have begged You for it day in and day out, I pay scant heed to You when You are good enough to give it to me. And if You do not, I am so apt to grumble and growl. How strangely impolite I am! But pardon me, dear Lord, for I promise to be more mannerly from now on.

THIRTEENTH THURSDAY AFTER PENTECOST

HE IS ALWAYS NEAR

I will not leave you orphans, I will come to you.
St. John 14:18.

SOMETIMES the isolation of the human soul comes home to us and carries with it a realization that hurries terror into our inmost heart. Between my soul and the souls around me there is a gulf so broad and so deep that all the powers of human expression cannot span it, when most it needs uplifting sympathy and buoyant encouragement. I have, indeed, my friends in the brightness of whose smiles my weary, care-worn heart is fed with strength and courage, but still it is fearfully true that my soul's deepest life is single and unshared. I live by myself—alone; alone, yet with an indomitable craving for one with whom to share all that lies nearest and dearest to me; alone, yet lashed on always by a vast fundamental yearning to pour out my heart and its most secret thoughts and fears and hopes to some one who will completely understand me. Friends we have whose love for us is as strong as our love for them, but friends they are with only a human power to help and so we are alone. Yes alone, alone and isolated with a bleak, blank road to death ahead of us, unless we know the blessed comradeship of Christ our Lord. He, the sweet Saviour, who trod the sun-parched roads of Palestine and furrowed the water of Galilee's lake in quest of souls, has eased, as only He can ease, this maddening fever of our souls. He knows the poignant griefs, which lie too deep and cut the heart too keenly for the telling. He knows the inexpressible racking pain of loneliness which beggars all description, and He has not left us orphans. He has stayed with us, He dwells with us, that we may come and tell Him all.

Mother may come and tell Him fears for loved ones that she dare not, cannot put in words; father can kneel and speak to Him of sharp struggles in the busy markets of the world and of the hungry little faces that will all too surely greet him in the nearing future, unless "the Keeper of little ones" quickly lends His aid. Sorrows of heart and fears of mind and terrors of soul, vague forebodings of shadowed days ahead and sharp grief for the hidden sins of days now gone, all, all may be told Him and we know that the telling will never be taken amiss, will never be misunderstood. But oh! the great strong solace, when strengthless from the utter pressure of the cross and speechless with the dread of all that is and all that is to be, we kneel in stricken silence before His tabernacle home. As toddling children we were wont to show our bruises to our gentle mother and feel relieved, if she but gazed on them—and what was mother's gentleness to His!

Jesus, knower of the human heart and all its boundless needs, I thank You that You have not left us orphans. Hard enough it is at times to pierce beyond the sacramental veil and catch the sight of Your own dear face, but life would be all too dark, life would be all too dreary and too frighteningly lonely, if You were not with us now. In Your own good wonted way You have met the deepest need of our lives, and Jesus dear, I thank You.

"Stay with us, Lord! Day is far spent!
The evening draweth on;
What could thy lonely children do
If Thou their Light wert gone!
Twilight is round about us cast,
We hear the night wind moaning past,
Oh! till temptation's shadows flee,
Mane nobiscum, Domine."

THIRTEENTH FRIDAY AFTER PENTECOST

BEGGING OFF

For which thing I thrice besought the Lord that it might depart from me. And He said to me: My grace is sufficient for thee.

2 Corinthians 9:8.

WE frequently lose our perspective in life and those who are most prone to introspection are liable to lose it more frequently than others. With my gift of faith I try to follow Christ and to carry out into my whole life those wishes He has made so plain to me. I feel that I am His friend and I cherish that conviction above all others, for to me He means more than life itself. Yet herein may lie a danger for me. Because of that conviction of friendship on the part of God for me, and the confidence of at least an abiding effort on my part to return it, does sorrow or trial come as a shock? "I have tried to keep God's law these many years, why should He treat me so?" Why? Well, when I feel thus, it might be wise to draw my eyes away from self and look out upon the millions of mankind. Let me go to the teeming cities and then out to the straggling hamlets and stop at each door of millionaire or pauper. Shall I find one that will be opened at my knocking behind which does not dwell a weighted heart? What life is there whereon the dark shadow of the Cross does not lie? Young and old, pagan and Christian, each has a sorrow tucked away to irk by day and smart by night. Shall I then, just because I am a friend of God and just because I have stood beneath the Cross, ask or even expect to be freed from the common lot of man? Have I not lost just a bit the right view of things, when I find myself wondering why, despite my services to God, my plans are balked, my dreams are shattered, my hopes are robbed of fulfilment? Were my life unflecked by sorrow, it would be a miracle among the lives of men; and have I the right to ask for miracles?

Of course there is a higher, broader way of looking at my crosses, the way the Saints are wont to look, for they are hungry to taste all sorrow, eager to gather in chips from the great Cross of Christ. But maybe at times such hunger seems an almost morbid thing to me and this eagerness almost a folly. Be it so, then at least let me take the crosses that all men and women bear and for the sake of my Christian manhood let me not sorrow where pagans often smile.

Dear Jesus, I often wonder at the way I look at life, and You must wonder too. When trials come, why do I lose my poise and fret? Why do I complain as though wrong were done me, when I must suffer pain of mind or body? All men must suffer thus, and yet not all know how to sanctify their cross by drawing it near to Yours. Oh, help me, Lord, to have a little sense and to take my share of suffering as a good soldier of Christ and not begin to whimper as a child.

THIRTEENTH SATURDAY AFTER PENTECOST

HOW DOES GOD STAND IT!

And he (Zacharias) did that which is evil before the Lord, as his fathers had done.

4 Kings 15:9.

And he (Manahem) did that which was evil before the Lord.

4 Kings 15:18.

And he (Phaceia) did that which was evil before the Lord.
4 Kings 15:24.

And he (Phacee) did that which was evil before the Lord.
4 Kings 15:28.

As we read the Old Testament, the two things that strike us are the unending rebellions of the Jews and the like unceasing patience of God. That was true from the time they left Egypt, but their rebellions and their sins became worse, it would seem, the more God showed His mercy. And then in "the days of the kings" we read the deadening refrain: "And he [the king] did that which was evil before the Lord; he departed not from the sins of Jeroboam, the son of Nabat, who made Israel to sin." Sin and yet sin, and sin once again, until we wonder how infinite patience itself could hold out. And yet it did—unto the end.

I may not have sinned as badly as Israel or as Israel's kings. I may not have forsaken God entirely and gone after false gods in my sinful madness. No, thanks be to God, from that I have been saved by God's plentiful grace.

But giving myself all the credit that is due me, am I not a sorry specimen? Just look at all that God has given me in the order of nature and of grace—and then look at my return.

First he gave me life from which so many have been withheld through His inscrutable decrees and from which so many others have been cheated by sinfully childless parents. And then He gave me health and strength of body and a sound mind within that body. He gave me eyes that drink in the beauties of His radiant world and ears that thrill to the music that surrounds us. He has given me speech whereby I share my joys and sorrows with others and pass on to them the secrets I have unlocked from His wondrous universe. He has given me to be born in a civilized land with opportunities for education and for culture.

And over and above all these things of nature, He has bestowed on me grace in lavish abundance. First it came in the waters of Baptism and grew strong thereafter in Confirmation. Penance, too, either increased it or brought it anew and He Himself came with it in Holy Communion. The great Sacrifice of the Mass flooded my soul with it and the gentle Benediction shed upon it a copious treasure. By day and by night, at home and abroad, at work and at play, that supernatural gift came plentifully into my life.

That is what God has been doing. And I? What a scant return I have made! Oh, I may have tried at times to show my gratitude; at times—but not too often. I did try quite bravely to catch up with God in His generosity. But really—most times have I not been downright unmindful of God and quite contented to jog along in a tepid, listless way? At best I have not offended Him seriously—but that is scant credit to me. I just did not try enough—and I jogged along in my own old easy-going way.

Dear Jesus, I wonder why You don't get tired of it all! I am sure I would if anyone tried my patience as I try Yours. I just would not stand for it. But You are God and Your patience is infinite—yes, that I know. Yet, infinite as it is—how *do* You put up with us? Dear Jesus, from my heart I thank You for Your patience. Just bear with me until I grow more grateful!

FOURTEENTH SUNDAY AFTER PENTECOST

FORGETTING GOD

If we have forgotten the name of our God, and if we have spread forth our hands to a strange god, shall not God search out these things? For He knoweth the secrets of the heart.

Psalm 42:21-22.

WE cannot afford to forget God. With most of our friends on this earth, when it comes to the last analysis, we can forget them and sometimes must forget them. But with God it is always otherwise. To forget Him and to hold out, "our hands to a strange god" is to wreck our lives, for life's ultimate stay is then gone. With God gone, life is blanked; it stops this side of the grave and is robbed of every motive that can stir a heart to noble deeds. Few of us are foolhardy and unwise enough to thrust God out entirely, but it were well to think how often we are discourteous to Him and harmful to ourselves by our discourtesy.

He has told me of zeal for souls, of interest in other men to bring them nearer unto Him, and I may know that He is calling me in special wise to be a saviour in my own small circle—yet I do my best to forget the call of God. He wants the pure, white souls of the little ones to be nurtured unto saintly manliness and womanhood, and yet some parents will stretch out their hands to the loud-mouthed god of worldly social-climbing and send their helpless children to schools, where God and all His sacred truths alone may find no entrance. He has told me insistently that I must be of lowly mind and unpretentious and quite averse to self-enhancing, but my ears have tingled with the siren's voice of flattery and I would fain be unreminded of humility and hidden ways. My hands are opened wide to grasp the gold that so bewitches men and I bow down adoringly before it in pagan wise, unmindful of the stern command: "Thou shalt not have strange gods before Me."

This idolizing of the things of time may be quite hidden from the gaze of men within the innermost chambers of our souls, but God is noting it. He marks our wayward love, our discontent with Him, our wanderings after alien gods; and can He help but charge us with our infidelities?

Jesus, my God, my only God, this truancy must stop. I really must not stray away again after that which can never hold my love and which must ultimately yield its place to You. And then again, dear Lord, it wrongs You so, who alone can claim my love with right indisputable. I give You now my heart to break therein each graven idol before which I have bowed. Just be enthroned within my heart—alone!

FOURTEENTH MONDAY AFTER PENTECOST

MIDAS-TOUCH

But He, laying His hands on every one of them, healed them.

St. Luke 4:40.

IT means a deal in life to be able to go and tell everything to a friend who "has been through it all." It will make the telling of our joys all the sweeter to know my friend has had like tasting and to show him the sunshine of my life will bring it new lustre, if so it be this own has been lighted alike. Sorrow's story, too, will be told more readily and words of cheer will come more encouragingly, when my friend has trodden life's dark ways and weathered blinding storms.

Such friends are rare, but to us all there is at least one such and He will never fail us. Be there the dull gripping of fears and forebodings on our mind, we have but to kneel by His side in Gethsemani and see Him grope His darkened way through three tense hours of prayer. And are we sad at loss of friends, who spurn us now, where once they welcomed? Then sit at the supper-board with Him and see the Judas nigh, or stand in Caiaphas' hall and hear a Peter swear to have never known Him. Again we find it growingly difficult to think much of others and little of self and self-borne trials, and then it is we must stand at the cross-roads and hear the self-forgetting Christ speak to the tearful women of Jerusalem. Proneness to unkindly thoughts and a soured outlook on the lives of others must bring us close to the Cross's shaft when our Saviour cries for mercy on His murderers, and stout rebellion against pain and physical discomfiture must find us keeping the death watch near the mangled body of our Friend.

Joys, too, must find us near Him, speaking each little happening to His Sacred Heart. When our hearts are strong with love for those we reverence as authors of our being, we must take into our confidence the little Christ a-playing in the holy house of Nazareth and let Him sanctify that love already sacred in itself. The joy of parents with child must be told to Him to whom the music of a child's fresh heart was the sweetest note discordant earth could sound. The peace and comfort friend gains from friend will find a counterpart in that great human Heart that loved His own and found deep solace in the comradeship of a Peter and a John. Then, too, the love of man and woman, hallowed by the sacramental bond of wedded life, must be brought near to the model of all such love, the love of Christ for His spouse, the Church, and gain therefrom new sanctity. When our hearts beat fast, because the praises of men are loud in our ears, we must hasten to the side of Christ, triumphant in His entry into Jerusalem, that He may teach us how to use such meed of glory prudently, and when the sun of life is very bright and there are cloudless skies, we must hurry on to Cana and ask the Master at the festal board to hold our hearts hard fast to Him, lest they be weaned by the very sweets He so kindly wishes us to have and to enjoy.

Thus with a Midas-touch, if we will only let Him, Christ will hallow each joy and sorrow that we can bring to Him and we ourselves will scarcely know our own poor hearts for they will be changed, as only God can change them.

Jesus, in childhood days, I read of the fabled king whose touch turned all into gold and in the day-dreaming of those young years I quite envied him his gift, but I felt sure it never could come true. Yet when years have passed, I find there is a truer, higher Midas-touch in life, and that You alone possess it. How kind of You to make my dreams come true! Teach me, dearest Lord, to bring all I have to You that You may touch it all, joy and sorrow alike, love and fear, sunshine and rain, life and death. Then and then only will the fairy tales of childhood have come true.

FOURTEENTH TUESDAY AFTER PENTECOST

TUCKING THE FUTURE AWAY WITH GOD

Sufficient for the day is the evil thereof.
St. Matthew 6:34.

SOME of us are always borrowing trouble. If we are human beings, we have difficulties and maybe many of them, for that is the lot of all of us here below. Tucked away somewhere in every heart is a thorn and hidden away in every family is a skeleton in some closet. Yet most of us are foolish enough not to let future trouble alone and, instead of facing the difficulty as it confronts us here and now and instead of solving it prudently in terms of our present knowledge, we give free rein to our imagination. We picture a tomorrow wherein more complications will arise, frustrating any solution we may now give. We see new crosses falling upon our already tired shoulders and fresh mishaps coming to those we love.

If this were only idle day-dreaming, it would be bad enough. But more than that, it is unreasonable to cross a bridge before we come to it, and yet even more than that, it shows a lack of trust in God. Through all these years He has been good, so very good to us and why suspect His love of waning in the future? Is it not reasonable, is it not square to our Lord to read His gifts of the past as so many earnests of help to be renewed in the days to come? Of course, crosses will be there and disappointments too, and many an anxiety for those we love, for we are still pilgrims in this valley of tears. But what of that? When the crosses darken our path, then the light of His cheering presence will be there to guide us. When disappointments spell the doom of hopes for whose fulfilment we had long waited, He will be to us our "reward exceeding great," making up for all we have been cheated of. Yes, and when we worry over those who by nature or by friendship stand close to us, He will tell us of His own greater love for them and bid us leave them to His care.

Tuck the future away with God and leave it with Him. It will bring sunshine and hours of joy and let us be merry then when they come. It will bring darkness too and many a tear, but let us weep then, not now. God alone knows what is the hidden freight of the days to come. There may be many more days of sunshine than of shadow. It may be that the tear-filled hours will far outnumber those in which we smile. Who knows? One only. So why not leave it all to Him and trust His love for us?

Dear Jesus, You know the weakness of my heart to reach out into the future and worry over what it may bring. It is a foolish thing to borrow trouble when so much is mine already, and worse than that it is not fair and square to You. My past is one long series of protecting acts from Your ever watchful providence and it is not right to feel You will be less kind than You have been. So, dearest Lord, to show my confidence in You, I shall take Your sound advice and let the evil of each day suffice me. I shall leave the days to come alone and here and now I tuck the future away with You.

FOURTEENTH WEDNESDAY AFTER PENTECOST

LABORING FOR THE WIND

What then doth it profit him that he hath labored for the wind?

Ecclesiastes 5:15.

THE Wise Man has been looking over the world and he finds it a mass of vanities which in the Hebrew text means "nothings." He finds toil and trouble, fever and anxiety, a mad race for wealth, a wild scramble for positions of power. He sees the one who hath "no child, no brother, and yet he ceaseth not to labor, neither are his eyes satisfied with riches," and yet this same man realizes that the covetous man "shall take nothing away with him of his labor" into the grave. Yes, and the Wise Man asks the further question even of those whose eyes are not dazzled by the glint of gold: "What hath the wise man more than the fool? and what the poor man, but to go thither, where there is life?" "What then doth it profit him that he hath labored for the wind?"

Indeed, to labor for wealth, for honor, for power, is to labor for the wind—and that is hardly profitable. Yet, foolish children of the world that we are, even we who know the better things of God, even we whose eyes have been lifted "thither where there is life," do we not at times "labor for the wind?"

Here is a mother and a father who love their little "keepsake for Heaven" and yet, that the child may be "fitted for the world," they will send it to a school from which Christ is outlawed or where at best He is but little known and that falsely. They do not think that in fitting their child to take its place in the society of this world, they may be unfitting it to take its place in the society of the Saints in Heaven. And is that not a vain "laboring for the wind"?

Again a man is seized with the desire for wealth and the ring of the coins is music to his ears and the feel of the crisp new bill is soothing to his hands. The hoard grows larger, yet "he that loveth riches shall reap no fruit from them," and though the world lays out its treasures before him and he eats and drinks of the finest from all lands, and clothes his body in softest raiment, "all the days of his life he eateth in darkness, and in many cares, and in misery and in sorrow," and his hungry heart gnaws away within him. He labors, yes, but he "labors for the wind."

Another would have learning and would peer into the depths of matter and snatch its whirling particles from their ultimate hiding-places. Yet another scans, night after night, the starry places of God's unsounded heavens and draws from the darknesses the unseen worlds and tags them with a name. The work is good and helpful too, but when the hands let the microscope and the telescope fall, what is there for that immortal soul to find—save God? And so it is with all the knowledge which "our thin minds that creep from thought to thought" can find—mere shadows of the one great Being who alone will ease the fundamental cravings of our nature. The rest is "laboring for the wind."

"Laboring for the wind," indeed, it is to chase the will-o'-the-wisps of time, no matter how real they seem, no matter how tangible. As well try to rest on the skirts of the fleeting breezes, as well try to cling to the mane of the thunderous storm-wind, as to find support in the things of time. Honor, and wealth and power and knowledge, yes, and the most unsubstantial of them all, human praise, these bend and snap under the weight of immortal souls.

Dear Jesus, You have been very good to me and You have taught me much about Yourself, and Heaven, and how I must hasten "thither where there is life." But I fail at times to hearken to Your goodly teachings and I listen to the siren call of the things of sense. They trick me into following them and yet I know full well how fleeting they are. Enough of my years have been wasted already and I would be done with this waywardness in seeking rest where rest cannot be found. Just give me grace, dear Lord, never again to "labor for the wind."

FOURTEENTH THURSDAY AFTER PENTECOST

JUST LIKE GOD

O God, who is like to Thee?

Psalm 70:19.

IT was in the dimly lighted ward of the great city hospital, whither the flotsam and jetsam of mankind drifted. On one of the beds lay a man's form just stilled in death, and near it stood a woman weeping.

Suddenly she looked up and spoke: "Father, did Jack get the Last Sacraments? Did he go to Confession? He's been bad, very bad! Oh, I hope he did! Did he?" And when the priest nodded his head in assurance: "Oh, isn't that just like God! Isn't that just like God!" was the joyous cry of gratitude that came straight from that sister's heart.

What a wonderful way and what a true way to put it! God can do, and He does do, "the nicest things" for us. First of all, when He created Adam, He gave him the greatest gift that lies within His omnipotence: sanctifying grace. And when Adam had wilfully thrown this gift away, it was "just like God," instead of leaving him alone, to have mercy on him and to give him a second chance. And the way in which He gave that second chance was a way that only God could conceive—the Incarnation.

And so it was "just like God" to choose a virgin for His Mother, and be born in a stable, and work as a carpenter, and die on the Cross.

And it was "just like God," when He had tarried here a while visibly, to be unwilling to leave us orphans. So He stays with us on our altars and comes to us to be the food and life of our souls whenever we so will it.

And in our own individual lives, isn't it "just like God" to put up with our peevishness and our rebellions, and after we have sinned, no matter what our sin may be, to accept us again, if only we be sorry and tell Him so? Only God could be so patient; only He could be so long-suffering; only He forgives and forgives, and forgives, not "seventy times seven," but on and on and on. Only God could remain a prisoner for nineteen hundred years, and wait for His loved ones to come to Him, and not be thoroughly disgusted with their discourtesies of neglect.

Dear Jesus, how good You are! Others are kind, but not so kind as You. Others are patient, but none endures what You put up with. Others suffer a bit of neglect and forgetfulness, but none forgives repeated "cuts" as You do. Strangely do I repay Your love; strangely do I try Your patience. Yet You are always my changeless Friend. It's all so wonderfully grand, dear Lord—it's "just like God."

FOURTEENTH FRIDAY AFTER PENTECOST

HIS BITTER DOSES

Passion of Christ, make me strong.
Anima Christi.

THE swallowing is hard, awfully hard, but I get comfort when I remember and think of your own bitter doses." Those were the lines penned far, far afield where God's missionaries fought His battles in the outposts of civilization; and they were the cry from the heart of a strong man of Christ. A few months back the call came to "go forth out of thy country, and from thy kindred—and come into the land which I shall show thee." The order came suddenly, quite unexpectedly; and it rocked the man, even though he had vowed himself to serve God wheresoever He willed, and fully meant his vow. And so he squared his shoulders and took the blow, and as the two priest-friends knelt in the great Cathedral before the final parting, they both laid his burdens at the feet of the Master. And then when months had passed and wide seas separated them, the word came back: "I think of your own bitter doses." Yes, the companion had had bitter, bitter doses, and they had come often and for long. Of these he had told his friend, for they were much united; and now the words came back that the taking of those "doses" in what was felt to be a manly way was nerving a fellow-soldier's heart to fight lustily ahead in a battle that was far harder.

"But I get comfort when I remember and think of your own bitter doses." How that thought should come home to us, as we kneel in adoration before our Lord! He had His "bitter doses," more bitter than human heart has ever known. At birth, He was an outcast, and His Mother found but a stable for His covering and a manger for His bed. And so it will help me to kneel at the Crib and remember this His "bitter dose," when the pinch of poverty makes me wince. It will nerve me to stand the slights of men, when I think of the "bitter dose" of rejection by His own and see the scorn on many a lip as the slurring query comes: "Can any good come from Nazareth?" To labor unrewarded by success, to be unsparing of self by day and by night and to garner but scant harvest from it all—is a trial that breaks many a stout heart. Yet, when that trial comes, it would ease the pain to think of the "bitter dose" of disappointment that was our Lord's, when after three years of journeying up and down the land of His own Chosen People He could find at the end so few, so very few that remained in any way true to Him. Yes, and of His specially picked Twelve, one betrayed Him, one denied Him, and all ran away! That indeed was a "bitter dose" of seemingly utter failure.

Sometimes, too, the very pillars of life seem to crumple beneath me and the very foundations seem to be moved. It may be, too, that men mock me for my failure and wag knowing heads over all the wreckage. What of it? Then above all times I must remember the "bitter dose" of Calvary and I must go out and stand long and prayerfully beneath the Cross in the gathered darkness. "My God, My God, why hast Thou forsaken Me?" will find an echo in my heart and yet will make that heart strong to keep close to its King, as He does stout battle unto death.

Oh, what comfort in our trials—no matter what they be—to know that the same "bitter doses" have been tasted by my changeless Friend and that He has shown me how to drain the cup of sorrow to its dregs! That is a consolation and a strength that no other faith gives and it is that I must gain, as I kneel before Him.

Dear Jesus, I do not like the "bitter doses" of life and the swallowing is hard. One day it is this trial, another day that; one day a disappointment and another day a failure; one day a slight and another day a sneer; one day false friends, and another day scheming foes. Oh, it is all so hard, all so discouraging! Yet I must face it all and see it all through manfully. And so I thank You from my heart for having gone before me and suffered so much for me. You drained the cup of sorrow that is pressed to our lips so often in this valley of tears. So please give me much grace in the hour of trial to remember Your own "bitter doses."

FOURTEENTH SATURDAY AFTER PENTECOST

YOU CAN'T BEAT GOD

Who is able to declare His works? . . . And who shall show forth the power of His majesty? Or who shall be able to declare His mercy?

Ecclesiasticus 18:2-4.

WE were driving down through the mountains just when autumn was touching with glory every leaf and tree. As the road dipped up and down and swung dizzily left and right around the shoulders of the hills, enchanting vistas of tempestuous colors opened up, and fold on fold of the mountains burst on us with a riot of radiance. "Look, Father! Look! You can't beat God!" Time and time again this cry burst forth exultingly.

No. "You can't beat God." No painter ever blended colors as He does. No sculptor ever molded beauty as He does. No architect ever builded as massively or as gracefully as He does.

But these sensible beauties are the lesser things in which God excels. There are other, better, finer things in which "you can't beat God."

Of His own goodness He has given us life, and no one but He could have given us that life. He has given us the plants and the animals for food and raiment. For our home He has given us the earth, and He has thrown about it the glories of the heavens, with the sun by day and the myriad stars and planets by night. And during every moment He sustains us in existence; for without His supporting hand we should instantly lapse into our original nothingness. "You can't beat God" in His generosity.

But greater than all these natural gifts, God has given us the power to know Him and His truths through His own Revelation. And He has given us His Church to teach and guide us, and all His sevenfold Sacraments to nourish and sustain the supernatural life of our souls. He came to us as a man, and He has stayed with us upon our altars. He has given us Mary His Mother to be our mother, and the Saints and Angels to be our guides and guards. "You can't beat God" in His kindness.

All this is in itself marvelous, beyond our thinking. But He has done more. When we have rebelled against Him and have forgotten His love for us, He tries to win us back. We violate His commands and add sin to sin, but so soon as we tell Him truly that we are sorry, He forgives and forgets completely. "You can't beat God" in His mercy.

And so it is with His justice and His power and His knowledge and all His infinite perfections—"You can't beat God!"

Dear Jesus, I am so happy that You are what You are—God without any limit to all You have: without limit to Your kindness, to Your power, to Your justice, to Your love, to Your mercy. Sometimes as a wilfull child I am displeased with You. I forget all You have done and are doing for me. I am truly sorry that I have ever wronged Your love and forgotten Your mercies. No one can ever equal You in all Your infinite perfections, and I am so glad of that. I am happy that "you can't beat God."

FIFTEENTH SUNDAY AFTER PENTECOST

I CAN ALWAYS GO TO HIM

Come to me, all you that labor and are burdened, and I will refresh you.

St. Matthew 11:28.

BUT why have you stayed away so long, Jack?"

"I say, Father, don't you know why? I wanted to come, wanted to, badly; but I realized better than I had before what a strenuous life yours is, and I didn't want to add to your burdens. But I will 'fess up that I was childish enough, the last time I was here, to want you to say: 'Jack, come again soon.' But you didn't."

And the priest's heart was heavy at the thought that a soul in need had been kept waiting.

That was most unfortunate, and how often it happens in life! Some one wants to talk, to unburden himself of something that is almost too deep to express and yet can and would be told to just one definite friend. But that friend may be far away or so overwhelmed with work that it is hard to get to him. Or it may be he has worries of his own, without burdening him with more.

That happens to all of us in life, and it were well to know, from our youngest years, that, however much we may be left without the help of human friends, there is always one Divine Friend to whom we can go at any time, in any place. Our Lord is never too busy to see us and to listen to our story. We can talk to Him as long or as briefly as we like, and He will understand. We do not have to ask Him in advance whether we may see Him; we do not have to know whether "any one is with Him now." He is never out, and He never has anxieties that crowd out ours.

That is one of the great consolations of our Faith. I can go to Him and always find Him, and, best of all, He understands. Even the truest of friends may read me amiss at times, may credit me with good I have not done, or condemn me for wrongdoing of which I have not even thought. They may misconstrue my motives and find selfishness where there was none, or pride where closest scrutiny tells me it was not present.

And when I have sinned I can go to Him—shamefacedly, yes, but confidently too; for "He knows the clay of which we are made." There is no sin that can put me beyond His mercy, and the more soiled and bruised my soul, the more healing will be His touch, with all "the tenderness of pierced hands."

And, best of all, He never changes. I may wilfully defy His laws. I may turn my love of Him into hate. But He loves me still: "For unto your old age I am the same, and unto your gray hairs I will carry you; I have made you and I will bear. I will carry and will save."

Dear Jesus, teach me to understand and realize Your love for me. By very reason of my human make-up I want to be understood and loved. Some of my friends do understand and love me, but my deepest thoughts and desires are beyond their reach. Then, too, when I need them most, they are apt to fail me, even through no fault of their own. But You do understand me through and through, and to You I can come any time and everywhere. Just help me to remember that when I need You most.

FIFTEENTH MONDAY AFTER PENTECOST

A ONE-EYED KING

What hast thou that thou hast not received? And if thou hast received, why dost thou glory, as if thou hadst not received it?

1 Corinthians 4:7.

WASN'T it glorious?" "And didn't she sing fine!" "Yes, and didn't he speak his line beautifully and act fine!" Thus was the crisp night air awakened in the little country place as "the folks" came out of the stuffy, cramped hall. The village singers had sung to their hearts' content and the country actors and actresses had stormed and fumed and screamed and cried in true and proper amateurishness. Yet the applause was long and loud and fully meant. For one who knew of better things it was an almost trying experience, but to these folks of narrow horizons and slender talents it was a night long to be remembered. It was indeed "a grand and glorious evening!"

"A one-eyed man is king among the blind" is the old French proverb which holds tucked away within it a deal of wisdom. Given a talent somewhat out of the ordinary or even a bit larger share of the gifts that all men have, and at once the lucky owner stands forth a marked man. To run a bit faster, to hit a ball farther, to dance more gracefully, to be a bit comelier, to have a quicker grasp on the things of the mind, to be able to remember better—that singles us out at once. Others show us honor and the more simple they are, the more they praise and marvel at our "wonderfulness."

Ought not that to help us in our temptations to pride, when the praise of men sounds sweetly and enticingly in our ears? Suppose it is all sincere —we scarce can know when it is—and suppose it is deserved—which may quite often be true—what then? Shall I forget my common sense and let pride swell my heart and head? If I do sing beautifully, what of it! The power to sing comes from God, and the song itself was probably sung better some time and some place. If grace and beauty of body is mine, what of it! That, too, came from God and it must not make me vain and silly, and forgetful that true grace and beauty is in the soul. Yes, and it might be well to draw the curtain of the future and look down into the narrow hold of the grave, when that same graceful, beautiful body will house devouring worms.

It may be that keenness of intellect is mine and the power to delve deep into nature's secrets. What of it? The sheer facing of facts will tell me that the poet was quite right when he described, "our thin minds that creep from thought to thought." We do learn a bit here and a bit there, but in the end and after long years, what scant harvesting is ours! And any way, did not the power to harvest come from God?

So a goodly proverb it is that "a one-eyed man is king among the blind," and a goodly thing, moreover, to remember that the "one eye" comes from God. The gifts of life and the praise that follows aptly on the use of those gifts must not unbalance us or make us act in witless wise.

Dear Lord, all that I have comes from You and I must use all well and for my good, and for helping others and for Your own service. Yet when I use these gifts, men are wont to praise and I am apt to have my silly head turned by their praise. I must not be so foolish. You gave me all the little that I have. Please give me, too, grace to use all well and, if the praise of men rings too pleasantly in my ears, the grace to remember that "a one-eyed man is king among the blind."

FIFTEENTH TUESDAY AFTER PENTECOST

STUBBORN

Be you humbled, therefore, under the mighty hand of God.

1 Peter 5:6.

JACK is an almost hopeless obstacle. I never heard of a man so thoroughly unpopular with every one—his family, his acquaintances, his fellow workmen. It's incredible." Well, it was not so incredible to anyone who really knew Jack, for an intimate friend had said of him: "He is the most stubborn human being I have ever met." Stubborn he was to the utmost degree, and when one had seen his stubbornness in action, one could regard no subsequent confusion as incredible.

Stubbornness is strength of will gone wrong. To have a strong will is to have received a great gift from God, but with its very strength comes a full obligation to use it aright and an attendant danger that it may get out of my control. A Twentieth-Century locomotive is a wonderful engine and can be used to devour mile after mile of the long road, but only if it be under control. But if it gets out of hand——!

An essential asset in life is humility enough to doubt, sufficient lowly-mindedness to be interiorly convinced that some time, somewhere, it is at least within the realm of possibility that I may be wrong. That is the minimum requirement of common sense, the slightest that can be demanded of me that my eternal salvation may not be wholly in danger.

Few of us, thanks be to God, are as stubborn as Jack. But we all grow stubborn at times in big or in little things. We may be right, and then our stubbornness is good. But equally we may be wrong, and then stubbornness will be either comical or tragic, as the case in hand is small or great. And so it were well to seek advice when we know that there are against us others for whose opinions men usually have a decent regard. The very fact that certain men judge me to be wrong, should make me pause and learn their reasons and weigh them well. After all, not every bit of wisdom has been tucked away within my own poor, small head.

And this ability to doubt one's own judgment is no immature attitude of mind. Quite the opposite. It is the outstanding trait of immaturity that it deems itself omniscient. And surely none of us wants to remain in callow youth. To doubt, wisely and deliberately, is a sure sign of maturing years; for youth does not stop to think, and so is wontedly stubborn.

To doubt in matters of earth is wise; to doubt in matters of our soul is very wise. For there we are in an unknown land, and the penalties of mistaking our way are far more serious. And that is why God has given us guides whom He Himself directs, that we may journey safely and directly to Him.

Dear Jesus, let me always have common sense enough to be convinced that I may easily be mistaken. That is sheer common sense, and it is true humility. I may know many things, and be quite capable to manage much aright. But still I can be wrong; I still can make mistakes. So give me grace never, never to be so stubborn that I refuse reasonable and legitimate advice, but to be ever mindful of my essential liability to make mistakes.

FIFTEENTH WEDNESDAY AFTER PENTECOST

HAPPY AND FORGETFUL

You have forgotten God, who brought you up.
Baruch 4:8.

SISTER, did you ever forget God, when you were happy? When I was lonesome . . . I prayed almost every hour of the day and now it is rather hard to pray; but I must." Thus wrote a young woman whose world was a supremely happy one in the love that had been sanctified a few months back by Holy Matrimony at God's altar. The world was very, very sweet and in the joy of her young, overflowing heart she penned those words to the Sister-teacher who had taught her much of God. She loved God—really, and with her heart—and she was trying hard to serve Him, and yet she knew she was not running to God as of old. "Did you ever forget God when you were happy? . . . now it is rather hard to pray, but I must." Fortunately for her, she realized that such forgetfulness was wrong and still more fortunately she made resolve to be done with it.

"Did you ever forget God when you were happy?" would be a right profitable question to ask ourselves—and how many of us could answer "No"? Just pause a moment and pass the days that are gone before our eyes. "When I was lonesome . . . I prayed almost every hour of the day." When sickness came and darkened the days of one we loved, down on our knees we fell and prayed with Martha and Mary—"Lord, he whom Thou lovest is sick," and long was our prayer and earnest, too. When men's tongues began to wag and say unkind things about us, injuring our work and hampering our efforts, we were quick to beg of God protection from their mischief-making. Yes, let but the slightest cloud veil the sunlight of our lives and like disappointed children we rushed to God and implored His help. We needed Him then badly and so we ran to Him.

But, children that we are, when all went well, we forgot God, even as child forgets mother when play-time is on. We did not feel the need of Him then. Our hearts beat fast with a happiness that seemed to satisfy so adequately, and it did for a passing while. Health was ours and all the buoyancy it brings; a competency of the world's wealth offset all fears of a nearing rainy day; and friends were true and most devoted. What was there then to ask for, and is it so strange that we failed to run to God?

Well, rather. Strange indeed it is that we do not go to God, like decent folk, to thank Him for His favors—for life and health and wealth and friends, and all the joys that go therewith. Surely a hearty "Thank you, dear Lord" would be quite seemly; would it not? And again—we have these gifts, but have we the power to retain them? Do we not need God's aid to keep the health that is ours, or are we fools enough to think that our refusal to hear would stop death's knocking at our door? The goods of time are ours, but are we quite satisfied with our ability to be ultimately successful in a game where the cleverest often lose? Honor may be ours, but others have been cheated of love and praise; and can I protect myself better than they? Yes, it is strange that we forget God, whose watchful protection we need so much each moment of our lives, and we must really try to be less impolite with God.

Dear Jesus, I know You understand this childish heart of mine. When I stand in need of anything, I always instinctively turn to You, because I know You always want to help me and can always help me. I beg and plead with You, and so You kindly heed my prayer. But then—off I run and, when the world smiles, I smile with it and scarcely think of You. This is not right and I am quite ashamed of myself that I treat You so. I need You always, Lord, need You badly, and even if I did not need You, sheer gratitude ought to make me never forget You.

FIFTEENTH THURSDAY AFTER PENTECOST

POP-CALLS

Where thy treasure is, there is thy heart also.
St. Matthew 6:21.

IT was high noon in the great city and far down in the heart of the section where men play the grueling game for money in the business world, the old Church held its doors wide open. Within was Christ our Lord in veiled majesty upon His altar-throne, for it was Adoration Hour, and around Him knelt a wondrous gathering of His folk. Here young women who had shortened lunch hour to say their beads before their King and there a woman on in years who told the sorrows, that lay nearest her heart, to her Friend from long ago. Strong steps, falling quite lightly, brought in young men who would whisper to their Captain Christ that their hearts were mindful of their pledge to be like Him, and far away in lowly adoration bowed gray-haired merchants who had learned these many years to prize aright the treasures of another world. All knelt before their King and told their varied stories and all rose up with new strength in their hearts to face life's stress and strain. And ever was the silent hush there, and ever did the silent forms come and go, and all day long the tapers burned themselves prayerfully away.

So come the friends of Christ, and do I come with them? As I pass before His door, do my feet instinctively turn and my hands reach out quite naturally that I may go within and have a word, just a word with my changeless Friend? In Southern lands friends often pay a "pop-call," tarrying just a moment to let the others know they are not forgotten. Thus their love is kept fresh and welded firm. Have we yet learned to give our best Friend the pleasure of a "pop-call"? Stress of work or other duties may make a longer stay impossible, but it will please Him so to see us for a moment and be told that He is loved by us still. Then for ourselves. If sunshine be upon our lives and joy be in our hearts, this will become a hallowed thing, for we shall share it with our Friend. Sorrow may be there, irksome in its newness or galling from its wonted frictioning, but that hurried call will bring, if not full freedom or even a respite, at least new grace to bear the crosses of our God's own fashioning. Yes, and if life be all quite colorless with little of the unwonted in its path, a fresh appeal will come from Christ our Lord to make this very commonplace life wholly His and to mold it into a rare and blessed thing by reason of unstinted love for Him. Only let us come, come and stay long and, if so we are privileged, chat quite at our ease; come and hurry away, if life's demands are heavy on our time—only let us come.

Dear Jesus, You must see more of me, for it is not right that I should be such a stranger in Your home. I come, I know, but surely did I realize that You are my dearest Friend, I would come oftener. Oh, I regret the neglectful past and I ask Your pardon for my lack of courteous friendliness. I do love You, dear Lord, and I would grow in love for You each day and so I promise now to visit You each time I may. And, dearest Lord, You will not mind, I know, if at times my visit be the hurried "pop-call" of a busy friend, for this very filching from my crowded hours will show You that I love You.

FIFTEENTH FRIDAY AFTER PENTECOST

DESPITE THE PAST

Lord, I suffer violence. Answer Thou for me.
Isaias 38:14.

NEITHER fire nor fagot nor scaffold shall separate me from Thee, O Lord," cries out the aged priest, as he stands upon the hurdle at Smithfield, where English martyrs bled. Brave words these are and sprung from a man's brave heart and yet in the past that same heart had quailed before the executioners. The love of life had been strong in him and the fear of rack and rope and cauldron and fire had set his nerves a-tingling—and he had signed what seemed a recantation. He had seemed to waver and to fall, as Peter did in years gone by, but only for a while. Then the old love of Christ, whom he had served so well, burned strong again and he was done with weaknesses. Beneath the fatal gallows he stands now and though he knows his fall and knows his faithlessness to Christ, he trusts his courage will not wane, because he has placed it in the hands of Christ.

What utter confidence in our Lord! The past was darkened by the unseemly fall, but what of that! Christ could take a weakling heart and make it strong. Christ could feed unyielding courage into a timid soul that once had failed. Christ, his friend from long ago, whom he had served these many years, could stand hard by His olden servitor and make his fight victorious, could answer for him now when he suffers violence.

A lesson, there, for me who lose so easily my confidence in Christ when I have fallen. It is a wrongful thing to sin. Of course it is. It is an ungrateful thing to fail Christ's expectations. Unquestionably. But does that change Christ? He knows my weaknesses; yes, reads them all discerningly. But what I must recall is that He loves me, not for what I am, but for what He would have me be and for His own undying glory. Then why this sense of helplessness? And why this thought of the utter uselessness of effort? And why this will to quit the fight because I know that I have fallen? It may be I have prayed amiss, or even cast my prayers aside. It may be I have loosed my tongue, and spiteful, hurtful words have sounded on the air. It may be I have thought me little of my Christian manliness, and have shown myself quite peeved and irritated when things have gone awry. It may be even that I have thrown God's grace away by deadly sin. It matters not. Jesus Christ, "yesterday, today, and the same forever," is waiting now to aid me, as he aided Peter of old and to nerve me, as He nerved the martyr of Elizabeth's bloody days. Sad, indeed, the past and dark in memory, but am I to win Heaven by my own strength or by the strength of Christ?

O Jesus, strength of wavering hearts, in days gone by You steadied many a man who found life's battle going hard against him. Strength had shown itself as weakness in the hour when souls are tested utterly, but Your own power brought them on to victory. Then help me now! My past is all a sorry sight. I have quit the fight and yielded as a coward yields. The fault is mine, mine only, and I am all ashamed. But, Jesus dear, just there is where Your strength must come and aid me.

FIFTEENTH SATURDAY AFTER PENTECOST

A CREDIT TO GOD

Blessed be the God and Father of our Lord Jesus Christ, who hath blessed us with spiritual blessings . . . unto the praise of the glory of His grace.

Ephesians 1:3, 6.

ST. Paul is writing to the Ephesians, who were quite ordinary men and women of their day, usually of no great wealth or social standing in their community but just a group of which each was just another specimen of "the man in the street." In the introduction to his glorious letter to the Ephesians he stresses the thought that each of them is to be a real credit to God because of what God's grace makes out of them. Commonplace men and women, they are by grace to grow so patient, so kind, so just, so pure, so outstandingly virtuous in a world of sinfulness, that men will marvel at the power of God's grace upon frail human nature.

What a thought to spur all of us on. Too often—or maybe most often—we take a quite selfish view of our spiritual progress. It is all a question of self—of self-improvement, of self-advancement, and finally of protecting oneself against an eternity in hell and gaining thereby a reward for self unendingly in Heaven. And it is always *self* very, very prominently in the picture.

But why not rather think of everything we do from God's side? If I can grow more humble, what a tribute to God's grace which is strong enough to bow pride such as mine! If I can leave off worldliness and grow enamored of the seemly things of God, what a proof that God's grace can steady even the giddiest of hearts! If, after having gone the way of sinful flesh, I grow pure again, will that not show men that God's grace can quench the fires of concupiscence, no matter how fiercely they may have burned?

A credit to God! The young man who walks straightforwardly through the snares of sin and keeps his Christian knighthood pure! The young woman who is every inch a real, live girl of her day, yet keeps her soul untainted! The husband and wife who remain firm in their mutual love and hold fast to the pledges made at God's altar! The business man who plays the game hard, but plays it squarely always! The priest or Religious who has sealed a heart away for God and lives an angelic life in a sordid world.

Dear Jesus, what a thought to spur me on—to be a credit to You and to the power of Your grace! Many a man and many a woman has been urged on and on to noble living by the thought of the happiness this would mean to a loving mother—and should it not drive me on, too? No thought of self here, but only of the glory it will be to You for men to see what Your grace has been able to do with me despite my frailties and defects. And Jesus, for all Your goodness to me, I do want to be a credit to You.

SIXTEENTH SUNDAY AFTER PENTECOST

PLENTEOUS IN MERCY

For Thou, O Lord, art sweet and mild; and plenteous in mercy to all that call upon Thee.

Psalm 85:5.

A QUITE unnecessary amount of harm has been done by over-insistence on God's justice. Just He is, infinitely so, and it is, indeed, a dreadful thing to fall guilty into the hands of the living God. Our Lord Himself tells us: "Fear ye Him who, after He hath killed, hath power to cast into hell. Yea, I say to you, fear Him" (St. Luke 12:5). When He punishes, His punishments are severe; but He punishes only when we force Him. In all His dealings with mankind "His mercy is above all His works," and this is written large over all the Scripture.

In the Old Testament we may sum up His dealings with the stiff-necked Jews in His repeated cry through the Prophets: "And why will you die, O house of Israel?" (Ez. 18:31). "Why then is this people in Jerusalem turned away with a stubborn revolting? . . . My sorrow is above sorrow; My heart mourneth within Me" (Jer. 8:5, 18). No matter how far they had strayed away, no matter how vile they had been, still He would always forgive them and take them back. Always pleading, always consoling, too, as when the prophet Baruch cried: "Be of good comfort . . . for as it was your mind to go astray from God, so when you return again you shall seek Him ten times as much."

And the one word that adequately sums up the New Dispensation is *love*: love shown at the Incarnation; love shown at Bethlehem; love shown at Nazareth; love shown in the three-years' ministry; love crying out aloud from the Cross whereon hangs the Divine Victim of love. Yes, the Son of Man will come again in majesty, "sitting on the right hand of the power of God, and coming in the clouds of Heaven," but He comes now daily in the frail whiteness of the Host to be our food and strength.

Surely the Lord is "sweet and mild, and plenteous in mercy" and we wrong Him much when we place our fear of Him foremost in our lives. He wants to be loved, not feared, unless, of course, we cannot find it in us to love Him. His whole plea is summed up: "Son, give Me thy heart." It is not the service of a cringing slave that He wants, no matter how exact that service be, but the dutiful attention of a loving child. Then, even though there are slips and faults, He is "sweet and mild" and will not take them amiss, if we regret them. Yes, even if we grow very rebellious and spurn His love, even then will He take us back into the intimacy of His children; for He is "plenteous in mercy," if we but call upon Him.

Dear Lord, how often we poor mortals wrong You! We measure Your love by our little love, Your forgiveness by our small sense of pardon. When men offend us often, we are only too apt to be done with them—and we think You are the same. Shame, Lord, for us not to know You better. The very meanness of our faults shows You "sweet and mild"; the very foulness of our sins proves that You are "plenteous in mercy." Just give us grace to remember that—always!

SIXTEENTH MONDAY AFTER PENTECOST

THE SILENCE OF DEATH

For we are the children of saints.

Tobias 2:18.

WHAT! That grand man gone!" were the words that came from many lips, when it was noised abroad that death had really come to one who was known far and wide for his courage and power and willingness to help. But did these words come readily to those of his own home? To the world at large his name was in benediction, but within his home there was the charitable "silence of death." Power he had, yes, but that power had been used too often to hurt and wound his very flesh and blood. Strong of mind, yes, but equally strong of tongue, he had made the one, whom he had chosen out of all the daughters of men as his companion in life, to feel the lash and sting of it often. Just he was in his business dealings, yes, but partial to one child more than another within the home. So, while the wide world chanted his praises, his own loved ones tried to forget the times of slighting, and moments of stinging rebuke, and the hours of pain. A grand man he was, and they knew it—but not too much so to them.

The charitable "silence of death"! Let me think. If death were to come to me here and now, would those nearest and dearest to me have to fight back memories they would rather not harbor? My lips would be cold and taut now, but would yesterday recall the uncharitable word that wounded hearts, and would another day throw back the echo of a scolding not deserved? My eyes are dead and lightless now, but would they think of the days they had craved just one look of recognition and approval, just one fleeting glance that told them of efforts recognized and appreciated? My hands would be stilled now, but as they clasp them for the last long time must the cry—"Oh, would they had been lifted oftener in benediction!" be smothered?

"He never caused an eye to shed a tear, until he died," was beautifully said of one who had spent life well; and would that it could be said of each and all of us! To leave behind us memories that will be fruitful of good, that will spur others on to higher, holier living, that will make them kind yet firm, gentle yet strong-willed for right, lovers of God and with their hearts set on eternity, yet facing squarely and solving fearlessly the problems of this world. These are the memories I must leave and not the biting, searing kind that the awful "silence of death" charitably tries to blank out.

It was such memories that old Tobias cherished of his parents—"for we are the children of saints." It was such memories that he handed down to his own son, for whose soul he had so goodly a care. Such are the memories I must hand down to loved ones, and friends, and acquaintances, and all the chance-met travelers on the road to God. But I shall never leave such memories unless, day in and day out, I press self and selfish aims under; unless I school myself to utter patience; unless I see beneath and behind the dross of life, and catch the true gold hid in every heart, unless I treat each man and woman as I myself would be treated; unless I love them all for God.

Dear Jesus, with Your grace I want to try so to live that, when I die, men and women will not feel that they must keep "the silence of death," lest they offend against charity. I want to lead a helpful life, a kindly life and an understanding life. But to do that I must keep very near You and I must learn of You to be "meek and humble of heart" and not to crush the bruised reed or quench the burning flax. So give me, Lord, much grace to catch the sweet contagion of Your ways.

SIXTEENTH TUESDAY AFTER PENTECOST

UPS AND DOWNS

Thou, O Lord, art a God of compassion, and merciful, patient and of much mercy and true. O look upon me, and have mercy on me.

Psalm 85:15, 16.

A RESOLUTION to amend and actual amendment are very distinct and different things. Here as I kneel in prayer my mind is flooded with light from the eternal hills and my will is stirred by that same Omnipotence at whose creative word the world sprang into being. I see the truths of time and of eternity in some way as God sees them. I weigh all things in the scales of God and I find my actions quite unfit to pass His scanning eye. Then with an onrush of my will's full power, I summon up a whole-souled act of sorrow for the times now gone, and pledge myself to see to it that the past be not repeated in the future. It is a wholesome act, this breaking in desire with the past, and when we have made it thinkingly and well, then we leave our prayer to go and make our pledge reality. The promise is made, the fulfilment is now to come.

Were it not well to realize the vital difference between these things? Our resolutions may be strong and very fervent and yet, frail mortals that we are, when the friction of daily life begins to wear and tell on us, we fail in our high resolves. Yesterday, as oft before, I told my Master I regretted much all my complainings against His holy will in days gone by, and that I really would strive to bear at least composedly the little trials He would send. Yet before the day had lost itself in darkness, I was loud in my rebellion once again. This morning I pledged my soldier's word to my Captain Christ to have done with pride and all self-seeking, and scarce an hour had come and gone, when I found myself a-strutting across life's stage to gain the plaudits of my fellows. And yet I really meant my morning words. So, too, with charity and so with prayer and so with all the virtues. Yet, in fairness to myself, I cannot say that I never did resolve to act a decent part.

Distressing? Yes, quite so, and almost enough to unman any but bravest hearts. I really love our Lord and I really want to serve Him, but the drag of poor old human nature tells against me. It is hard to walk ahead courageously when I know that I fall and rise, only to fall and fall again.

It is wearisome work this endless righting of myself and it hurts my pride, yes, hurts it very much. Yet how else become a Saint and how else get to Heaven? Patience, then, a deal of patience with myself, and a constant thinking on the things of God, until their utter attractiveness so wins my fickle heart, that it swerve no longer from the upward path, wandering after creatures and the little comfort they can give.

O Jesus, what a tangle of contradictions I am, "one day eager and brave, the next not caring to try," one hour resolving and the next hour acting as though I knew not what a resolution meant! Frankly, it is discouraging, almost too discouraging, until I remember once again that in You and You alone I must find my strength, for "Thou, O Lord, art a God of compassion and merciful, patient and of much mercy and true." Therefore will I fight on, dear Lord, fight in the dawn-light, fight in the shadows, fight on, because I know my changefulness will be borne with, and pitied, yes, and one day done away with by my changeless Friend. "O look upon me, and have mercy on me."

SIXTEENTH WEDNESDAY AFTER PENTECOST

SWIFT HOLINESS

Forgetting the things that are behind and stretching forth myself to those that are before, I press towards the mark, to the prize of the supernal vocation of God in Christ Jesus.

Philippians 3:13, 14.

OH, yes! Being a Saint is fine, I suppose, but it is the getting there that is too much for me," were words that might have been on the lips of anyone of us. Most of us want to be Saints, but what galls us is *becoming* Saints. In our witlessness we think of a Saint as placid and undisturbable, devoid of human passions and affections, whose life is not and cannot be ruffled by the mere things of time and we all feel that such a state would ease us of pain, and so we want to *be* Saints.

But the shoe hurts much, when we try to put it on. A Saint must be patient, yet it is far from pleasant not to let frayed nerves have their way. A Saint must be calm, but so many circumstances arise "that would make even a Saint mad," that storms do find ample space in our lives. A Saint must be humble too and willing to be unnoticed and never thought of, but just let some one slight us in the least way and our blood is set a-boiling. A Saint can take the rough and tumble things of life quite handily and will stand up like a real man when crosses weigh most heavily, but the smallest cheating of our hopes and the tiniest pain that snaps the pleasure of our lives bring tears to our childish eyes.

Of course it costs much to become a Saint, even as it costs much to become proficient in anything. Should we, could we expect it otherwise? To be a Saint is to be a real, honest-to-goodness man or woman, with all unruly tendencies whistled to heel and all good qualities used to their full, with life managed capably and consciously, so that when we leave the world itself at death, or a bit of it and its folks each day as the chance and change of life demands, the men and women of the world will be the better for our tarrying. But that large conquest of self is not made in a day —and "there's the rub."

There may be indeed crises in life, great, nerve-racking, will-straining crises that will, if we manage them rightly, bring us on breathlessly to sanctity. But these crises come not every day, and when they do come most of us do not yield our lives utterly to the swift winnowing of sorrow's wings, nor let ourselves be caught up by them unto higher realms of holiness. Poor fools! We grow afraid just then when our "becoming" Saints would be quickly done.

Then how become a Saint? The way we learn any other profession. A lawyer must study now this book, now that; a doctor must learn the function now of this organ, now of that; a musician must practise today and again tomorrow and let the music grow more difficult slowly. Then why have it otherwise with holiness, which is none other than the complete mastery of the hardest of all subjects—one's own undisciplined self? Holiness means a checking of a mean impulse here, and the furthering of a generous desire there. It asks of us to let die on our lips the unkind word that would hurt one who would hurt us, to speak the gentle word that would soothe an aching heart or nerve a soul that is quite beaten in the battle of life. Sanctity means self-control and self-control means the daily, hourly measuring up to those fine standards in all the big and especially in all the little things of life that make God's own gentle men and gentle women—His Saints.

Dear Jesus, what a strange creature I am! I really want to be a Saint and if by a single act of my will, utter sanctity would be mine, I would make that act right now. But it is not thus that I am to reach holiness. Today a try and then tomorrow another and maybe a slip in between, and it all hurts so—this endless trying—and, when all is said and done, with so little progress that I can see. I cannot be swiftly holy, I see that clearly, and so, dear Lord, give me patience, much patience to keep on trying, so that one day I may *be* that which there is so much labor in *becoming*—a Saint.

SIXTEENTH THURSDAY AFTER PENTECOST

BIG HEART, BIG PURSE

Come to Me, all you that labor, and are burdened, and I will refresh you.

St. Matthew 11:28.

BUT Margaret's heart is bigger than her purse." Thus ends the story of one of New York's "Hundred Neediest Cases." A child had been orphaned of parents and the bludgeoning of a hard world had left it without home or food, and slowly but surely disease twined its hands chokingly about the little life. A piteous waif, friendless and in want, in that great whirling mass of men! But one there was who took the child unto herself in motherwise and sheltered it and nurtured it unto health again, until——. And there the story ends for Margaret's heart was as big as it had ever been, but Margaret's purse was empty.

That child was needy, yes, so needy that all men were told of its need; yet every man and woman in this world has greater need than that wee orphaned one. Ours is the need of a breaking heart, the need of a beaten will, the need of a wrecked life. Ours is the need that springs from problems that tax our waking moments and toss our heads nervously when sleep should hold them still. Ours is the need of a cheering word when the warfare of life is waged lustily and we would be glad to run away and seek a coward's place. Ours is the need of a soothing word when anger burns within our hearts and impatience bids us rip aside all opposition. Ours is the need of a steadying hand to help us over the rough places of life and to shore us up when crosses fall most heavily.

These are our needs, as broad and as deep and as vast as life itself. What an awful thing it would be, if in our hour of darkness we were to go to one whose heart was bigger than his power to help! Yet some have tried it so. When life's ways were dark and life's burdens very heavy, they sought their respite out where foolish men and women throng, out where grasping men fight for filthy money from filthy hands—and they found no help. Men and women, the companions of their noisy hours, may indeed try to reach a helping hand, or to speak the enheartening word, but who that flits upon the surface of life and swings lightly on its passing waves, can reach down into the depths, into which the wrecks of human lives are sinking, or send a word of cheer over the roaring torrent that would engulf the derelicts? A hollow mockery is life if from such our help must come.

But, thanks be to God, it is not so! There is One to whom we can go, One to whom we must go, and His heart is not bigger than His purse; for He is God and the riches of His gracious help are infinite. We go to Him, all sick and sore at heart, and He will find the soothing balm that will ease our smarts. We go to Him, when the night of the soul closes in upon us, so tangible, so felt, that our hearts grow frightened at the darkness, and just by our side we hear His voice and round our hands we feel His own clasped encouragingly. We stumble forward till we fall prone upon our faces at His sacred feet and look up pleadingly from beneath the crosses that life has thrown full on us, and with "the tenderness of pierced hands" He lifts us up and feeds into our soul that courage that was His. No, since He is "infinitely rich to heal the wounds of our souls," we have no dread that we shall tax His strength or ask a healing that He cannot give or plead for help beyond His reach.

Dear Jesus, great God of Love, how I thank You for Your helpfulness! Life is a bitter thing at times and our poor hearts cry aloud for sympathy, for help. These we may find indeed from men and women suffering like ourselves in this valley of tears, but sooner or later the day comes when all human help is powerless. Then it is we rush to You; then it is we learn to love You most; for then it is You prove Yourself our truest friend. Dear Jesus, we are glad you are so very rich, for that means help in all our trials.

SIXTEENTH FRIDAY AFTER PENTECOST

GIVING MISERLY

I will not offer to the Lord, my God, holocausts free cost.
2 Kings 24:24.

DAVID stood on Moriah's summit on the solid rock of king Areuna's threshing floor and asked the price that would make it his, that he might build thereon an altar to the living God. The Jebusite made answer that the rock was his for the asking. Then swiftly, strongly came the answer of the man, who loved God so well: "Nay, but I will buy it of thee at a price and I will not offer to the Lord, my God, holocausts free cost."

Thus it is that whenever friend gives to friend, it is always a gift that costs. Gifts, that are rare to find and hard to purchase, speak of the unselfish seeking of a wealthy friend, and the trifling keepsake, bought where all may buy, tells of a friend, who stinted not in his poverty. It is not the wont of those who hold each other in true affection, to exchange in token of their love what things they hold not dear.

Then why act otherwise with Christ? We tell Him that we love Him, and we do; yet why so scant in all our giving unto Him? We give Him gifts, oh, yes. Before and after the day's long work, we say our prayers, provided there is time left from all else we care to do. We sometimes stop in church and give Him the pleasure of our company, so be it this entails no sacrifice of a chat with another friend. We try to be like Him and follow Him in His holiness, if only He asks but little of us and the way is not too rough. These we give and other like—but do we "give until it hurts"? Yet there is room for ample giving in our lives. If we would hold our tongue and have a tender care for the goodly name of others, if we would check the earliest risings of impatience, if we would wrench all pride from out our actions, then we should have gifts that Christ loves well and prizes dearly. Again we please Him much (because He reckons well the cost), when we are quite resigned though the cross of His sending be full athwart our lives, or when we down the nagging jealousies of life and envy none success, and most of all, when with sleep made short, we kneel each single morn about His sacred altar and let Him be our Guest within us.

Jesus, with heavy heart I kneel before You as I think again of my unsightly past. Long lovers we have been, and from Your side the love has been so true, so selfless. But I have been so niggardly in all my gifts, so selfish in all my ways. But, Jesus, dear, this is the past, the now relinquished past; for with Your kindly help the best I have, the all I have, shall be Your undisputed own, until I give myself and all my petty wares into Your hands at death.

"And must I be giving again and again?"
"Oh, no," said the Angel (his glance pierced me
 through),
"Just give till the Master stops giving to you."

SIXTEENTH SATURDAY AFTER PENTECOST

GOD HAS NO CLOSED MIND

I am He that searcheth the reins and hearts, and I will give to every one of you according to your works.

Apocalypse 2:23.

BUT won't he look at facts? Won't he see them staring him in the face?" was the final cry of one who was being horribly wronged. "No," the answer came, "no, I am very much afraid the facts won't count. Facts will mean nothing, simply because he will not see them. He has a closed mind." And with that, despair numbed the heart of the defenseless lad, against whom the dice of life were loaded—and all his "straight playing" was absolutely useless.

How often—tragically often—such injustices occur in life; and there just does not seem to be any remedy for it at times. Even good men and women have "closed minds," not through any wish to do wrong or to injure others. No, but it may be a "know-it-all-ness" that afflicts some who have not learned to listen; it may be an unrealized unwillingness to revise a judgment once formed or a decision once made; or it may be a native inability to take a broad, inclusive view of a situation. But whatever the cause, the "closed mind" brings much anguish into this world.

What an assurance, then, it is to know that Christ, our Saviour, has no "closed mind"! He never misjudges; He never misconstrues; He never leaves one iota out of the picture. That is why my destiny is so safe in His hands. "He can neither deceive nor be deceived." He knows all that is right and all that is wrong, all that is good and all that is bad in everything I think and say and do. No thought tucked too far down for Him to find and catch its slightest shading; no word so colored that he does not see it in its true light; no deed so secret that He does not know it, and whence it sprang, and whither it tends, and what it will bring about.

What confidence and trust should not that bring into my life! My eternity depends on what I do now, and what I say now, and what I think now—and it would be a dreadful thing to know that a "closed mind" might misread even one of my acts and penalize me for eternity as a result. After all, no matter how I am misjudged now, a few short years will bring the injustice to an end. But suppose, after that, we had to face God and He had a "closed mind"!

But He has not—and so with utter trust, I can commit my life to Him with all its goodnesses and all its badnesses. He knows the clay of which I am made—and He allows for it. He knows I am "compost of Heaven and mire"—and He knows that He made me so. He knows that I am "a thing of whim and wavering"—but He knows, too, that deep down beneath it all, I do want to be steady in my love for Him. "He knows our needs; to our estate no stranger"; and so, human like ourselves, He has pity on us brethren of like flesh and blood as He. He knew no sin, of course, nor any frailty, but He did permit Himself to be tempted, and to feel discouragement, and to dread oncoming pain, and to have the waters of desolation surge upon His soul as He neared death. He came through valiantly, yes; but He *knows*. And it is in His hands that our eternity lies.

Dear Jesus, men misread and misjudge me at times, and this is a bitter cross. But I know You never do and never can misjudge me. I am not always what I should be; rather, sad to say, I am hardly ever what I should be. You know this, but You know, too, the good that is in me. That makes me contented, dear Lord, fully contented. And please give me grace to keep this contented conviction throughout my life, that, when death comes, I may cry with utter confidence and perfect trust in Him: "Father, into Thy hands I commend my spirit."

SEVENTEENTH SUNDAY AFTER PENTECOST

ENCOURAGEMENT

Take heed, brethren, lest perhaps there be in any of you an evil heart of unbelief to depart from the living God, rather encourage one another every day, whilst it is called *today*, that none of you be hardened through the deceitfulness of sin.

Hebrews 3:12, 13.

MUTUAL encouragement is one of the greatest assets in any walk of life. Our poor human hearts are so fickle and our spirits so prone to droop after a short display of strength, that sooner or later we fain would give up the trying. Be our task in life what it may, that of individual progress as a student, or that of training others as a dutiful mother or teacher, that of the professions or that of the laborer, not many days go by before the inevitable frictioning of mortal ways awearies us. Then it is that the companion who stands by our side can nerve our hearts anew and can spur us back into our wonted stride, if he but find it in him to say the inspiring word. Encouragement is the boon most human hearts crave and need.

So in the life of the spirit. To those who really have a care for their souls, who really find the task of treading the walks of sanctity engrossing, the path steepens often and the music that was in their hearts, when the way first broke on them, becomes quite hushed. Then the wish is strong to sink slowly back into the abandoned valley of half-hearted service or at least to stand and make no effort to reach the higher goal. The weight of mortal flesh is all too heavy for the upward path. Just here must come the word that will straighten our shoulders beneath the load and snap our wills back into place. A father, tired of struggling against the sharp practices of the business world, who now feels almost forced to yield to ways and means that God forbids, must hear the voice of her he loves, telling of the land beyond the grave where the just of this world hold unlosably the wealth of God. A mother worn by wilfull ways of little ones and the seeming ingratitude of growing boys and girls would fain rest from her God-sent task of molding pliant lives; then must father recall the little home of Nazareth, where God's own Mother did like work as she. Here the young folk begin to find the way of God hard and there they find the music of the world a bit too sweet. Then a true companion must tell them that the narrow way leads back home and the music is the siren's lure to doom. To others wonted prayer becomes a distasteful task, perseverance in kindly ways of thought and speech and act, an irksome gag, fidelity to plighted ways of service to our King, a chafing restraint. Oh, then for the friends who will "encourage one another every day, whilst it is called *to-day,*" so long as this mortal life holds men exiles from their true home, bringing once more into bold relief the dimming outlines of eternity, re-lighting within each other's heart the flickering love of our changeless Friend!

Jesus, the one Friend who ever spur us on by Your insistent grace, oh, give us earthly friends also to further on Your work within our hearts and do You teach us, too, to do like service unto others. Though Your grace is full strong enough, yet we really need at times a human, audible voice to rouse us, our faintheartedness is so great. So send us inspiring friends and make us be such to others, for it will mean that Your love will grow much within our hearts.

"O child of love, be not still sad,
    But change the sigh to happy song,
For you can make the Saviour glad
    By loving Him who loved you long."

SEVENTEENTH MONDAY AFTER PENTECOST

SAY SOMETHING THAT WILL HELP ME

Lord, I suffer violence. Answer Thou for me.
Isaias 38:14.

FATHER, say something that will help me," were words that sprang deep from a heart that was sorely tried and tempted to quit the fight. The forces of life seemed leagued against her and anguish of mind and heart and body had been her portion day after day, and night after night the hours were measured and tolled off only by the stabs of pain that dug into soul and body. Fighting, splendid fighting, there was, but tonight a sense of utter futility seized upon that wearied heart and did its best to make it quit. But quit it would not, and from the inmost recesses of that quivering, pain-shot life came that cry for help, yes, for help that God's priest was willing to give and for which the frightened soul yearned so. "Father, say something that will help me." And God's priest tried again—and the soul was helped.

Thus it was that night in the great city hospital wherein the bodies of men are racked with pain and their souls are torn with sorrow. Thus many another night and many another day from many another heart goes up the cry to Heaven: "O God, say something that will help me."

Men are playing the hard, unyielding game wherein victory means more of this world's unsatisfying wealth, and one is crowded to the wall and finds his business gone, his savings seized upon, and life—his own and the lives of those he loves—is blanked. Now this plan fails, now that, and soon, as he kneels in prayer, his soul cries out to God: "Say something that will help me."

A mother pleads with the child of her love, the girl on whom she has lavished all her time and all her affection, pleads with her to stand her ground and be done with following the siren call of pleasure, but youthful wilfulness is strong and headlong—and mother's prayers fall on deaf ears. Then tears come fast from mother's eyes and her heart eats itself out in bruised loneliness and her hands are lifted high in prayer ever calling, calling loudly: "O Lord, say something that will help me."

So too when anger comes and rips our soul apart and rends the very fibers of our being. Huge impulses drive us on to wreak our vengeance, yet all the while we realize that restraint is wisest in the storm, and in our fear lest we be hurried into acts that we shall quickly regret we beseech our Lord: "Say something that will help me."

Again the pleasures of the world beckon most pleasingly and its music sounds very enticingly and we feel our feet are slipping, slipping slowly but surely, along a primrose path that ends in death. Can we deafen our ears and steady our gaze? We know not and our fright at impending ruin throws us on our knees and we plead with God from whom these temptations would tear us: "Say something that will help me."

That is the cry that must be on our lips when the cross weighs all too heavily; the cry, too, when the joys of life would filch our love away from God and give it thievingly to perishable things; the cry, too, when the tangles and snarls of life are too much for our unraveling; the cry when all is wrong and life itself awry. And always will the cry be answered and our Lord will always "say something that will help us."

Dear Jesus, sometimes, You know, my heart is so numbed with pain and anguish it cannot pray. Sometimes the crosses of life seem thrust too full upon me and bear me down too mercilessly. Sometimes, in other wise, the world with its pleasures is quite too attractive and bewitches my silly heart, so that it would fain stray from You. O Jesus, in those hours let me always run to You, and let me always cry to You—as once that soul did to Your priest: "Lord, say something that will help me." And Jesus dear, please always say that "something".

SEVENTEENTH TUESDAY AFTER PENTECOST

LISTENING

Speak, Lord, for Thy servant heareth.
1 Kings 3:10.

A VISIT to my friend does not mean that I must do all the talking. I speak, of course, but, unless I am wholly selfish and quite inconsiderate, I listen a deal and let him, too, speak out all that lies nearest to his heart. His views are welcomed by me, all his aims are eagerly seized and his slightest healthy aspirations readily encouraged. Thus it is from day to day, and yet ever and anon, other times come, times that only true, tested friendship knows, when we sit and neither talks, and thus the hours pass, and with never a word between us, yet all the while we know the deep unison of our hearts. We enjoy each other's silent company and find strength therein, though we scarce know how or why.

Is this our way with our Lord? It seems not so with most of us. A visit to Him seems an endless prattling on our part. Halt our prayer but for a moment, we deem that moment lost. Prayer, true prayer, is a conversation, and a good conversationalist is "one who listens as much as he speaks." Rather a bad test for our chats with our Lord, isn't it? A steady stream of petitions and supplications, a ceaseless murmur of word on word, and never the slightest chance for our Lord to make reply. Would it not be well to be as polite with Him as we are with earthly friends? Would it not be wise and very profitable to listen awhile at times? Oh! not out of laziness nor slackness of will nor failure of purpose, but just that we may hear Him better and learn a deal from Him. Yes, it would be well and rather polite, too, to give Him chance to speak, to allow Him, at times, the privilege of ordinary conversation.

Then again, when friendship's test comes round, how are we found? Today we find it hard to speak, so heavy lies the cross athwart our shoulders or maybe the very buoyancy of our joy outstrips all words. How act we then? Are we wont to stay and feel quite at home, yes and more, quite soothed and comforted by the very presence of our Friend, to the beatings of whose Sacred Heart our own has been long since attuned? Have we learned to read in His silence the answer that cannot be put into halting human words and can be caught only in the dumb language of love? Blessed are we, if we have, for we have indeed reached unto close intimacy with Christ. Whether it be fear that cripples our tongue or joy that leaves all words behind, let us learn just to kneel before our Friend that He may read our very hearts, yes and ofttimes read them best, when our lips are sealed.

Jesus, my Friend, as I look over the times that we have met in the past, how strange my attitude is shown! I quite forgot that prayer was a chat with You and I have always made it so one-sided. It must have pained You much, dear Lord, that I should act so thoughtlessly. Indeed, it pains me now, and I am sorry for it and ask Your pardon for my lack of courtesy. Oh, let this laggard scholar grasp some day the lessons that should have been learned these many years now gone.

SEVENTEENTH WEDNESDAY AFTER PENTECOST

EXPECTING GOD TO COME ACROSS

They have turned their back to me, and not their face: and in the time of their affliction they will say: Arise, and deliver us. Where are the gods whom thou hast made thee? Let them arise and deliver thee in the time of thy affliction: for according to the number of thy cities were thy gods, O Juda.

Jeremias 2:27, 28.

THE young lady was quite excited, and quite angry with God, too.

"Why, I prayed all night—I begged God all night long to help me—I certainly prayed just as hard as I could. And—and—look! Did I get it? You bet I did not. And yet you tell me to pray, Father!"

A quiet pause and then:

"Mary, when was the last time you prayed to God? Honest, now; when?"

"I can't remember, Father. You know I'm not much on praying. But it has been a *long* time."

Again a pause; and Mary became restless.

"You've got your answer, Mary. Think it out."

Mary did not have to think too hard; she was much too honest for that. The answer was simply that she wanted God "to come across" just because she wanted something very badly. She forgot all the months that she had forgotten God; and she expected God to forget them too.

We may not be as negligent of God as Mary was, but we often act as she did. We suddenly make up our minds that we want something very badly or we find ourselves in great trouble and at once we turn to God and "pray our heads off." It is fine to turn to God in prayer, but what about the many times we have failed to say any prayers at all? We said "Good morning" to every one else but had no time to say it to God. What about the hasty, thoughtless way we sped through our prayers on the mornings when we did get them in? And our night prayers—how lazily, drowsily, impolitely said; and how often have they been cut short because we were all "done up" by the day's work and pleasure!

Grace before and after meals—it may be we scarcely remember there are such prayers. The *Angelus?* Yes, we do recall that we said some such prayer when at school. The beads? If we had as many dollars as there are times that we said those beads, our purses would be very flat.

An exaggeration? For many, yes; for many others, no. Yet it is true that few of us pray consistently with fervor. It is so easy to pray out of routine. It is so easy to be present bodily at Mass and to be far, far away in mind. It is a simple thing to drop into a church, kneel a few moments, "rattle off" a few prayers, and leave without a real lifting of the mind and heart to God. It is even possible to walk up to the Communion rail and receive Christ as our Guest and proceed at once to forget that He is within us.

But when we want something or find ourselves in serious danger to soul or body—well, then it is different.

Suppose God answers us as He did the Jews in the days of Jeremias? They had forgotten Him for false gods and had violated His law constantly and seriously. But when their enemies attacked them, then and only then did they cry to Him. And God's answer was: "Where are the gods whom thou hadst made thee? Let them arise and deliver thee in the time of thy affliction."

God will never answer us in that way unless we have grievously and wilfully and continually cast aside His love; and even then His chiding will be for the good of our souls, that we may recognize our evil ways and repent. "If thou wilt return, O Israel, saith the Lord, return to me." Even to the stiff-necked Jews of old, Jeremias had that word of comfort. God is only too ready to hear our prayer; but sheer decency requires that we do our part. We do feel free to run to a close friend for a favor; but we hesitate to ask the same of one we have treated shabbily. And do we not often treat God shabbily, very shabbily, yet suddenly rush to Him with an immediate demand? Hardly polite, is it?

Dear Jesus, I am quite ashamed of myself when I realize how shabbily I have treated You. I have not forgotten Your love and I have kept to my prayers. But there is little for me to be proud about there. And I am ashamed that my fervor usually came only when I wanted something very badly. I ought to be more decent with You than that. So give me grace to say my prayers at all times fervently, respectfully, politely.

SEVENTEENTH THURSDAY AFTER PENTECOST

ALONE WITH MYSELF

I am become burdensome to myself.
Job 7:20.

IN my bitterness I deliberately turned from God but the anguish and torture of living alone with myself forced me back to Him to find peace and rest . . . and I wish to add that a void long felt in my life disappears entirely, when I try to give my best to God."

Thus wrote one whose soul had been seared and scarred in its struggle against God. God it would leave, God it would ignore, nay more, God, it would stoutly affirm, was non-existent. Yet all the while, go whither it would, turn this way and that as it might, it was always pulled up short, face to face with self, petulant and peevish and fretful; and slowly but surely the very awful, lonesome intimacy with its miserable self hurled it back to God—and when it knelt to God, "a void long felt in life" was gone.

Most of us, thanks be to God, are spared this stern experience. Thanks to His grace, few of us turn with such fierce deliberateness away from Him. But we do turn from Him, now in this way and now in that, and do not our own hearts tell us that when we do, the only thing we find is our miserable selves?

It may be we hear the voice of God calling us to more fervent prayer, to a closer intimacy with Him in His Sacramental presence, both when we visit Him and especially when we receive Him in Holy Communion. But that means added effort, and maybe we do not want to make it. And then? Are we happy in our self-won listlessness?

Again, we realize that some fault is spoiling much we do and that it cuts straight across the plans that God has for us and others. But it will cost a deal to dig and root out, and it will hurt. It is so much easier to "let things slide," even though that "sliding" makes for much friction. So we do "let it slide," and then—! Bickerings here, and raspings there, and a growing disgust with self when in our moments of quiet we face that same ugly self.

To find self away and apart from God is to find a most unattractive thing—"of all man's clotted clay the dingiest clot." It is bad enough to know myself and all my faults and weaknesses and at the same time to know that God's nerving grace is always helping me to make myself a little less selfish, a little less mean, a little less wilfull and self-contained. But take God away, and the stark realization that "I am one of nature's little kings, yet to the least and vilest thing am thrall," the numbing consciousness that "my life's a pain and but a span, my sense is mocked in everything," bite into my very soul. No wonder then that with the poet I would conclude that to be a man is "a proud and yet a wretched thing": proud, because of an immortal soul; wretched, because it is the plaything of moods and the dupe of the gewgaws of time.

Dear Jesus, I need a true realization of self, if I am to make any progress at all, if I am to grow up in any way. But do not, I beg of You, let me see myself away and apart from You! It is hard enough under Your gentle chiding to look myself squarely in the face. But if You are not there, what then? Self, miserable self, and only self—and, in sheer irritation at the unseemly parody on myself as I ought to be, I lose all patience and do not want to try any longer. So please be very near me always and let me know myself and see myself only with You as teacher.

SEVENTEENTH FRIDAY AFTER PENTECOST

HE'S GONE AHEAD

If I shall go and prepare a place for you, I will come again, and take you to Myself; that where I am, you also may be.

St. John 14:3.

THIS world seems quite a fair and happy place at times and for the moment our hearts think perhaps to have found their rest; but it is for only a moment, and then the illusion fades. For our joys are always fleeting and our sorrows are wont to linger, and even when they go, their shadows are long and they darken many a day. At best the world is a place of groping where tears fall fast and laughter's ring is quickly hushed. How can an immortal soul love a tarrying place like this? How can we help but feel a thrill of joy when we hear that it is not to be our home forever? Isn't it a cheering word that tells us that "there remaineth therefore a day of rest for the people of God"; that the shadows will one day pass away, that we but wait "until the day dawn and the day-star arise in our heart"? Surely it is right good news to hear that one day and that not far away "God shall wipe away all tears from our eyes, and death shall be no more nor mourning nor cry, nor sorrow shall be any more for the former things are passed away."

Even though we have Christ Jesus with us now, that cannot make us content. He is with us—yes, and thanks be to God for that!—but He is hidden from our eyes. He is in disguise and when the day grows dark and our eyes are held, we find it hard to pierce behind the veil and catch the face of Him we love so much. Even Jesus Christ in disguise cannot make this poor lodging of ours a lasting comfort. His nearness may nerve our hearts to bear the trials of our darkened pilgrimage; through His dwelling with us our exile may grow less hard; but it will never, nay for the very added reason of his concealment, it can never seem like home. Home is to be with God face to face; to see Him as He is, and not in the cloudy mirror of time; to be with Him with never the fear of separation there where "the man Christ Jesus" reigns as "the first fruits of them that sleep," where Mary is Queen and Mother, too, of all her ransomed children, whither some we have loved "have preceded us in the sign of faith" and keep an eternal Sabbath with the choiring angels. There is home! How our pilgrim hearts yearn to be there, yearn to have Christ come again and take us to Himself! "For, yet a little while and a very little while and He that is to come, will come and will not delay."

Jesus, elder Brother, how good You are! You saw the sorrows of our pilgrim days, the tear-stained eyes, the broken heart, the "arms outstretched with love of the farther shore," and You have lighted up the twilight of our tarrying. You have come and dwelt amongst us and oh! that makes it so much more like home—yes, but so much more that we yearn with greater longing to end our exiled days. You cheer the days away from Heaven, away from those we love and our best Father. But, Jesus, it is not home. That lies far beyond. It seems so very far. Yet You are with us now and You will guide us aright and some day, dear Jesus, You will lead Your exiles home.

SEVENTEENTH SATURDAY AFTER PENTECOST

RESCUED

And who is the God that shall deliver you out of my hand?

Daniel 3:15.

THE king's command had gone forth and all Babylon had obeyed it—all Babylon except the three Jewish young men, Sidrach, Misach and Abdenago. True to their Faith, they had refused to fall down in adoration before the king's statue. Die they might, but disobey God they would not. "Then was Nabuchodonosor filled with fury and the countenance of his face was changed against Sidrach, Misach and Abdenago and he commanded that the furnace should be heated seven times more than it had been accustomed to be heated. And he commanded the strongest men that were in his army to bind the feet of Sidrach, Misach and Abdenago and to cast them into the furnace of burning fire." Helpless, they were hurled into the midst of the flames and the words of the king rang mockingly in their ears: "And who is the God that shall deliver you out of my hand?"

Small hope there seemed and yet we know that "the Angel of the Lord went down . . . into the furnace and he drove the flame of the fire out of the furnace and made the midst of the furnace like the blowing of a wind bringing dew, and the fire touched them not at all nor troubled them, nor did them any harm."

What a lesson in this miracle! There are times in the lives of all of us when humanly speaking hope is gone utterly. All is so dark and so foreboding that everything within and about us cries out despairingly: "Who is the God that shall deliver you out of my hand?"

It may be that a habit of sin has fastened itself upon us and, though we do want to break away from it, we slip and fall again and again. We would like to find some way out, but we are weak and temptation, when it comes, proves too strong. It is then that the enemy of our souls keeps dinning insistently into our ears: "Who is the God that shall deliver you out of my hand?" If only he can get us to feel the wrecking despair that would be bred in our souls by hearkening to that question, then victory is his unendingly.

Or it may be that, despite all we try to do, stark poverty seems to lie ahead of us for ourselves and those we love. The gaunt specter stands astride our path. No hope seems left anywhere. Yet, if we but go to Him in whom are hidden the riches of the Godhead and plead our case with Him in full confidence, in vain will the tempter whisper to our souls: "And who is the God that shall deliver you out of my hands?"

No matter what the crisis is in life, no matter how great the doom that lies ahead, no matter what the crushing sorrow that lies full upon our hearts, if we but go to Him, we shall be safe. We know His mercy and His love better than did the three young men of old and with them, no matter what the darkness of our souls may be, we must answer: "Behold, our God, whom we worship, is able to save us from the furnace of burning fire, and to deliver us out of thy hands, O King. But if He will not, be it known to thee, O King, that we will not worship thy gods, nor adore the golden statue which thou hast set up." Yes, and even more than that, we must find echoing in our hearts the words of holy Job: "Although He should kill me, I will trust in Him." It is that trust which will steady our souls and bring us peace—and victory.

Dear Jesus, amid all the darkness of this valley of tears I am apt at times to forget Your infinite power and, more than that, Your infinite readiness to help me. My road grows very rough and steep, and difficulties beset me so that I would quit the fight and give up all struggling. But would that be right? Would that show confidence in You? You so loved me that You died for me. Shall I not trust You for lesser gifts? Just let my clasping of the crucifix be always my answer, when the tempter cries: "And who is the God that shall deliver you out of my hand?"

EIGHTEENTH SUNDAY AFTER PENTECOST

HAPPY SERVANTS

Happy are thy men, and happy are thy servants, who stand always before thee and hear thy wisdom.

2 Paralipomenon 9:7.

IT is far back in the days of Solomon and into his kingdom and unto his palace has come the Queen of Saba to verify the wondrous tales then current about the king. Long discourse she has held with him and varied have been the topics of discussion. Much has she seen of all his enterprises, his wealth, his servants, and all his glory. Expectation has been more than realized and the queen, in utter admiration for all that her eyes have seen and for all the wisdom she has heard from Solomon, cries out:

"The word is true which I heard in my country of thy virtues and wisdom. I did not believe them that told it, until I came, and my eyes had seen, and I had proved that scarce one half of thy wisdom had been told me: thou hast exceeded the same with thy virtues. Happy are thy men, and happy are thy servants, who stand always before thee and hear thy wisdom."

Solomon was wise, unquestionably so, for God Himself had gifted him with wisdom in answer to his prayer. Yet there is One before whose wisdom Solomon stands as ignorant. We need not travel afar to chat with Him, for He is with us always. Uncreated Wisdom, incarnate in human form, our dear Lord, dwells so near to all of us that none can plead excuse of distance for not visiting Him. Go into the church at break of day and kneel within His home. See men and women break their fast on the Bread of Angels and then go with them to factory or office and are they not happy with a strange, strong happiness as the mills of the business world grind out their very lives? Go into the home at eventide and before the shades of sleep hold fast "tired eyelids on tired eyes," kneel in prayer within the circle of the family, as father and mother and little ones bid goodnight to God in unison of heart and lip. Are not they, too, happy with a happiness not found in other homes? Steal into those larger homes where cloistered lives are sealed away into the sole service of God, where men and women literally stand always before their King and hear His wisdom and what find we there? Read it in the face of the old whose eyes are lighted with holiest expectation, as they look across the grave to their nearing Friend beyond. Catch it in the cheerful ways of the younger servitors of God, who hasten to spend themselves in some new work in the Master's vineyard. Happiness! Can there be found in all this great wide world a happiness that can compare with this peace and joy that is born of God?

Dear Jesus, who can tell of all the happiness there is in being near to one so wise as You, so great as You? Joy of the mind there is in knowing You, joy, rich joy of the heart in loving You. Other friends may come and go, but You are always with me, and as the years swing by and life and all life's problems take on sterner aspects, the single thought of Your abiding love and its unfathomable wisdom is all-sufficing. Oh, truly happy, happy beyond the telling, are Your men and happy are Your servants who stand always before You and hear Your wisdom, and use the grace You give them to hearken to Your wise counsels.

EIGHTEENTH MONDAY AFTER PENTECOST

A GRAB-BAG SOUL

I therefore so run, not as at an uncertainty; I so fight, not as one beating the air.

1 Corinthians 9:26.

"THE whole trouble with her is that she has a grab-bag mind, a helter-skelter mass of knowledge, which keeps tumbling out as each chance provokes." A rather hard but still an accurate description of the mind of one who was packing now this, now that bit of knowledge, but not getting order in it at all, nor consistently following up any one line. The result? A medley of facts and opinions and rumors which piled out disconcertingly into conversation to the exclusion of other folk's chatting.

What was true of that person's mind is often true of our souls. Instead of forming them along definite lines, we jump now at this new devotion, now at that, and continue our loyalties briefly. Instead of examining our souls carefully in prayer to find out what may be the root-trouble therein, we pluck at one defect today and at another one tomorrow, not stopping to see whether there be any more of even that one defect to be corrected. We read a book and we are quite sure that patience is what we need, and off we go a-chasing patience; then we hear a sermon and a fresh conviction surges over us—and all thought of patience is tossed aside, and charity or prayer or humility is the object of our pursuit.

All well and good, is it not? Are we not practising virtue? Hardly. To practise virtue means to develop a habit, a skill and ease gained from repeated exercise of an act. This we are not doing, most emphatically. We place a few acts of this virtue or of that, or even a few handfuls of acts and then—off to another snatched-up group of good acts. And the result? A grab-bag soul, a medley of half-formed habits, habits almost begun, habits just begun, habits half-persisted in, all of which make us most uncertain commodities of goodness.

Too bad, is it not, that so much real effort, so many good intentions should all land up on a scrap-heap? With the same amount of trying, if the trying were only orderly and systematic, we should have been saints long ago. Instead of that, neither we ourselves nor anyone else is certain how much of goodness or what kind of goodness may be expected of us a day hence. From the grab-bag soul as from the grab-bag mind anything may come—and no one can predict the value of what comes.

Dear Jesus, I am getting along in years and I really ought to be making something out of myself. I want to, but—! If ever a phrase hit off my soul it is that—a grab-bag soul. I have tried to be good, now this way, now that. I have tried to avoid now this fault, now that. But it has all been a hit-and-miss attempt. So give me grace now to study my soul and to form a definite, abiding plan of self-conquest and of self-improvement, and let me stop once and for all this helter-skelter way of acting that makes me have a grab-bag soul.

EIGHTEENTH TUESDAY AFTER PENTECOST

HE WILL NEVER GIVE ME UP

> **Even unto your old age I am the same, and unto your gray hairs I will carry you. I have made you and I will bear; I will carry and will save.**
>
> **Isaias 46:4.**

YOU won't ever give me up; will you, Father?" was the cry that sprang from a heart that was frightened at its own weakness, terrified at the thought of losing the one strong grip that kept it from slipping utterly into the quagmire of sin that surrounded it. The poor young chap had struggled, had given up much, very much at the priest's word and yet the dice of life seemed loaded against him. Down, deep down in that quivering heart there was a real desire for good and the friendship of God's priest was cherished above all else the world could give, yet "it was all so hard." And God's priest knew it thus, and meeting the anguish of that struggling boy, the words came strong and sure and most kindly.

"No, Jack, never—never, till I see you safe with God."

As poor Jack cried out for the help of God's anointed priest, we who know God better than Jack knew Him often cry out to God Himself: "You won't ever give me up, will You, my God—no matter how bad I am, no matter how forgetful of Your love I may be?" And ever the answer comes: "Unto your old age I am the same, and unto your gray hairs I will carry you. I have made you and I will bear, I will carry and I will save. Go, child, where you will, follow what will-o'-the-wisps you will—but you are My child and with more than a mother's love I will follow you and win you back again. No, child, I will never give you up."

What a consolation to realize this! And yet we sometimes doubt it. In our moments of holy living we fondly think that God loves us for all we are, and then when sin comes again and much forgetfulness of our "tremendous Lover" we feel that He must hate us now and loathe us for our inconstancy and ingratitude. But all the while we forget that God loves us precisely because we are His and wants our love just because we are His handiwork—not because we merit that love by any worth that is ours. Oh, yes, He is pleased when His children are well mannered and bethink themselves of Him, but when our petulancy comes and our rebellious moods, He loves us still because He is our Father. No prodigal ever was met by expectant father as our wayward steps are welcomed back by God. No matter where we go, no matter if our sins are as red as scarlet and as many as the sands of the sea—our Father loves us still, because and just because He is our Father.

So when the devil tempts us to discouragement and shows us the blackness of our sins and all the baseness of our ungrateful ways, let us for our own soul's sake cry to God and run to Him. He is never far away but always just waiting for our cry. Nay, rather it was His own good grace that brought that cry. He is there just waiting, just yearning for His children to come back home and bring Him their love once more. So let us run to Him and we shall be safe.

Dear Jesus, oh, what strong comfort it brings to my poor, weak heart to know You are my changeless Friend! The changing days bring changing moods and one day I really want to try and really do try, and then the morrow comes and with it much forgetfulness and many imperfections and maybe sin. And then my soul grows fearful lest it has lost Your love forever, lest You may have grown tired of my childish, wilfull truancy. But Jesus, dear, in those dread moments when I realize my sins and all my wilfulness, just let me always realize that You love me still and only want me to quit my truancy and to run to You again. For my own soul's sake in hours of darkness, let me always remember this one fact that You will never give me up!

EIGHTEENTH WEDNESDAY AFTER PENTECOST

ACCEPTING ALL AS FROM GOD

Father, if Thou wilt, remove this chalice from Me; but yet not My will, but Thine be done.

St. Luke 22:42.

THE saintly old Sister was dead, and now her Superior was going through her effects, that were very scant indeed. There was a worn, frayed prayerbook, the pages of which had been thumbed again and again. It evidently had been the Sister's favorite through many a year. Tucked away therein was a bit of paper, yellowed by the passing years, and on it just two lines: "Lord Jesus Christ, I here and now accept as from *Your* hands *whatever* the future may bring." It was signed and dated. The date told everything; for, as the Superior checked back, she recalled the story that at that very time the Sister, then a young woman, had been misunderstood and misrepresented in matters of serious import. Often had she been seen in the chapel during those searing days when her life seemed about to be laid in ashes, but only a few then knew of the cross she carried. But there, after death, was the mute witness of her resignation when the burden was heaviest and the outlook darkest: "I here and now accept as from *Your* hands *whatever* the future may bring." The future came, and it proved to be quite bright; but, from her side, the fullest resignation had been made.

Untoward things happen to all of us in life. My soul may not be harrowed as was the soul of that Sister, but trials greater or lesser do come and they strain my courage and virtue at times. It is so easy to rebel, so easy to ask why God should permit such a cross to be thrown on *my* shoulders. But that never helps, nor, if I grow peevish and resentful, does it win more grace from God or a lifting of the cross.

God knows what is best for me, and God watches over me. He, Himself, does not always send the trial or the pain or the misfortune, but at least He permits it to come. If no sparrow falls to the ground unless He knows it, surely He has a more watchful eye over my immortal soul. He did not die for the sparrow; He did die for me.

Then why not trust Him? And why not leave my cause in His hands? That does not mean that I must sit with folded hands and do nothing to help myself. To act thus would be presumption. "God helps those who help themselves." He expects me to do all I can, but if and when I have done all I could, then I leave the rest to Him and I await the future as a gift from His hands. If it is a gift I like to hold, then I shall readily thank Him for it. If it is a gift that it hurts to hold, then even through my tears I shall let Him know that I accept it and, if I am very brave, I shall even thank Him.

On His knees in the Garden of Gethsemane our Lord faced a frightful future. Every least detail of the Passion stood out before Him. He dreaded it as I or any other human being would dread it. He would have liked to have been rid of it. But His prayer was one of utter resignation, and He repeated it and repeated it to show us the extreme agony of His Soul and to give us an example: "Father, if Thou wilt, remove this chalice from Me; but yet not My will, but Thine be done."

Dear Jesus, even the brave souls that loved You most found it hard to resign themselves to the trials of life. And did not You Yourself fall into an agony as You foresaw the Cross? And was not a sweat of blood the answer to Your massive act of resignation? If You and Your great Saints found it hard, what about poor me? I do not have Your strength or their courage, and yet I do want to accept life and every part of it as coming from Your hands. So, please make me braver and give me more strength to be resigned—always.

EIGHTEENTH THURSDAY AFTER PENTECOST

IF ONLY—!

Yet now Christ hath reconciled you by the body of His flesh through His death, so as to present you holy and blameless and irreproachable in His sight, if only ye hold by the faith, well-grounded and steadfast.

Colossians 1:22, 23.

SOME of us do a great deal of worrying about death and Heaven and hell; all of which is about as profitable as worrying whether the sun will shine tomorrow or not. Of course we should be deeply concerned about death and Heaven and hell, but our real and principal concern should be about the thing on which they depend, and this is how we live here and now.

Our full accent ought to be on *this* life, or rather on this *day,* this *hour,* this *minute*. A minute is all I have at any time, and any minute may be my last, and on the condition of my soul when my last minute has come, will depend my whole eternity.

If I am driving an auto, my concern is not about the hill five miles away; it is about the curve I am rounding now. If I am at the wheel of a boat, I am not thinking about the billows on the other side of the bay, but on the waves just in front of the bow of the boat. It is the present problem that should be solved, not the one that is the tenth or the one-hundredth one away.

Why not act then in the same way in the life of my soul? On the present depends the future, necessarily and inevitably. So, if I take care of the present, the future will take care of itself—rather, I am taking care of it myself right now. St. Ignatius put it well: "Man is created to know, love, and serve God, and *by so doing,* save his soul." Be concerned about knowing and loving and serving God now—which in plain English means merely doing my job in life the way God wants me to—and I need not worry about my soul's salvation.

St. Paul put it in another way. Christ wishes to have us "holy and blameless and irreproachable in His sight" for all eternity. And how will that be brought about? *"If only* ye hold by the faith, well-grounded and steadfast." If ever a man had both feet on the ground, St. Paul had, and so his accent is on the "now." He tells me that I shall be holy and blameless and fit to see God face-to-face for all eternity *if only* I know my Faith and adhere to its commands and hold to its practices.

Could anything be more consoling than this doctrine? It is disquieting to think about death and hell, or even Heaven, it seems so unreal and far away. And to think overmuch about them is to put the accent where it ought not to be. My job now is to think about the work I have to do now, the prayer I have to say now, the pleasure I am to have now, the book I am to read now, the movie I am to see now. It is all so simple: do each moment what I have to do; and when the next moment comes, do what I have to do then; and if some "next moment" the thing to do is die, well, I shall do that the way I did everything else—and I shall wake up in Heaven.

Dear Jesus, thank You for this consoling fact of faith, and let me daily grow in the realization of its importance. I wish to be with You in Heaven, of course I do. Then what I ought to do is to attend to each present duty and fulfill it as best I can, and in the way You would wish me to. If I do that always, then, when Your summons comes, I shall be quite ready to come home.

EIGHTEENTH FRIDAY AFTER PENTECOST

BOUGHT WITH A GREAT PRICE

You are bought with a great price.
1 Corinthians 6:20.

WE take great care of precious things and we measure the worth of things by the labor and gold they cost. What any chance comer may find, that we count as nothing worth and guard not at all; but that which has been garnered by dint of constant toil or bought with a deal of gold for which we slaved, that we hoard and guard, lest it be lost or filched away from us by pilfering hands.

It was of this that St. Paul would have us think, as he sped his letter off to Corinth. "You are bought with a great price." He would have us note the value set upon us, not in the great trading marts of the world, where values rise and fall as played by skilful hands, nor yet again, the worth appraised by fleeting word of mouth, but the value set upon us by the deeds of God. We have been "bought" and the price was not that which any one might pay nor was it paid by one who guessed awry the value of his purchase. "You are bought with a great price"—and straightway before our eyes come Bethlehem and Nazareth and the Mount of the Beatitudes and then, across the shortening span of years, Gethsemani and the Governor's hall and then, the shameful tree on whose limbs outside the walls the final purchasing was done in blood. "A great price." Yes, the greatest of all prices and it was fully paid by Him who cannot be deceived nor tricked by false valuation.

Yet, do I really realize my worth and by my actions do I really show a merited regard for my priceless value? Are my ways as the ways of men whose hopes and aspirations are bounded by the grave, my thoughts as theirs, my words as theirs, my deeds as theirs? Do I hoard and guard within me the things of God, the gifts of faith and hope and charity and all the panoply of virtues which go to make the fullness of that life which Christ came that we might have and "have it more abundantly?" Oh, it is a saddening sight to see some folk of God, for whom He died, so giddy and so thoughtless that they carry about unguardedly the priceless treasure of their soul, nor ever exert a decent care to keep what Christ won for them by dint of mighty striving. "Bought with a great price!" To watch them, one would deem they judged themselves to be as "flies of a later spring, that lay their eggs, and sting and sing, and weave their petty cells and die." "Am I of this careless folk who set no value on the price which God once paid?"

Jesus, You have paid the price for my own soul and only You can tell the value of Your purchase. You gave "until it hurt" and all for me and to win my soul another chance for Heaven. Oh, teach me then to guard this soul for which You died, teach me to be afraid of sin which cheats You of this purchased soul, teach me to be most greedy for the means of grace by prayer and frequentation of the Sacraments and the daily practice of the virtues. For, Jesus dear, it is not right to squander what Your precious Blood has bought.

EIGHTEENTH SATURDAY AFTER PENTECOST

DARN LITTLE FOOLS LIKE YOU

For He knoweth our frame. He remembereth that we are dust.

Psalm 102:14.

AND why were you so good to me, Father? You did not know me! Why were you so kind?" That was the question asked of the old priest who held the door-knob, ushering the young man out. And the old priest smiled and said ever so eagerly: "Because Christ loves darn little fools like you." Rebellion there had been in that young heart, and a deal of hatred of God and His Church; but it all had been poured out now, and God had given His priest to see far down into a soul that was at war with its best self and was slugging itself away into radical ways of thought in sheer desperation to find a way out. "Because Christ loves darn little fools like you."

That boy was a fool—yes. But are not most of us, who try to find a way out from God and His law in great or lesser things? "Who hath resisted Him and hath had peace?" Job asked long ago. Surely, no one. Yet, time and time again, though we know God's law and recognize His designs in our regard, we try to turn a deaf ear and seek for a way to escape from Him.

When I know that God wants something of me, and my judgment is backed up by those into whose care I have placed my soul, what a fool I am to refuse to give in to God! It may be only a small thing He wants, but to deny Him that small thing may quite disturb our friendship—even as such denial would play havoc between earthly friends. And if the thing He asks be really big and its refusal mean a serious violation of His law, then holding on to it means full severance of His love.

What "darn little fools" we are! And yet, because of His love, and, too, because of His understanding of our witlessness, Christ can still pray for us: "Father, forgive them, for they know not what they do." Of old His psalmist said: "He knoweth our frame. He remembereth that we are dust." That is why His anger is restrained; that is why He can still love us—because we are "darn little fools."

But why play the fool? And why put the love and understanding of Christ to the test, to see just how much He will stand from wilfull, foolish children? Do properly behaved children act thus toward earthly parents? Just a bit of thinking about all He does for us, just a spark of gratitude for favors received, just plain, everyday decency should make us grant His wishes. Yet, He understands!

Dear Jesus, I am glad You are big enough and good enough to understand me, and to love me still despite my foolishness. I hope I never so play the fool that I thrust Your love aside completely. But I know my weakness and my selfishness, and I fear my cowardice—and even that can happen. So give me grace to value Your love above all things and to give You always what You want. But if I do play the fool, please love me still.

NINETEENTH SUNDAY AFTER PENTECOST

"BUY AN ICE-BAG"

But He (Jesus) held his peace and answered nothing.
St. Mark 14:61.

SORRY, Father; couldn't get an ice-bag. Thanks, really." So read the telegram that was handed to the priest as he was about to give Benediction, and back of it stood the story of one who had found life at home intolerable. Long had he and the priest talked it over the day before; calmly and yet forcefully had the priest cautioned against a too hasty move: "Buy an ice-bag, Jack, and put it on and keep it on your good old hot Irish head." The lad promised to try to cool down, and to come back on the morrow—and the morrow came, but no Jack; only the telegram that told its own stark story. Jack was "headed West."

"Buy an ice-bag" was a splendid bit of advice, and one that we all need from time to time. Life goes hard against us, as it had gone against Jack; but is it wise, or is it brave, to run away from the fight? And is it prudent to lose our poise, and maybe our temper, too, when "all goes wrong"?

Of course it is hard to hold our tongue and to keep sharp check on our nerves when every single thing is all awry and the dice of life are all loaded against us. But does it remedy matters to get all excited and to fret and fume and storm? When all is upset, calm judgment is needed and a sureness of viewpoint that takes in all the angles of the situation and all the complications therein. But frayed nerves and a vision clouded by anger are the last things in the world to help thereto.

Suppose some one is irritating, and loses his temper frequently, and is utterly inconsiderate in every act—is losing my temper going to calm him down and make him more thoughtful of my interests? Does one fire cool down another fire?

Suppose my plans have been upset, maybe deliberately upset, by one who does not like them—is peevishness on my part likely to make him more kindly disposed, or less ready to upset my next apple-cart?

Of course it is hard not to give vent to one's irritation—but anyone can get riled; it takes self-control to keep one's poise. Of course it is easy to "fly off the handle" and "say what I think," and "give a piece of my mind"—any undisciplined child can do that; but it takes a strong will "to stand and be still" and to utter never a word.

And was it not most irritating to our Lord to be made a fool before Herod, and to be the butt of their jokes as they hailed Him as an upstart, deluded king? And did it not hurt to have Annas and Caiphas and Pilate question and accuse and insult Him? And was it easy for Him to sit out the night in Caiphas's servants' quarters and have them play the rough Greek game of "blind man's buff" with Him?

Dear Jesus, I have often messed things up in life because I have failed to keep my poise. You know, as well as I do, that life can be very exasperating at times and that others "get on my nerves" dreadfully. It is hard for me to hold myself in then, and very hard not to say and do nasty things. But it just makes matters worse—and life is bad enough at best without my knowingly making it worse. And it is so untrue to all the examples You have given me. So please give me the grace to keep "cool, calm, and collected" all the time, and to keep an ice-bag on my heated brain when the temperature rises too high.

NINETEENTH MONDAY AFTER PENTECOST

WITH A PERFECT HEART

And he did what was good in the sight of the Lord; but yet not with a perfect heart.

2 Paralipomenon 25:2.

WHY, of course, whenever I travel, I make certain to say Mass every day. It means inconvenience, yes, and a deal of planning as to trains, but, if the Mass is what it is, it is worth a deal of trouble, isn't it? Surely if God comes down from Heaven at my words of consecration, isn't any discomfiture on my part too small to count?"

Thus answered the old priest, who often said that the one thing about our Catholic Faith is its splendid logic, and, in consequence, the one thing that same Faith ought to bring out in our lives is the terrible logic of holy living.

The terrible logic of holy living! There is a sweet fierceness about it, and a kindly severity that repels none, but rather attracts all. We all respect "a man of his word"; and the man who carries out his principles of holy living into everything is merely a man of his word with God.

But, honestly, am I that sort of man? Or am I like King Amasias who did, indeed, "what was good in the sight of the Lord, but yet not with a perfect heart"? There can be no excuse for me. I can serve God "with a perfect heart" anywhere: in the cloister or out in the world, married or single, in youth or in old age.

I can serve God "with a perfect heart" and yet have much of human love in my heart and much of the pleasures of this world. For the world is good, and its true pleasures are good, and human love is most to be treasured. And so, if it be God's pleasure that I should find Him in this way and through another's love, then I must learn to love Him in all these things and to love them all in Him alone. Nor will this take one iota of happiness away; nay, rather it will make it all the sweeter, all the more lasting.

I can serve God, too, "with a perfect heart" within the cloister walls; indeed, that is then the very profession of my life. Priests and Religious are the great lovers of God, pledging their lives away entirely to Him; and God, with them, is a very jealous lover. The pleasures of the world are not for them, nor human love; for these, though much to be desired, have been left aside for God. So, if God has thus chosen me, the sheer logic of my life will have me give myself undividedly to Him with no thought of creature comforts, or of easeful living or of human affection. Others may have these lawfully and become very holy thereby. But I cannot, else I shall not serve God "with a perfect heart."

Dear Jesus, in my own poor way, I do want to love and serve You well. Whatever I give will be poor enough and most unworthy of You. But still You are good enough to want it, and I, too, want to give it to You. So help me, please, by Your strong grace, each day and every hour of each day to serve You always "with a perfect heart."

NINETEENTH TUESDAY AFTER PENTECOST

GOD DOES NOT HOLD OUT ON US

Now therefore saith the Lord: Be converted to me with all your heart, in fasting, and in weeping, and in mourning. And rend your hearts, and not your garments, and turn to the Lord your God: for He is gracious and merciful, patient and rich in mercy, and ready to repent of the evil.

Joel 2:12, 13.

SOMETIMES our sins stand so vividly before us that they literally strike us in the face. The sins of our youth, and the sins of our maturing years, and the sins of the level years and of the years that are sloping downwards. Sins of thought and word and deed. Sins of commission and of omission. Sins alone and sins along with others. What a mess it all is! "All my sins rise up before me; all my virtues disappear." And it may be that before that gaunt vision our hearts fail within us and we grow quite fearful of God's mercy.

Yes, God is just and His punishment of sin is terrifying. But He punishes only when we force Him, only when we deliberately and wilfully refuse to let Him forgive. God never "holds out on us." He wants us to repent and be truly sorry—and the moment we are, He forgives and forgets. And even the grace to repent and to be sorry comes directly and thoughtfully from Him.

It makes no difference what my sins may have been; no matter how vile, no matter how utterly insolent. If we but rend our hearts "in fasting, and in weeping, and in mourning," if we are really sorry, wishing we had not done them, and are really determined now not to do them again, and confess them, as Christ bade us, God being "gracious and merciful, patient and rich in mercy," will forgive the evil we have done and blot it out completely.

But, for most of us, in all frankness, our sins have not been so very heinous. There is no use of painting black blacker. And even humility must be curbed within the bounds of truth. I have sinned, yes, very often, and with scant regard for God's love. I have fumbled life's duties and played free with its privileges; I have acted with scant courtesy to God in my prayers, and have violated the duties of decent charity towards my neighbor. Where good example should have been given, I have so far failed as not to have led men and women nearer to God. There is little I can be proud of in my life and much, very much that should make me hang my head in shame. All right! But what then? Not despair, nor discouragement, not a sense of frustration. That were the veriest folly—and most untrue to God. The only thing to do is to drop on my knees and cry out from my heart the sorrow that is there—and then await God's grace. And that grace will come as surely as I plead for it, and it will work into every nook and cranny of my being, healing and cleansing and strengthening unto a newer life, closer to God.

The worst sin we can commit is ever to suspect that God will "hold out on us" when we come to Him with true sorrow. "A contrite and humble heart, O God, Thou will not despise."

Dear Jesus, at times when the past stands out before me in all its sheer sinfulness, my heart grows numb within me and it is all I can do not to give up in despair. By Your grace, I may have been saved from more heinous sins. But I did sin "in thought, word, and deed." I am sorry now for it all and I ask Your pardon for it all. And I know You will and do forgive, for You never "hold out on us."

NINETEENTH WEDNESDAY AFTER PENTECOST

WORKING HARD—FOR GOD

Labor as a good soldier of Christ Jesus.
2 Timothy 2:3.

MOST of us must work hard in this world, whether we like it or not. In that we have little choice. It is work at home such as mother does, or it is work in the office, or factory, or classroom, or out in the fields. It may be work by day, or through the night. It may be work alone, or along with others. With few exceptions, each and every one of us fulfills the primal curse put upon our parent culprit: "In the sweat of thy face shalt thou eat bread."

But I have a choice: whether I shall do all this "as a good soldier of Christ Jesus" or in pagan-wise, taking it dumbly and uncomplainingly as part of the game of life. I can shoulder my burdens daily, and drop them again at night as does the pack-horse. Or I can pick them up and lay them down with the full consciousness that every ounce of burden is known of God and every step of my fettered way is measured by Him—and I labor in His sight and for His sake.

Thus would St. Paul have Timothy do. Timothy was "his own son in the Faith" and was taught by Paul to know God and to serve Him well. Timothy was one of the front-line fighters in the onward march of Christianity, and lusty battles were to be his in making Christ known to men. And Paul's pithy advice is: "Labor as a good soldier of Christ Jesus." Paul had done so, and would do so until the end. And he would have "his own son" be as brave a soldier as he.

And so can we all—no matter where our days are cast. Mother at home can cook breakfast, can rouse the children and see them off to school, can make the beds and tidy the house, and do it all for Christ; and take the many, many trials incident thereto "as a good soldier of Christ Jesus."

Out in the busy world of office or factory or school, there is many a hard knock and many a wrong against which there is no redress. The very struggle of competition, the very necessity of doing my best to hold my own lest another supplant me—these wear me down, and often wear me out. And yet they are part and parcel of human life in the world that lies about us. We cannot change it. All we can do is to put up with it:

grudgingly, grumblingly or even stoically; or taking our share in its trials and hard knocks "as good soldiers of Christ Jesus."

There is no way out. Stand the drubbing we must, unless we want to lose our very manhood and renounce our maturer years and be thrown aside as one of life's misfits. Shall we stand it only because we cannot avoid it? Or shall we take it all for God and with God as His good soldiers? It is hard; of course it is. But when was a soldier's life easy? And we became soldiers of Christ in Confirmation, and His grace is with us always, nerving our hearts with His own courage.

Dear Jesus, truly "the life of man upon earth is a warfare and His days are like the days of a hireling." It is all so endless, so wearying, so discouraging. Yet there is no way out. If I am going to manage life at all aright, I must stand its friction, I must put up with its trials. It is not right for me to do this just dumbly and uncomplainingly, as many do who know You not. I am *Your* soldier. I am pledged to carry on *Your* battle in life. I should be untrue to You did I not fight the fight of life with and for You. So give me grace at all times and in all places to take my share of labor as Your good soldier.

NINETEENTH THURSDAY AFTER PENTECOST

ANOTHER TRY

Be of good comfort, my children, and cry to the Lord . . . for as it was your mind to go astray from God, so when you return again, you shall seek Him ten times as much.

Baruch 4:27, 28.

AND you know, Father says I can begin all over again," were the words that came hopefully from the lips of the little girl, as she sat in the clinic of the great hospital and told her story once more to friendly ears. Upon her young soul the world had laid its soiling hands; she was but one of the flotsam and jetsam tossed about amid the millions that thronged in the whirling metropolis, and for years there had been none to care what life might bring to her. But one day in the great city hospital a kindly eye fell upon her and a supporting hand was held out to her, and with patience for her childish wilfulness, true friends nerved that poor little heart to fight again for what is right and true and good in life. The priest had told her of God's love and won her once again to prayer and Mass and new fires were relighted in her heart, and then came those words from the heart that told of lessons that were beginning to be learned—"And you know, Father says I can begin all over again."

Would to God that each and every one of us always said those words! For we need them, all of us need them when the hour is dark and the worthlessness of "another try" seems quite apparent. God Himself has spoken them to us, for He has told us that we can never outstrip His love nor face an hour of trial wherein His grace will not be plentifully present. It does, indeed, seem strange that God should have such patience with us. Yet did we ever watch a mother teaching her little one to walk? She does not mind the falls, but lifts up the tot again and kisses its bruises, so they will not hurt, and smiles as it stumbles ahead once more. So too with God, whose love reaches far beyond the love of tenderest earthly mother. He knows our falls, our weaknesses; He knows the plentiful failures of our lives. Yet He still calls to us, as He did to the Jews of old: "Be of good comfort, my children, and cry to the Lord . . . for as it was your mind to go astray from God, so when you return again, you shall seek Him ten times as much." And across the history of the world of souls is written large: "And Father says I can begin all over again." That is the message that has come from Heaven to us, as we stumble and fall and rise again with the growing conviction of the uselessness of it all. Of course, it hurts our pride to know that our lives have been spoiled in larger or lesser part. Of course, it is discouraging to look back over the lost years and to realize they might have been much otherwise. But despite it all, Father who is in Heaven tells me I can "begin all over again."

Thus when our anger has flared up again, or our patience has played out sooner than it should, or our tongue has once again sped barbed arrows that wound our neighbor's heart, we must recall God's own encouraging words and we must make "another try." Again, when our prayers have been forgotten once more or said with accustomed impoliteness, when our visits to the Blessed Sacrament have been poorly made or omitted entirely, we must again resolve to treat our Friend more courteously. Yes, even if graver sins come anew into our lives and we have violated once more God's high commands, and cast His good grace out of our souls, we must pluck up our courage again and listen humbly and with great confidence to our infinitely good God who tells us that despite our sins we can "begin all over again."

Dear Jesus, patient and enduring in Your love of us, it seems almost impossible that You should have such patience with me. And yet again it is not strange, for Your Sacred Heart is ever kind, ever forgiving, ever encouraging. I know this well and yet at times when I have again forgotten Your love and once more played truant to my promises to You, it seems not true. It seems impossible that I should return and seek You "ten times as much." But even if I do not seek You "ten times as much," just let me return once more to You. Just give me in those hours of soul-weakness the grace to remember that You still think it is worth while for me to make "another try."

NINETEENTH FRIDAY AFTER PENTECOST

GUARDED PETS OF GOD

And He (God) kept him as the apple of His eye.
Deuteronomy 32:10.

WE all know what is meant by a pet; one who is specially beloved and tenderly guarded and shielded, one on whom many good things are showered. Not all pets are "spoiled," but all are the objects of unremitting care and love.

Do we ever think of ourselves as "the pets" of God? Yet we Catholics are. That is precisely what our Faith means. If our Faith is true—and it is—then we Catholics are the objects of God's untiring love and care. If it be false, then we are the most foolish people in the world for believing what we do.

And how are we God's "pets"? Let us see.

First, He has made us members of His one, true Church and lets us share in "the Faith once delivered to the Saints." The constant guidance and teaching of that Church has been given us at home, from the altar, in our classrooms, and in the books we read. Thousands of men and women have never heard of our Faith, thousands hate it, and thousands fear it.

Again, in that Church He has given us grace both actual and sanctifying. By His holy inspirations He enlightens our minds to see what is right and moves our wills to do it. He fills our souls with His habitual grace which makes us "holy and pleasing to Him and heirs of Heaven" and forms us into living temples of the Holy Ghost. Daily He increases that sanctifying grace, if only we do not fall into mortal sin.

Within that Church too, He has given us seven great channels of grace in the seven Sacraments that smooth our way to Heaven from the cradle to the grave. Through them our lives are made holy, and all we think and do and say is made pleasing to Him from the day He accepts us as His children in Baptism to the last moment when He seals us unto Himself in Extreme Unction. Guarded pets of God! Could even God do more for us than offer Himself in the Mass, and come within our bodies in Holy Communion, and make us one with Him in His Mystical Body?

Then too, at home and at school, at work and at play, alone and when with others, sleeping and waking, in childhood and youth and maturing years even unto the grave, not only does He watch over us by His Providence, but He has given us a companion from Heaven, whose one sole duty is to "watch and guard, to rule and guide" us all the time. With this Guardian Angel we go through life, watched at every moment, guarded in every place, helped in every act.

And more than a Guardian Angel—He has given us the tenderest, sweetest, holiest Mother, the very one He chose for Himself—and surely He chose a most perfect one. To her we are most dear, and all the love she had for Him she shows to us—because He Himself has asked her. When He did not keep His Mother for Himself alone—does not that prove we are His "guarded pets"?

Dear Jesus, let me learn more and more of Your love for me. In some slight, dim way I grasp it, but not fully, not as I should. If I once just got to a complete realization of what it means to be Your "guarded pet," my life at home, at school, at work, at play would be so different. I just could not do some of the things I do now. So please give me grace, at all times and in all places, from now until You call me home, to be intimately conscious that I am Your "guarded pet."

NINETEENTH SATURDAY AFTER PENTECOST

CHEATED OF THE PROMISED LAND

Thou shalt see the land before thee which I will give to the children of Israel, but thou shalt not enter into it.

Deuteronomy 32:52.

MOSES has led the children of Israel for forty years. Up and down the desert, pleading with them, chiding them, praying for them. At God's command he had led them "out of Egypt and the house of bondage"; at God's command he had gone to the top of Sinai and there, amid thunder and lightning, had received the Ten Commandments; at God's command he had been leader and father to that great multitude of stiff-necked people, and now, after all he had done and suffered, at God's command again, he was to "go up . . . unto Mount Nebo . . . and see the land of Chanaan . . . and die . . . in the mountain."

To see—and not enter in! What a bitter dosage of disappointment, and yet how often it comes in our lives! We may work hard and, when the time comes to rest and enjoy the fruitage of our labors, it is someone else that has the enjoyment.

It may be that father and mother have labored long and self-sacrificingly to bring up their little ones well-mannered before God and men; yet, perhaps, just when they may expect a lifting of the burdens of life, sons and daughters leave home to make their own homes or maybe are called by God to serve Him within cloistered walls. Is it easy to let them go? Ask father and mother who have long looked forward to the promised land of a bit of repose from life's labors—and now cannot enter in.

A job has been given me and with uncounted generosity I have played out every ounce of strength to make it go well. Yet how often I am shifted to another post exactly then, when I might have a respite from constructive work and a bit of comfortable ease in running a well-planned job. This happens in the business world, in the school world, in professional life, yes, everywhere. One sows, another reaps.

What shall I do? Complain and grumble? Hardly. Not if I would act manfully, as Moses did. There was no least murmur from him but "Moses went up from the plains of Moab upon Mount Nebo . . . and the Lord showed him all the land . . . and Moses, the servant of the Lord, died there in the land of Moab, by the commandment of the Lord." To die within sight of the promised land is a bitter pill—and it takes a full-grown man or woman to swallow it without making faces. Moses did it. Do I?

Dear Lord, You must have been much pleased with the great, old leader of Your chosen people. All through the forty long years in the desert, he proved himself a man; and, when You gave Your last hard command, he did not flinch a bit. Hard things come to me, too, in life, and not the least hard is being cheated, like Moses, of the enjoyment of the fruit of my labors. Sometimes it is in small matters, sometimes in great. But it always costs me much to take the bitter dose without complaining. So if and when this trial is mine, give me the grace to measure up as Moses did, when he was cheated of the promised land.

TWENTIETH SUNDAY AFTER PENTECOST

THANKING GOD FOR CROSSES

Giving thanks always for all things, in the name of our Lord Jesus Christ, to God the Father.

Ephesians 5:20.

HE was a hard-headed specialist, one of the greatest authorities in his line. He had seen service at a leper colony, and had cared for the four thousand patients there. While there, a Jesuit chaplain was stricken with the dread disease.

"When I told him, Father, of his condition, he looked at me and then slowly lifted his eyes to Heaven, saying: 'Thanks be to God!' I just couldn't make that out—and I can't make it out yet. Thanks be to God for leprosy!"

It did seem strange; and it didn't seem to make sense. Thank God for leprosy! Thank God for the "gray death" that is so feared by man!

Yet, once we have caught the real, inner meaning of life and the full providence of God over us, we know how to thank Him for everything. Any one can thank Him for health and wealth and happiness and success. Any one, even most casually acquainted with Him, can thank Him for bright days and joys and a road through life that is broad and smooth and sunny. Even a dog will bark and a cat will purr when food is given them.

But when the hard things of life come, and the days are dark, and every road leads steeply uphill—then it is that only a strong faith can bring a "Thank You" to our lips.

Yet if we believe in God's Providence, we know that nothing happens to us without His knowledge and consent. It is not correct to say that all that is hard or painful is sent to us directly by God. No, much of it comes from our own mistakes or perverseness, or the mistakes and perverseness of other men. In those instances, God merely permits hard things to happen to us. Thus, when they actually do come upon us, they come with His full knowledge and permission, and we can, therefore, accept them as His will. He could have disposed things otherwise, but in His wisdom He did not; and thus here and now I bear my cross because it is His will.

But to a Christian there is a higher reason. Christ could have come upon earth and never have suffered a pain, and never have had any opposition. He could have had all the wealth He wanted and made Himself the honored ruler of all mankind. Certainly all that lay easily within His omnipotence. But instead He came in want; He met opposition and enmity throughout His life; He knew hunger; and often had not whereon to lay His head; and He died in the worst form of agony man's cruelty has yet invented.

So when we are in want, when we are in pain, when crosses weigh us down, we can accept them—yes, and will accept them—with a heartfelt "Thank You." They are hard to bear—of course they are; and our nature will rebel—of course it will. But we will realize as the great Catholic poet realized that it is "shade of His hand outstretched caressingly." He knows what is best, and if He hurts or allows us to be hurt, He does it as the surgeon does, to heal. And we thank the surgeon, don't we? And we thank the doctor that gives us bitter medicine or restricts our food, don't we? And we are more like the Man of Sorrows in our days of darkness and our hours of pain. We love Him, don't we? Well, "love either finds or makes alike." Surely then a real "Thank You" will spring from our hearts and hang jubilant upon our lips for each untoward thing that makes us more like Him.

Dear Jesus, let me learn to say "Thank You" for *everything* that comes to me in life. It is easy to be grateful for what is pleasant and to my liking. But it is hard, very hard, to be at all thankful for pain and disappointments and crosses. You know it; You Yourself found it hard. Yet You were thankful nonetheless. So give me much grace to say "Thank You" for *everything*.

TWENTIETH MONDAY AFTER PENTECOST

ONE OF THE KING'S OWN

They that fear Thee shall see me and shall be glad, because I have greatly hoped in Thy words.

Psalm 118:74.

THE lamp of life had flickered lower and still lower for years and fainter and fainter for months, and now the young Jesuit priest had gone home to God. His had been a fight that called for the bravest of hearts and never once, as eighteen long years swung slowly around, did even his closest friends see a flinching. Gifted with a mind that had few peers and with a heart that reached out for souls, he had heard and hearkened to the Master's call to come aside and sit well within the shadow and fold toilless hands, when life had scarce blossomed into manhood. It seared his heart, this word of high command, but to none did he tell the aching. Silently and manfully and with a soldier's will, he took his lonely watch and never left it, and now as his bowed companions knelt about the lifeless clay, they knew a saint had left them and there was one more victor man-at-arms in God's eternal court.

Were I to lie now at the hour of my dying, and were I to gaze back with one last, long, lingering look on the days that were gone, could the words of the Psalmist rise to my lips: "They that fear Thee shall see me and shall be glad, because I have greatly hoped in Thy words"? In my life there have been joys, whose tasting was very sweet, and maybe many a lengthening shadow; but whether sunshine came or shadow fell, did I so stand the test of light and shade as to give pleasure to the friends of God? When life was very happy and the cup of its wine was richest, did I always show that my heart was firmly set on the imperishable treasures beyond the grave? The world was indeed a pleasant place, but did all still know that I felt an exile's cravings? Then, when the light we loved so well was torn away and darkness with its frightening shadows fell, did light from another world light up my eye and guide my steps and cheer my heart? Oh, it is a goodly thing to see a valiant, fearless soldier stand the brunt of battle well nor fail from highest aims in times of peace. Is this the spectacle my life affords to angels and men, who are the friends of God? God grant it is!

And for the future? Why not feed new steadfastness into a heart about to hearken to the insistent call of sin by the thought of the credit we shall prove to God and the consequent joy we give His friends, by standing our ground and flinching not? And when the night of the soul with its peopled darkness comes on, as please God it will, shall we not find our strength and courage, when we bethink ourselves that others will gain new joy and help, if they see the old hopes still burning bright in our hearts and our trust in God no jot or tittle weakened?

Jesus, my God, would I were like Your valiant, vanished knight! He never once belied Your trust in him. But what of me? Oh, it is a grievous thing to see my cowardly past and I see well that I need every motive to nerve me on. So let me think, in sunshine and in shadow, of the joy I will give Your friends, if I measure up well to Your calling. Then, when I stand on the outgoing threshold of life, in all humility I may cheer my heart and say: "All these things have come upon us and we have not forgotten Thee." "They that fear Thee shall see me and shall be glad, because I have greatly hoped in Thy words."

"The days grow shorter, the nights grow longer,
The headstones thicken along the way;
And life grows sadder, but love grows stronger
For Him who walks with us day by day."

TWENTIETH TUESDAY AFTER PENTECOST

TRAILING SOULS AFTER US

He (Mardochai) sent word to Esther again, saying: "Think not that thou mayst save thy life only, because thou art in the king's house, more than all the Jews."

Esther 4:13.

FEW of us can get to Heaven uncompanioned. There may be some such men and women, whose lives are quite islanded off from fellowship with others, but for most of us the threads of our lives are so interwoven with others that Heaven for ourselves means almost inevitably a drawing of them with us. Human lives, especially in these days, are so intertwined that there is a continuous exchange of example set and example followed, a steadily growing current of influence and counter-influence whose markings can be easily read. We cannot avoid it, and thus day in and day out we bring souls nearer to God or drive them farther away from Him.

We may be quite free from personal responsibility for others because of our years or the isolated way of our lives, but we cannot go unattended to Heaven. The young man with his chance companions or with those with whom he whiles away many an hour always lifts them up by clean speech and fair play or pulls them down by a foul mouth and underhand ways. The young girl by her modesty and poise makes men respect her and through her the womanhood of her sisters, or by her frivolity and forgetfulness of her own outstanding dignity, lowers herself and those she meets, blurring the ideal every decent man has of a woman he would really love.

This is more than true for some of us who are "in the King's house more than all" others. Father and mother cannot go to Heaven unattended, for "the keepsakes for Heaven" that are theirs must go with them, led on ever gently but ever firmly, more by holy deeds than by harsh chiding, more by the example of self-restrained, God-fearing lives than by insistence on "do's" and "don'ts." Down in the business world the man who stands at the head must play clean and straight and his word must be his bond, that those around him and under him may learn that "honesty is the best policy," and that fair play in the game of life is as fine a thing as fair play on the field of sport.

In the classroom where dozens of little eyes drink in example and retain it so lastingly, teacher must mirror forth in a competently controlled life the discipline that must be instilled into the growing children. Out from the class they go each day, and, when many a day has passed, out from the school itself into the world which will tax so heavily their new-won strength, and back they must be able to look and cherish memories of one who taught by deed and by word that it "is only noble to be good" and that only by being good will God's blessing be won in life.

The wider our scope of authority, the higher our eminence among men, the more outstanding the gifts of mind and heart with which God has enriched us, the more impossible it is for us to go to Heaven alone.

Dear Jesus, what a terrible responsibility this is to know that I must not come home to You alone! I so often think of my salvation as something purely personal, something that affects myself alone. Yet it is not so and cannot be so. My life affects the lives of others and none can stay the influence. So help me, Lord, at home, and in the hours of my recreation, and at work, yes, everywhere, help me to trail souls after me.

TWENTIETH WEDNESDAY AFTER PENTECOST

A FRIEND'S WISHES

You are My friends, if you do the things that I command you.

St. John 15:14.

I AM always anxious to prove to my friend my love for him. He may be quite sure, and so, too, may I, of the depth and height and breadth of our mutual affection, but show it I must. Now it is a thoughtful word, and now it is a little deed done when the hour is dark, and yet again it is a kindly omission of an act which would offend. I often catch myself day-dreaming of new ways that will manifest what I hold so much to heart. And if my friend makes known to me each little thing which pleases him, will words come easily to tell of all my joy? Could trouble or pain or time prevent my giving it to him?

I often want to show my love for our Lord, in fact it is my one enduring thought. I love Him, yes—both He and I are sure of this—yet, as with other friends I must keep proving it. Would I be pleased to know just how I best can give Him joy? Of course I would, and this He knew, and so with wonted thoughtfulness He told me long ago: "You are My friends, if you do the things that I command you." And what are His commands? To serve Him first and best, because I hold Him dearer than all else. To pray to Him within my home, but best of all to come and chat with Him within His home, wherein He silently waits for me. To count my fellow man His brother, and so to be kind to him in thought, word and deed. To lend a helping hand when others fall, and to shore them up when they lean heavily. To count myself of little worth save only when I do His will in every least detail, and even then to realize that it is His aiding grace that saves me. To think of Heaven as my real home, and earth but as my place of pilgrimage, wherein I prove my right to a welcome home when death summons me. Thus it is He tells me how my love can show itself. But do I always give Him the gifts He asks?

Dear Jesus, friend whom I love so deeply, I thank You for Your thoughtfulness. I would have found it hard to know just how to show my love for You, for You are great and I so very small. Yet love would not endure without some proof. I thank You for the secret You have told me, and I shall try hard to give You what You want.

TWENTIETH THURSDAY AFTER PENTECOST

GOD'S SILENCES

For thus saith the Lord God, the Holy One of Israel: If you return and be quiet, you shall be saved: in silence and in hope shall your strength be.

Isaias 30:15.

THE hurly-burly of the great cities had been lost in the distance and now the man, who was forever driving himself hard, sat out in the silence of God's country-spaces and, as evening came down upon the landscape, he gazed out over the quieted waters—and thought. There at that old mission-house, on whose porch he sat, saintly men had lived and done their work in a peaceful way and souls had come to them so unhurriedly and gone away with like lack of haste and all the while the great world of men had been roaring on its forgetting way and down in its crowded cities men had fought for gold and honor and pleasure and all the tawdry tinsel of time—as though it mattered much who won the most—and their cries were loud and their wrangling strong. It was in that world this man of energy had been working, and now in God's own silences he asked himself: "And when the hurly-burly's done, what then"?

It were well for us to go apart thus from time to time and to test out our souls in the silences. The poet has sung: "The roar of the world is in my ears. Thank God for the roar of the world," and well may we, too, for down into the throbbing fastnesses of men we must go, some of us to earn our livelihood, and some to lift a hand to salvage human wrecks, and some to bring surcease of pain to ailing bodies, or better still to call down God's grace into bruised souls. But then the roar of the world must cease and from time to time we must go aside and rest awhile and listen to God alone.

No matter where our lives are cast, no matter what is our vocation, we need God's silences. Sometimes we can go apart and find silence indeed of body and of soul, far separate from our daily routine of life and then we can plentifully steep ourselves in that quiet which has been rightly called "the bath of the soul." But such privilege can be rarely ours and yet we need imperatively that solitude which is indeed "the homeland of the brave," and we gain this solitude and silence when we kneel in prayer and all life falls away from us and God alone remains.

It is to prayer we must go, when our hearts are numb from the bludgeoning of the world. It is to prayer we must go, when anger reddens our eyes and we begin to see things awry. It is to prayer we must go, when loved ones worry us because of their waywardness and wanderings from God. It is to prayer again we must go, when the very bottom of life seems to have fallen out and the world seems all out of joint. Then, when we have gained the silences of God and abide alone with Him and listen to His view of things, we shall come back to life refreshed and shall face our problems more squarely and we shall realize that the hurly-burly of of life will pass quite swiftly and then will come rest and much happiness with God.

Dear Jesus, Giver of all good gifts, give me the grace to come to You always, to gain respite from the roar of the world. I must needs work amid that roar and I must bustle amid its turmoil, while the weight of the crosses of life are thrown full on me; but I must not forget where alone I can find my comfort and abiding strength. The noises of time would almost shut You away from me and yet this must not be. And so I shall run to You and pray to You and seek in the silence and solitude of prayer the help that can come from You alone; and best of all, I shall bring my troubles to You in Your earthly home and pour out my heart to You in the silence of Your Sacramental Presence. And when I come, dear Lord, just talk to me and set my heart aright amid Your silences.

TWENTIETH FRIDAY AFTER PENTECOST

WHERE THERE IS BITTERNESS

There is no understanding, where there is bitterness.
Ecclesiasticus 21:15.

I ALWAYS treat her as a lady, and why this insolence to me now?" were the words spat out from quivering lips in the parlor of the rectory. A man, fretting and chafing, with eyes flashing with uncalled-for anger, with tongue and teeth biting off harsh words, made charge after charge, and all the while the priest sat quietly and listened. It was useless to argue here. There was a grain, a small, wee grain of truth in some things said, but everything was seen awry, twisted and distorted and thrown completely out of perspective, because of bitterness long harbored in his heart. A misunderstanding here, a misinterpretation there, again an insolence detected where none existed and yet again a conviction of an attempt to thwart his plans exactly there where a special effort, known to the listening priest, had been made to cooperate! And so the turgid heart relieved itself of all save the bitterness, which alone should have been emptied out therefrom.

"There is no understanding, where there is bitterness." How true that is in the lives of all of us! So much misunderstanding and consequent unhappiness come from the fact that we cannot "see straight," because of the poison that is swelling within us. At home, at school, at play, at work, the venom eats away. Here an angered wife sees her husband plotting to torment her, deliberately coming late when she would have him return early, cunningly cheating her of her least desire—and all because she let herself become querulous, and now with twisted gaze sees wrong intended when none was even thought. Here a husband, out of sorts because some trifling thing has gone amiss, shouts out his anger, as time after time he finds new offenses given, new causes for displeasure about the home, where none exist at all. Everything is misconstrued, everything misread, because there is bitterness to spoil the sight of everything. Again, between friend and friend things go amiss and ever wider grows the chasm between them because of fancied efforts made to irritate. Unthinkingly a word is not said in passing—and this means an added insult. Unwittingly a kindness is left undone—and this means a new discourtesy cunningly contrived. Without the least intent to tease, a pleasantry is passed, and sensitiveness reads therein a fresh attempt to wound deliberately. Put on yellow glasses and all has a sickly hue; put on red glasses and all is afire; place upon the mind the lenses of bitterness and all is distorted. No matter what is said, it is all awry. Poor foolish creatures that we are! Let us empty out the venom from our souls and all the world will be sweet again.

Jesus, dear Saviour, would that I had Your gentle Heart for reading all in kindliness! To all of us poor sinners, despite our faults, despite our wilfull sins, You show abiding gentleness. Then why cannot I, Your pupil, learn this virtue from You? Why do I harbor bitterness and thus find faults where none exist, and take offense where none was meant? When shall I grow to man's estate and have a bit of sense? When shall I learn to keep bitterness far from me, that I may not misunderstand?

TWENTIETH SATURDAY AFTER PENTECOST

WE ALL LIKE IT

For every man that eateth and drinketh, and seeth good of his labor, this is the gift of God.

Ecclesiastes 3:13.

"WE all like it; we might as well admit that," were the words of comment passed by one on the applause he had won. "Only we must not work just to get it."

Wise words, those, and splendidly true. To be frank with ourselves, deep, very deep down in our hearts we are all very glad to hear the loud praise that caps off our efforts in public or in private, and it warms our very souls to catch the smile of approval from those for whose opinions we care. That is saying no more than that we are human, and it were well not to try to practise self-deception and fool ourselves that we do not relish it decidedly.

It is hard to work on unnoticed, to slave from early morning until the growing hours finally force us to our beds and yet never once have a

"Well done!" said to us. To work silently and lonely, away from the plaudits of men and to realize that scarce anyone ever takes particular note of what we do is to all a trial and to some a staggering cross. And so it is good for us to have a kindly, spurring word whispered in our ears. It makes us want to try again, when men and women tell us sincerely that our words of tongue or pen have nerved them on in life's hard moments.

Good, yes, yet very bad and quite destructive of our meriting, if we make this the motive of our striving. To eat ice cream or candy is very pleasant, and yet, if we are right-minded, we do not eat these sweets wholly and solely because they are sweet. We take them for health's or recreation's sake and along with the taking comes the pleasure—and we like that, too.

Yes, and it were foolish, too, to let pride creep in and rot out the wholesome goodness of our deeds. Whatever powers we have come from God, and if in using these powers we strut about peacockwise, showing off our feathers as though they were of our own creation, then are we fools indeed. Today we have those gifts, because God so wills; and tomorrow? Maybe felling sickness comes or robbing accident, and then, try as we may to hold them, these selfsame gifts will slip from our grasp. So why be fools and let our poor, silly heads be turned! Men like what we do and praise it. Well, that is good and we are pleased that they are pleased and that we have been nerved to make another effort; glad too, yes and gladder, that, by some little thing we did, God's cause has been helped, and our Lord made better known.

Dear Lord, may I not be frank with You and with myself and admit that I am pleased, when my efforts are applauded? I hope it does not mean that I am vain and proud, but only that my poor, old human heart is what it is: hungry for fellowship with others. I must not work for this applause and recognition, nor must I let it turn my head and make it swell with pride. No, that would be wrong and quite unreasonable. So, if and when it comes, let me take it for what it is; but let me ever be mindful that praise from You is the only thing worth working for.

TWENTY-FIRST SUNDAY AFTER PENTECOST

A FORGIVING SPIRIT

Father, forgive them, for they know not what they do.
St. Luke 23:34.

FORGIVENESS of those who have wronged us is a virtue that costs us much. Revenge holds out to us such a snug sense of satisfaction and the spiteful poisoned words promise so adequate a balm to our wounded feelings! Then, too, does not a proper respect for our rights, as men and women, demand that we put the offenders abruptly back into their place and give them much to think about concerning their own ill-trained, misshapen characters? Isn't it quite the time for someone (and who better suited for the task than our clear-sighted selves?) to place their straying feet back on the straight and narrow path from which they, rather than we, have so evidently wandered?

When thus we feel, and our quickened pulses would speed us with hurrying feet on our errand of would-be charity, let us stop for just one moment in the home of our Friend to ask Him what He thinks of our purpose. He will not keep us waiting. "My child, what did I, your Friend and Leader, do, when My own folk had nailed Me to the cross and were hurling blasphemies and curses at Me as I hung dying before their gaze? Will you go now and act in otherwise? And you, too, my child! 'I forgave thee all the debt, because thou besoughtest Me; shouldst not thou then have had compassion on thy fellow-servant, even as I had compassion on thee?' "

Shall we? There will be no less manhood in us when we have done what the Son of God did so repeatedly. We shall have lost no jot or tittle of self-respect by stamping our souls with the image of Him, who was the most perfect of men. The fleeting satisfaction of having stung our brother in return, the questionable pleasure of showing him what faults we find him out to have, these will not be ours. No, thank God, they will not. But in their stead the consciousness of a soldier's part well played, the joy of having followed Christ when "the lead" was hard and our nature stoutly rebelled, yes, and deep down within our souls the new-won grace of God, by which we claim a higher place in Heaven throughout eternity because of the little victory we have won. Can there be question of a hesitant choice?

Jesus, oh, how glad I am that I have paused to ask You what You thought and how You looked on what I wished to do! The tempest of hurt feelings was surging in my soul and I would fain have struck back in my anger. But You have shown me where true knighthood lay and how my soul could grow more like Your own. I thank You for the lesson, O my God, and I beg Your grace to make my life like unto Yours.

"I ought to be kinder always,
For the light of His kindly eyes,
I ought to be wiser always,
Because He is just and wise;
And gentler in all my bearing;
And braver in all my daring,
For the patience that in Him lies."

TWENTY-FIRST MONDAY AFTER PENTECOST

I'M SO AFRAID OF ME

Keep thyself, therefore, and thy soul carefully.
Deuteronomy 4:9.

I'M so afraid of me" was the ending of the letter which came from one who, having been a truant far and long from God, was at length trying hard to serve Him wholeheartedly. Where once there had been much of pride and self-will, now there was a suppression of self and a really humble seeking for advice and guidance. The young chap was once quite certain he could guide himself, was once quite definite that others were all wrong when they pointed out his wrecking faults. But that was gone and in its stead was a fine sense of personal distrust. Victory, a splendid victory, in one of life's hardest battles was summed up in that self-revealing phrase: "I'm so afraid of *me.*"

So many of us have yet to learn to be properly afraid of self. There is an improper timidity, a lack of due confidence in self, which does much harm to us and affects a deal of good work. But a calm, moderated self-assurance is perfectly compatible with fear of self; rather, it will never be adequately *moderated,* unless there is this fear of self. Self-assurance without fear of self is on the broad high road to self-assertion and arrogance, than which there is little more disgusting in flawful man.

And this fear of self, what is it but a fundamental distrust of our own unabetted judgment on ourselves and on our virtues and faults? The Saints of God warn us that we are poor judges of ourselves and of our own causes, no matter how skilled we may be in directing others through the tangles of life. We are too far within focus to get a right perspective of ourselves, too close to see our good and bad qualities in proper proportion. We *may* see them aright, but there is at least equal chance that we may see them awry.

Shall we, then, not study ourselves? Is all that is said and written about self-examination merely advice not worth the heeding? Not at all! But when we have studied and probed and tested, then it were ordinary, healthy common sense to submit our findings to someone else, someone who knows us and knows human nature, someone who really cares to see us true and straight, and to bring us close to God. Then, if we have read ourselves amiss, our mistake can be corrected. Then we can go ahead with our work, with our prayer, with our recreation, with our comradeship with others, with all that self-assurance that must be present, if success is to attend our efforts in any line.

Dear Jesus, I need to have this fear of self, not a cramping, numbing fear, but that healthy distrust of my own judgment about myself and all my good and bad traits. With Your grace I will try both to analyze and know myself and then to go with humility and common sense to someone else, that I may be checked up on my findings. Teach me to be rightly self-confident and self-assured and to that end to be properly "afraid of me."

TWENTY-FIRST TUESDAY AFTER PENTECOST

FIGHTING TO THE END

But I fear none of these things neither do I count my life more precious than myself, so that I may consummate my course.

Acts 20:24.

IT is St. Paul's farewell to "the ancients of the Church" of Ephesus. He has told them and will tell them again the story of his labors for them, how he has "kept back nothing that was profitable" to them but has spent himself for them, and has for that been the object of Jewish conspiracies and has been hunted by his enemies. Yes, and more than this he tells them, for he is off for Jerusalem and there more tribulations await him. What they are he knows not, "save that the Holy Ghost in every city witnesseth to me, saying that bands and afflictions wait for me in Jerusalem." Yet he does not shrink nor draw back like a coward.

No, not St. Paul, the fighting Saint who would place the world as spoils at the feet of his Captain Christ. His one cry is—"But I fear none of these things; neither do I count my life more precious than myself, so that I may consummate my course."

Paul was determined to die fighting as a true soldier of Christ, flinching at nothing, quailing before no man. What boldness! What fearlessness! And yet ought not that cry be upon the lips of each and all of us? Duty calls me to stand my ground and hold a post that is fraught with much anxiety and maybe real danger, and surely encompassed with much toil. It may be I have to guard myself against those who play themselves to be my friends, and yet manoeuver strangely when they think my eyes are away from them. It may be that those placed over me seem underhanded and say one thing, and mean and do another. But what of that, if God calls me to abide where I am! Am I going to play the quitter because puny men fight against me? Or again, I find God beckoning me on to work that seems to draw with it more than I feel I can bear and yet His call is clear. It would be so easy to stay where I am, so comfortable to refuse the proffered chance to make new and harder efforts in His service. But shall I then fight a man's fight when I run away and shirk the call of God? Of course, it is hard on poor human nature but what of the thousands of men and women who know not Christ as we have known Him and yet who face the hardest things of life and grit their teeth and see them through! Of course, it is hard to throw my shoulders back and nerve my arms for fresher battles. Yet that is what His Saints have done and that is what brave St. Paul did for our Lord who fought the hardest fight that ever any man fought and died upon the Cross the hardest death that any man ever died.

Dear Jesus, You know, as no one else knows, how often my poor old heart begins to fear and to want to quit the battles of life. It is hard to keep on fighting, fighting always and it is harder still to see still fiercer fights ahead. Then teach me by Your grace to fear none of these things and not to count my life more precious than myself. Just let me, "consummate my course," as a true, fighting soldier of my unbeaten King.

TWENTY-FIRST WEDNESDAY AFTER PENTECOST

NO PAROLE

And after they had rest, they returned to do evil in Thy sight: and Thou leftest them in the hand of their enemies, and they had dominion over them. Then they returned, and cried to Thee, and Thou heardest from heaven and deliveredst them many times in Thy mercies.

2 Esdras 9:28.

THE fourth-time offender ought not to be paroled" was the deliberate judgment of one who had had much experience with criminals, and his opinion was acknowledged just by most men. After all, men at large must be protected, their lives and their properties made secure. For the first, for the second, even for the third offense we may suspend sentence, or, after a period of imprisonment, grant parole if we feel that reformation can be reasonably expected. But then the day comes when justice must have its way and mercy must be set aside, lest life itself and the ordinary way of life be all undone.

Thus, too, it is between friend and friend, between child and parent. The day comes when offenses will be no longer brooked, when friendship will be denied because trust can no longer be placed in the one that has been loved. Only when we come to God does this law of often repeated offense break down. Patient, infinitely kind, we have learned to abuse His patience and to play upon His abiding kindness. Because He is so ready to forgive we seem to be all the readier to offend. Years back we have learned to take the name of God in vain, and day after day has heard His Sacred Name bandied about on our lips and He forgives and forgives again our rudeness, and waits for us to treat Him with a common reverence. Our prayers, if we find time to say them, are hurried through with scant attention and devotion, yet every morning and every evening He waits to have us grow a bit polite with Him. A wagging tongue is ours, which tastes its words most sweetly when these are seasoned to hurt another's goodly name, or to vent our spite, or to while away our time gossiping; yet all the while He waits to have us learn a wee small bit of Christian charity and elemental kindness. Irritability and sensitiveness, selfishness and pride, have been stamped out boldly on our lives, and yet, though earthly friends take all amiss and rightly so, God puts up with it all. Thanks be to God He does! Suppose God took the stand that we feel is eminently just when man deals with his fellow man!

Dear Jesus, I kneel before You with all my sins upon me. I know the past and You know it too. Long, long ago, what earthly judge would not have sentenced me for life if I had violated civil laws as I have broken Yours! But Your thoughts are not our thoughts, nor are Your ways our ways and You have pardoned, pardoned, pardoned, until my life is but one massive interweaving of sin and granted pardon. Jesus dear, surely You are "much for pardoning" and I thank You from my heart for all Your many, many mercies. Just grant me now the grace that I may not be rude enough to call upon Your mercy quite so frequently.

TWENTY-FIRST THURSDAY AFTER PENTECOST

IN THE BREAKING OF BREAD

And they told what things were done in the way, and how they knew Him in the breaking of bread.

St. Luke 24:35.

BACK to Jerusalem, Cleophas and his companion had come in haste. A few hours back they had gone forth disconsolate, with all hope gone. As they told the Stranger in the way: "We had hoped." *Had* hoped! And yet, when they had come to Emmaus, He "took bread and blessed and broke and gave to them" and with the Bread "their eyes were opened and they knew Him"—and hope returned. "In the breaking of bread"—at the Communion Table they looked deep into the mind and heart of our Lord—and the world was a changed place for them.

"They knew Him in the breaking of bread." How that story has been renewed down the ages. It is the story of sanctity within the Church of God. In the quiet of His Presence, or, better still, with Him within them at the altar-rail men and women, young and old, know the mind of God, and their hearts are attuned to His.

But what of myself? Do I visit Him as frequently as I might? Or do I pass His door when, if it were the door of a merely earthly friend, I should surely stop in? Do I receive Him as my Guest as often as I can? Or does day after day pass and I fail to welcome Him? Surely, if I really "knew Him in the breaking of bread," I could never be so impolite and heedless of His friendship.

And if I do receive Him daily and visit Him as often as I can, am I growing always in His love and service? Is my preparation for His coming, no, not worthy of Him—that could never be—but at least not too hurried, not too thoughtless? Maybe I must admit to myself in all candor that I hardly look forward to His coming at all. And then those few tremendously rich moments when He is "really and truly and substantially" with me, am I quite rude to Him and scant in my attention? Maybe I even rush at once to eat my bodily food for which I seem to have a greater relish than I have for the Food of my soul!

Of course, I need not stand on ceremony with my Changeless Friend. But in all honesty, does this excuse my rudeness?

Dear Jesus, would that I knew You in the breaking of Bread! I do, of course, in a way, but not intensely, not convincingly, not overpoweringly. For if I did, I should be a saint—and that I am not, sad to say. But I must know You; for to know You is eternal life, which is companionship with You forever. So I will try by greater fervor and by more attentiveness each time I come to You, to know You "in the breaking of bread."

TWENTY-FIRST FRIDAY AFTER PENTECOST

BE MINDFUL OF MY BONDS

The salutation with mine own hand, Paul. Be mindful of my bonds.

Colossians 4:18.

HIS secretary had taken down the letter; yet before it started on its long way, Paul, in his Roman prison, reached out his heavily shackled hand, and, as best his fettered fingers might, wrote briefly: "Be mindful of my bonds." All his story, all Colossae's story was there. That his love, the love of the convert Jewish Rabbi, who once had despised the "Gentile dogs," might bring him always to the folks of pagandom, he had braved the storms of unleashed Jewish hate and found as a reward manacled hands and tethered feet. The Colossians must, even as he, read in his bonds the charter of their freedom, children now of God and co-heirs with Christ Jesus.

As Paul to the new-born Christians, so Christ our Lord says to each of us from off the Cross: "Be mindful of My bonds." On Calvary's top that high noon of the first Good Friday with a binding that Paul never knew,

His sacred Hands and Feet were riveted to the tree of shame, and as He hangs, "placarded" before the world, He looks out over the centuries and says to me, to me, the wayward heart, whose love He would have solely His, as though no other heart might love Him: "Be mindful of My bonds."

When the road of life runs through rough places and the burdens of life fall crushingly upon us, we must bethink ourselves of the Lord of all, who went out beyond the city, carrying His own hard cross. When the world with the sound of music and of mirth tries to bring us into sin and to steal our hearts from God, we must remember our Friend who redeemed them by His own blood-letting. Success comes and with it the lure of pride and the ringing applause of fickle men. Then, if we would stand true, there must swing before our dazzled eyes the Way of the Cross, that pressed so closely on the heels of Palm Sunday's merry-making throng. "Be mindful of My bonds. Think you of My nail-dug feet, that your own may not go a-straying; of My fastened hands, that your own may not reach forbidden fruit; of My darkened eyes, that your own may not soil your soul; of My spear-rent Heart, that yours may open to none save Me. Be mindful of My bonds, for they gave you liberty, that you must not lose, for the loss would be eternal slavery."

Jesus, ransomer of our souls, "if we have forgotten the name of our God, and if we have stretched forth our hands to a strange God, shall not God search out these things?" Oh, what a search You would have to make, then, of the past! Days and weeks and months we have set up strange, petty idols in our hearts and made slaves again of the souls You had redeemed. But, Jesus dear, this must not be again and with Your helping grace it will not be again. Come failure or come success, come joy or sorrow, we will ever hearken to Your voice: "Be mindful of My bonds."

"Christ as a light illumine and guide me!
Christ as a shield overshadow and cover me!
Christ be under me, Christ be over me!
Christ be beside me on left hand and right!
Christ be before me, above me, about me!
Christ this day be within and without me!"

TWENTY-FIRST SATURDAY AFTER PENTECOST

GONE NATIVE

Hence we must all the more earnestly give heed to what hath been heard, that we may not drift away.

Hebrews 2:1.

HE was a wreck of a man. Years back he had stood high in the business and social worlds, but long years of mingling with the unkempt, listless natives had sapped him of his moral strength. He had lost the snap of his race, he had worn through the fiber of his manhood and had cast his lot in with the very people he had been expected to uplift and save. Travelers have one phrase for that, a telling phrase: he had "gone native."

Few of us ever get a chance to "go native" in that sense of the word, but there is a sense in which it may be applicable to us, no matter where our lot may be cast. We who have been taught the higher culture of God's true Faith, who have been nurtured in the family of the Saints, are, nevertheless, living among men and women who are strangers to our ways. Their principles are not ours, nor their thoughts, nor the manner of their lives. In matters of Faith we talk a different language; in matters of morals we stand for a purity in public and in private life that seems to many of them a hypocritical impossibility. Yet we must live with them and be friends with them and interthread our lives and theirs, and there is no little danger that we may "go native." For the children of God have many a time in the past "gone native" with the children of the world.

Youth and maid have pledged unending love before God's altar, and God has blessed them. Holy they are to be and holy must their children be. And they are—for a while. But then! They breathe more deeply of the worldly atmosphere; they learn a deal more of its unholy principles; and then, forgetting that their wedded love is a symbol of Christ's love for His fruitful Church, they "go native" and join the children of a pleasure-loving world.

Within the cloister-walls men and women have pledged to God a love to do and dare all things for Him and Him alone. In the heyday of early maturity it was not hard to give Him all and to serve Him most generously. But the slow-footed years go by and the world becomes a thing more attractive than the God who had won their young love. Here a little concession to self-comfort, and there a yielding to petty vanity, and there again a more serious taking-on of the worldling's ways—and maybe before long, despite the outward habit of a Religious, they have "gone native."

So it is in the business world, in the political world and in the world of thought and letters. Men and women begin with principles that would keep them saints, but soon the daily, hourly friction against the world wears down their spirits and breaks their morale—and they "go native" to the ways of the children of time.

Dear Jesus, by Your good grace, I have enjoyed the intimacy of Your company, and Mother Mary's, and that of the Saints and Angels. Nurtured with them, I have learned Your truth, and the holy ways of living You would have us follow. But many of the children of the world, who rub shoulder to shoulder with me each day, are strangers, nay rather, are hostile to all this. Their ways are easy ways and make strong appeal to me at times; and therein lies the danger. But I beg Your grace most earnestly that I may never forget the nobility of my calling and "go native" in the ways of the world.

TWENTY-SECOND SUNDAY AFTER PENTECOST

WEARYING OUR LORD

Jesus . . . being wearied with His journey, sat thus on the well.

St. John 4:6.

FEW pictures in the New Testament are so well remembered as that of our Lord seated at Jacob's well at Sichar in the Samaritan territory, worn out by His seeking for souls. He had left Judea and was on His way to Galilee, and the rough walking over the ill-kept roads of Palestine, over hill and down into valley and then up again, had quite exhausted Him—and added thereto was the disappointment, growing daily, that men were not listening and were not going to listen to Him when He spoke to them. He was "wearied"—wearied physically, wearied mentally, at the seemingly useless efforts.

Have we ever wearied our Lord? If we are not saints, we have. Of all of us, except the Saints, the strong lines of "The Hound of Heaven" are unfortunately true: "I fled Him, down the nights and down the days: I fled Him, down the arches of the years." We have not given in to our Lord. That is clear; else high, very high sanctity would be ours at this moment. And yet, though I fled Him, He did not let me run away but "with unhurrying chase, and unperturbéd pace . . . came on the following Feet."

When am I going to stop wearying our Lord?

His grace has been insistent that I grow more kindly in thought and speech, that I forego the cutting word and the rehearsing of gossip; and yet I still offend Him by my uncharity.

He has asked me to be less self-seeking, and to think of ways of helping others. But I go my lonely, isolated way, thinking largely of what I can get out of life, and not what I can put into it for others.

Closer union with Him by reason of prayers well said and a spirit of larger recollection throughout the day—this He has sought from me for many years. Yet my prayers are dashed through and frequently shortened; and I rarely think of Him at all during the time of either business or pleasure.

No wonder He is weary of pursuing my soul! Would I have His patience if another had thwarted me all these years?

Dear Jesus, I am sorry that I have wearied You so much these many years. It was truly good and merciful of You not to give me up to my own wilfulness. And the worst shame of it is, that all that You have asked me to do was for my own benefit—not for Yours. And yet, even now, dear Lord, despite Your love and all You have done for me, I find it hard to be definitely, seriously, explicitly determined to be a saint. I want to be, but—! Yet You know my weakness, and so have patience with me, even though I may weary You a bit longer.

TWENTY-SECOND MONDAY AFTER PENTECOST

TIRED

And they marched from Mount Hor by the way that leadeth to the Red Sea, to compass the land of Edom. And the people began to be weary of their journey and labor.
Numbers 21:4.

IF the journey be long, we often tire of it, even though home be at the journey's end. So it was with the Jews as they traveled up from Egypt and Sinai and on through desert wastes to the Promised Land. They began to be aweary of the homeless life, to be tired of a morrow and yet again a morrow that seemed to bring them no nearer to the home that God Himself had chosen for them. They would rest their weary feet, they would be done with travel that meant a day of wandering followed by a night which was but a sleeping span that ushered in another day, only to find themselves far from home. Mary, the sister of Moses, was dead and gone, Aaron lay buried on Mount Hor, and many of their dear ones who had crossed the Red Sea lay cold in death beneath the desert sands. Why journey on to a goal that seemed "to fade forever and forever from their view"?

Can we not see herein a likeness to ourselves as we go on a-pilgrimaging back to God? The way is long, now through sunny places, but oh! how often are our footprints stained with blood and our eyes bedimmed with tears—and we begin to be weary of the journey and the labor of our homeward path. Heaven, the goal of all our aspirations, ever beckons us on and those dear ones that stand upon its blessed shore call to us with longing arms and yet at times we, too, grow weary of the long and seemingly lengthening way that leads back home to God. Once on a time it seemed so easy to make the journey Heavenwards and the costs were counted slight indeed. To serve our Lord with utter loyalty and follow all the inspirations of His grace, to give our wills to Him without one single thing reserved for self, to have Him reign within our hearts as life's sole King—that was the dream of our waking hours and the prayer that tired lips formed. But now how seems the way? Has the appeal of home grown less to us, precisely because we have thought of it so long? As the journey's end draws nearer, are our feet more loath to travel on? We once bethought us of the joy of our welcome home, were we to come with our hands heavy laden with the wealth of holy deeds, and maybe now we find the little virtues hard and the great virtues quite beyond our gaining—and so again the folk of God begin "to be weary of their journey and labor." Oh, let us stir our hearts and make quite fresh again the thought of our home beyond the stars. The journey's end may not be quite so far away, as the shadows seem to show, and it would be a shameful thing to come there empty-handed, or be found a-loitering on the way.

O Jesus, the journey home seems at times so very, very long! The way is rough, the clouds are dark, and my vanished earthly friends have left me alone in my pilgrimage. Yet I must not slacken in my onward path. You call, and Mother Mary calls, and all the saints are calling, and all my holy dead. So I shall try each day and many times within the day to make my soul quite as You would have it be, when You come to call me home Just keep a wayfarer's weariness away from me.

TWENTY-SECOND TUESDAY AFTER PENTECOST

REMEMBERING THE PAST

Remember that thou wast a slave in Egypt and the Lord thy God delivered thee from thence.

Deuteronomy 24:18.

AND when you condemn these others, do you ever think how far you, yourself, have fallen below your ideals, and how far, far away from them you are at present?" were the words that cut straight across a deal of censure that had been peevishly spat out. "Yes, others have fallen and they ought not, and others have been untrue to lofty aims and yet why carp at them? Just look at yourself, and all the tale you have come to tell and yet see what you ought to be! Stop and look!"

And then the head was bowed in shame and from humbled lips came contrite words:

"I'll never talk that way again!"

So it was of old that God spoke to the Jews of the slaves and the poor among them. To these unfortunates they must be kind, and of their needs they must be thoughtful. And why? Because years back they themselves had been held in bondage and had known the pinch of poverty. Yet to them in their poverty and bondage God had come and He had delivered them. So, too, now, remembering the toil and sorrows that had once been theirs, kindliness and mercy will live in their hearts for those whose ways are still rough and irksome.

And so with each of us. If we are mindful of ourselves and our days of trial and doubts, and the hours of our sorrows and the times when we ourselves have mishandled our problems, and faltered and failed and fallen, we shall not be too hard on others. If parents will think of the pranks they indulged in when young, a larger patience will be theirs to bear with the tantrums of the little ones. If when youth is bright and active, and the age-old craving for a larger but unwise liberty comes to their boys and girls, if mother and father will then bethink them of their younger days and how they found the call of the world most enticing and how they balked at advice from older heads, then they will read aright and understand well these tugging souls that they must rule and guide. Then they will hold the confidences of their maturing children and save them from life's pitfalls.

So, too, in the classroom, if the teacher will recall the dreariness that was over a little life not so very many years ago and how the bell that rang for school had a doleful sound and how its peals were merry when it rang for play, then will she bear with the youngsters' restlessness; for they like study no more than she. Their restiveness is but their springing spirits snapping out through healthy bodies that chafe at the bit.

So, too, when others grow peevish and fling their answers back, the sharp rebuke will die on our lips, for we remember how such harsh words are wont to make our own querulousness more rebellious. When sin comes into other lives and makes them fear to tell us of their truancy, we shall say the kindly word that more than once broke down our own reserve. Remember, only let us remember, the ways of our poor heart and a healing touch will be ours when others stand in need.

Dear Jesus, did I but "remember," how different things would be! But I do not, and just there it is that so much friction and unpleasantness arise. I would be more patient with others when they are mean and nasty, if only I thought of my own surly moods. Their crosses would be lifted more by me, if the hours of my own cross-carrying came before me and I recalled how gentle was the touch that brought me surcease of my pain. But I forget, and lose my self-control and then others suffer more and matters are much worse. Yet this ought not to be. So give me grace, dear Lord, just always to remember the past and all will be much better.

TWENTY-SECOND WEDNESDAY AFTER PENTECOST

LOVED

I have loved you, saith the Lord: and you have said: Wherein hast Thou loved us?

Malachias 1:2.

IT was a dark hour for the Jews and their enemies were pressing them hard from all sides. Each day brought its weight of sorrow and trial to burden hearts already sore with pain. Thus day in and day out the shadows darkened and the problems of life thickened until utter desperation seemed the logical sentiment for all. Then it was that God, through His prophet, spoke to them of His love and told them how near and dear they were to Him. "I have loved you," saith the Lord. And querulously they answered Him: "Wherein hast Thou loved us?" They forgot Egypt and Sinai, and the miracle-fed years in the desert, and the day that Jordan stood asunder, and the evening that the sun went not down in Ajalon; they forgot Hebal and Garizim where the twelve tribes stood and swore to love and serve their God for all His loving kindness to them; they forgot it all and cried: "Wherein hath He loved us?"

Can we not catch more than a faint resemblance to ourselves in this? When joy is in our lives we are quite willing to admit God's love for us but when the shadows fall, what then? I had dreamed a dream for years and just when it should come true, it vanishes into thinnest air. The little one God gave to cheer life's hours with tinkling laughter, has now its lips close sealed in death and all the merry noise is hushed. The hard-earned savings of days when I labored and toiled and stinted myself against the leaner years, are swept away from me and I find myself facing life's downgrade with scant assurance for my livelihood. I have sought hard to fight the battles of life aright and to play my part as a man should play it, and now I find myself quite helpless on a bed of pain or crippled. Then some one comes and tells me of God's love for me and tries to lift my eyes beyond the darkened present. What say I then? Is all the past forgotten? Do I complain, "Wherein hath He loved me!" Wherein? What of the gift of life itself and the gift of warming sun and cooling eventide! What of the gifts of bird, and beast, and flower! What of the gifts of Holy Mother Church, of Baptism, Confirmation, Penance, of the greatest gift of all, the gift of His own dear Self to be my food! "Wherein hath He loved me?" Roll back the scroll of time, slowly, yes very slowly, for every moment was His gift, and each hour came freighted with His graces, and when I have unrolled it all, can I then ask "Wherein hath He loved me?"

Dear Jesus, changeless lover of my soul, please never let the darkness grow so great that I lose sight of all Your love. You know how prone I am to lose it. You had Your hour of shadowed agony in Gethsemani and again upon the Cross and then it was You deigned to feel the dreadful depths of my poor soul's darknesses. Just help me, Lord, to take the crosses as I take the joys of life and grant that I remember always wherein You have loved me.

TWENTY-SECOND THURSDAY AFTER PENTECOST

WANTING TO BE GOD

And the serpent said to the woman: No, you shall not die the death. For God doth know that in what day soever you shall eat thereof, your eyes shall be opened, and you shall be as Gods, knowing good and evil.

Genesis 3:4, 5.

THE craving to be like unto God was the cause of the fall of our first parents. It was a sinful thought, sprung of pride for they would satisfy this craving wrongfully, and it brought its penalty swiftly. Lured on by the hope of wider vision and of knowledge that would teach them all things, so be it they ate the forbidden fruit, Eve reached forth sinful hands towards the tree. "She took of the fruit thereof and did eat and gave to her husband who did eat." And then the wider vision came indeed! Yes, a vision came, but it was dark and full of pain and moist with tears that flow unto this day.

Thus man fell and when God came to place him back into his high estate, He acted in a wondrous way. Man fell because of woman, and God made a woman bring about redemption. Man fell by reason of a tree, and God redeemed him by the tree of shame. Man fell by reason of his desire to be like God, and God—we almost tremble at the thought—has deigned to have it so. What once brought sin is now a holy craving, what once brought death now brings man life and brings it most abundantly. Is not that the meaning of the Blessed Sacrament? That we might reach up unto God, God has stooped down to us, not merely to abide hard by our homes, but to be our daily bread, that we may be nurtured unto godliness by food that is very God Himself. He has taken man at his word and changed its sinfulness and made it "truly right and just and available to salvation" to crave and yearn for likeness unto God. Indeed He pleads with us to come and eat the Bread of Angels. Nay more, reversing the command of old, He threatens us with loss of life unless we ease this craving for our Heaven-sent food. "O the depth of the riches of the wisdom and of the knowledge of God! How incomprehensible are His judgments, and how unsearchable His ways!" With this fundamental yearning within me for all vision and all knowledge and all holiness, a yearning as vast and as broad and as deep as life itself, I yearn inevitably to be like God, for only in possessing Him can that longing be stayed. So now Heaven is begun upon this earth, for God is with us always.

O Jesus, most considerate of friends, with rarest delicacy You have changed what was a sinful craving into highest virtue. In the dim and distant past man would reach up and pluck Heaven down to him in sinful wise and now when You have punished him for that same fault, You grant the object of his petulancy. Did ever parent act like this with forward child? How good You are, dear Lord, how very thoughtful for our weaknesses! I thank You, dearest Lord, for letting it be right for me to want to be like God.

TWENTY-SECOND FRIDAY AFTER PENTECOST

WILLING SPIRIT, WEAK FLESH

The spirit, indeed, is willing, but the flesh is weak.
St. Matthew 26:41.

IT was a westside tenement, gloomy and crowded, and far back in the darkness lived a young boy and girl across whose lives much sin was written. Bereft of their mother years back, they had fought their way in the strange big world and much had they known of its sordidness. But now helping hands were held out to them. God's priest had told them of His commandments and of the need of prayer, and they had begun to turn again to God. This night, as the priest once more spoke to them of God, down from the wall the young girl took a large crucifix she was buying with a weekly pittance. "Bless it, Father, will you?" was her request. Living lives of sin from which they were not yet won, yet from their poverty, they buy the sign of redemption! And Christ looked down from that wall and grace did come into their lives.

Continued sin and yet with hoarded pennies a costly crucifix is bought! Strange human heart, all craving for the right, yet weak to do the wrong. What patience we must have to read it all aright. Scolding was not in place nor angry censuring, but the patience of Him who hung upon the Cross and died thereon to win our love by His long suffering; patience to find the inmost craving for good of their poor soiled souls, and to build thereon. Patience! How we need that in this life! Patient understanding of wife for husband and husband for wife, to know indeed the little daily frictions that come and go, and more so the unwonted discontents which arise, yet all the while to see deep down the old love still enduring. Patient understanding of parent for child whose growing years spell renewed rebellions and an impatient plea for larger liberties, yet underneath it all, to catch the eternal cry of youth for the worthwhile things that can hold its leaping heart, and the same true love for mother and for father which will bring tears bursting to their eyes, were sickness or sorrow to come to either of them.

Sin, great sin there may be in life, and much wreckage strewn in seeming or in real wilfulness, but underneath it in man and woman, youth and maid, we must reach down and find the finer stuff still there and see the ceaseless craving of the heart to know where God may be and how His law may bring them happiness. Patience, we need it all; patience in the home, patience in the classroom, patience in the business world. Patience, yes, and not mere patience, not mere negative sufferance, but a sympathetic reading of that strange thing the human heart which can do the wrong yet crave for the right, can seek the false yet kneel in prayer to ask a love of truth. Yes, we must have a warmth of true, strong encouragement that will insist on the heinousness of sin, yet tell all the while of God's enduring love which brings forgiveness and an abiding strength to walk in the way of His commandments. Good there is in the worst of men and we must find that good and bring it to the front and foster it until its very growth stifles the bad—and then we have won another soul to God.

Dear Jesus, infinitely wise to understand the contradictions of our human hearts, infinitely patient to unravel the strange puzzles of their desires, grant me the grace to read aright the hearts of all my fellowmen! But above all, let me understand the hearts of those You have committed to my care. So much depends on how I deal with them; for I can lead them nearer to You or send them far away. Let me indeed know the wrong they do that I may guide them away from all that harms them, but let me know, too, the fundamental goodness in each heart that I may nurture that and make it strong. I beg You, dearest God, to give me patient understanding.

TWENTY-SECOND SATURDAY AFTER PENTECOST

IN THE LONG-AGO

Who will grant me, that I might be according to the months past, according to the days in which God kept me, when His lamp shined over my head, and I walked by His light in darkness? As I was in the days of my youth, when God was secretly in my tabernacle?

Job 29:2-5.

WHEN I look back on the past! What a vision to make me sorry and hang my head in shame! Then, Father, I served God joyfully and it was a pleasure to pray—and to do kind things—and to do my job in life well. But now—!" Once again the old, old story was told—and yet the man was not quite square to himself. In the past he had been more merry as he walked in the way of God's commandments, and there had been more music in his heart. That was true; but now—though the music was gone, and his feet were leaden, he still walked faithfully according to God's law. It was hard plodding now, for the road was rougher and darkness folded in on him often.

Job had such thoughts when he looked back over his life. Days there had been when all was well with him, but now he had been bereft of all: children and wealth and friends and health. Yet, more determinedly than ever, he kept to God's law, for "till I die I will not depart from my innocence."

To each of us come moments when the past comes back with the days of our early fervors.

Years back at school, we made our yearly Retreats with ardor, and said our Angelus daily, and visited the Blessed Sacrament often, and, all in all, found a thrill in pious practices. But today the thrills are gone, and the difficulty of "getting in" these and other exercises of piety is very real. And yet—we *are* trying to serve God in a maturer way and with deeper conviction than before.

To others the vision comes of the happy morning at God's altar when two hearts pledged undying love, which was entwined with God's sacramental blessing. That day, and many a day thereafter, God was very near and the days of Paradise seemed almost back again, for God seemed to walk with them as the hours rolled by. But now—? The world has swung its sterner realities against them and it costs much more to serve God when life's friction is hard against them. But serve Him they do, with a more reasoned compliance to all the duties He has placed on them.

To others again the memory comes of the days when first they turned their backs upon the world, and walked so airily and lightly along cloistered halls; the day when first they, too, knelt at the altar and tremblingly swore the triple oath of undying fealty and love. All was music then, and each least thing added its own sweet note to the harmonies of a life that was lived for God alone. But now—! There's little music now, and many things irk. Yes; but then, is it not true that our love for God has grown deep and is more consciously and deliberately inclusive of each item of life? The earlier love rather carried us along; now, with surer grasp and maturer conviction, we rather take that love for granted and feel no longer its pulsing surge. (And is not that the way when human love has grown together many years in the marriage bond?)

Of course, it may be that we have gone far astray from those early days and have been truant to God's love. If so, then may we truly hang our heads in shame for the unfaithfulness of our love. But even then the vision should cheer and encourage us; for though we have changed, the vision comes from our changeless Friend who loves us now just the same as He did when our own love was strong.

Dear Jesus, I sometimes get discouraged when I think over the past. Like Job I look back to "the days in which God kept me, when his lamp shone over my head and I walked by his light in my darkness." Those joyous days are gone; and yet, may I not truly say that I am trying to serve You and do what You want me to do? There is less thrill in Your service, but is not that the way with human love?—and I am just a human lover, even though You are God. And even if I have been faithless, Your love is true and constant. So, faithful or faithless, I am sure of Your love—but, Jesus, just help me to be more like Your faithful self.

TWENTY-THIRD SUNDAY AFTER PENTECOST

OUR HOME BEYOND

But our country is in the heavens, whence we eagerly await as Saviour, the Lord Jesus Christ, who will transform the body of our lowliness, that it may be one with the body of His glory.

Philippians 3:20-21.

MOST dreadful of all things is death, for it is the limit, and for the dead man there appears to be no further good nor evil left." So wrote one of the greatest geniuses of Greece and in so writing he gives us the clue to the pagan world. If death is the last and closing act of the drama of life, rightly did the revelers of old cry out; "Let us eat and drink; for tomorrow we die." If after death comes non-existence, if the grave's narrow bounds be our lasting resting-place, it were quite sensible to catch the sunshine and the flowers as we may, and gather in life's gold with clutching hands with little care about our fellows. This fitful span of life is all we have, and we are fools, utter fools, to stint ourselves in aught, if the yawning maw of oblivion is to engulf us wholly.

So thought the pagan world and so it acted. But we know otherwise. This life is quite a transitory thing and yet a real and vital thing. We have not here a lasting home and yet upon the manner of our living now will depend our future happiness. Today, a speechless child, tomorrow buoyant with youth's tingling years, again a morrow and life is faced with the steady gaze of rounded maturity and then—! Yet, all the while, I know this passing fickle thing is the gauge of an eternity, and that is what consoles my heart. Riches may be mine or poverty, it matters not, so be it that I am garnering richest harvests for the life beyond. Friends may yet abide with me or may be fast numbered with those that sleep beneath the sod, but what of that, if they and we so live that we shall meet unendingly beyond the stars! Ambition may have won complete success, chance may have placed us high before the gaze of men, or we may travel ways that no man notes or cares to note, yet all the while, upon the heights or down in the darkened valleys, the one thing necessary is to see that we are journeying on to God. "Life is real, life is earnest and the grave is not its goal," and so we labor hard and labor patiently, biding God's good time. Nor do we slacken in our toiling, for we must traffic well, that, like exiled merchants who ply their trade in foreign lands, we may come richly laden with our wealth, when He comes to call us home.

Dear Lord, how can I thank you for the vision of home beyond the grave! I know You have given me a very real work to do before death comes; but, thanks to Your good teaching, I know its worth is reckoned only as it counts for Heaven. This life is real but it is passing, and how it passes must be my great concern. Grant me then the grace to live and labor so, that when You come, as comes the thief at night, to call me from my toiling, You will find my eyes fixed full upon my home above.

TWENTY-THIRD MONDAY AFTER PENTECOST

HURT FEELINGS

The learning of a man is known by patience; and his glory is to pass over wrongs.

Proverbs 19:11.

IF they only gave you credit for being thoughtful," was the pained remark of a man who had planned and schemed to serve other's moods and desires, only to be completely misunderstood. He had studied their times of work and their hours of leisure, had teased out as best he could the tangles of their character and had then adjusted and re-adjusted with scheming hands the work in which many were needed to cooperate. Yet, when all was done, some were offended, because they felt they were treated inconsiderately!

Hurt feelings are the cause of so many, many quarrels in this poor sick world of ours, and feelings are hurt so very often because we imagine that others have been inconsiderate. We are so far within our own focus that we ourselves bulk out of all proportion to every other object in the world, and on our majestic, disproportioned selves we would have all mankind dance attendance. Then when they do not, or when we think they have failed in any least way to show us proper respect and required honor, our quivering pulse registers each moment of outraged feeling.

Is not that a pity? There is so much great work to be done in this world and so little time to do it in, that it is a sad, sad thing to waste precious moments nursing our imagined woes. But suppose we are really slighted! Are we not bigger men and women, when we rise high enough to be able to stoop very low? What earthly use is there in carrying quivering nerves through life to rasp our own souls and cause much irritation in others!

Slights do come, but, most often, much is due to our imaginings. Sensitive and wincing at every touch that does not come most gently, we sense a slur where none was intended and feel a hurt that was never inflicted. Does that help life—our own and others—to be more smooth and gracious? Surely it does not. Then why not try to tuck our feelings away and keep the even tenor of our lives, not getting pained at every contact?

Dear Jesus, how much good is spoiled in my own life and in the lives of others by my hurt feelings. I grow peevish and quite out of sorts, when others pass me by or merely seem to overlook me, and then my work suffers and maybe health itself, if my sensitiveness reaches undue bounds. This is all a pity, Lord; so help me to get over it! Children fret and wince at everything, but I am supposed to be full-grown. So give me grace to take life, as it is, quite manfully and not to give way so frequently to hurt feelings!

TWENTY-THIRD TUESDAY AFTER PENTECOST

INTERESTED IN OTHERS

Have they made thee ruler? Be not lifted up: be among them as one of them. Have care of them, and so sit down, and when thou hast acquitted thyself of all thy charge, take thy place.

Ecclesiasticus 32:1, 2.

HE'S not interested. That's all." This was the answer given to the young man who was complaining that his "higher-up" never asked about the health of anyone, never said a kind word of praise, never made a remark about anyone's work except to point out a flaw. There was no positive unkindness—that was true, and that was something. But there was never evidenced the slightest interest in what those under him were doing, no least question about their aims and ambitions. And that was hard for all, but doubly hard for one who by nature needed to realize that somebody did care.

A defect of character, one may retort. Well, maybe, but then it is a defect that is very prevalent and one from which very few are entirely free. We are by nature social beings and meant to live in one another's company. Inevitably this supposes that we are to have a seemly regard for their opinions and expect them to have a like regard for ours. Rare is the man or woman who does not care what others think.

What is harder than for a husband to feel that nothing he does is of even slight interest to his wife; that she takes so little interest in what he does that he might just as well be an utter stranger? And if a wife feels that all her care to please, all her efforts to think out the problems of the home to a solution, are passed by unnoticed, what a wrenching of the heart there is!

Children may feel that parents are glad to be rid of them and pack them off to bed in their earlier years, and then later on to boarding school, just so that they may be "out of the way." Yet mother and father are to stand to them in the place of God and they are the ones who should visibly manifest to the children God's loving Providence over them.

In school or in the office the story is the same. The consciousness that work well done is noticed, that faults, while not overlooked, are not the only things that are marked, that a decent regard is had for the human dignity of each and every man, woman or child—that and that alone will create a spirit of loyalty, an atmosphere of contentment, an eagerness to study or to work.

No matter where I am, no matter how humble my position in life, there will always be a chance for me to take interest in others. Of course, if my position is one of authority, especially of authority whereof the main spring is supposedly deep-seated loyalty or love, then my clear duty is to be interested and the scope of my influence very broad and very deep.

Dear Lord, the one great privilege in life is to help others. We all need at least the help of encouragement and that costs very little, yet is valued so much. My field of influence may not be very wide but I do want to do all the good I can. So I shall try to make all those over whom I am placed feel that I am properly interested in them and their work and all that happens to them.

TWENTY-THIRD WEDNESDAY AFTER PENTECOST

DOING THE WORK OF GOD

And next to them the Thecuites built, but their great men did not put their necks to the work of their Lord.
2 Esdras 3:5.

THE Jews had just returned from their captivity and were rebuilding the walls of Jerusalem. Every man of them was needed for the work and "the heart of the people was excited to work." Name after name is listed by the sacred writer. "Of them that built on the wall and that carried burdens, and that laded: with one of his hands he did the work, and with the other he held a sword." Thus did they toil, but not all of them; for "next to them the Thecuites built, but their great men did not put their necks to the work of their Lord."

What a condemnation! The work of the Lord was to be done, and after all His favors to them the Thecuites refused to do it. Quick, indeed, we are to condemn them, yet a glance at our own lives may halt the words on our lips. Just let us ask ourselves how often do we not refuse to put our necks to the work of God.

The little ones need us, as parents, as teachers, as older brothers and sisters, and we let them go their way unadvised, unassisted. And then maybe we condemn them for not being better. The young have a right to help from us and it may irk us somewhat to give it. But is not the work of God in the forming and fashioning of their lives worth this bit of trouble?

Others in need reach out an imploring hand. Do we spurn it? Here it is the call from the poor, that they may have the very necessaries of life. There it is the floating wrecks of men that might make harbor, if only we steered them a bit. Again, it is one hungry for truth, which only we in the Church can give. Do we spurn them? Do we just go our unthinking way and leave them to themselves in all their helplessness?

The work of our Lord is to be done at home, in the school, in the business world, and out where the world is at play. I can do that work first and foremost by being what I ought to be, by letting the grace of God shine out directingly from my every word and act. The sermon of my life will do more to build up men's lives than all the words I might ever speak. And, thereafter and thereby, I can do it by actually helping others over the rough ways of life. For so many the rough spots are very,

very close together. No matter what my walk in life, no matter how narrowed the radius of my daily ways, I can in a very real way put my neck to the work of the Lord.

Dear Jesus, I never want to be like the Thecuites. You have been too good to me for me to shirk the task of making my own soul pleasing to You and, thereafter and thereby, helping others to draw nearer to You. It is hard at times and I do not like the task. But help me, Lord, always, and everywhere, and in every way, to put my neck to the work You would have me do.

TWENTY-THIRD THURSDAY AFTER PENTECOST

A FRANK FRIEND

And they healed the breach of the daughter of my people disgracefully, saying: "Peace, peace," when there was no peace.

Jeremias 8:11.

WE all need a friend who will be brutally frank with us. Try as we may to examine ourselves, we can never know ourselves accurately by unaided self-analysis. We are too far within focus to see ourselves in proper perspective, and our known motives color our actions too distinctly for us to discover clearly the more hidden and radical sources of our general run of actions.

Nor is that a true friend who soothes our soul by assuring us that "All is well," that "Things are going fine," that we "are great." Thus the false prophets and priests did centuries back to the people of Jerusalem, who were steeped in the abominations of idolatry. Many did not realize the heinousness of their ways. Those who should have awakened their souls failed to do so, and taught them to cry: "We are wise, and the law of the Lord is with us." Yet, in very truth, the law was far from them; and so God sent them Jeremias, who pitilessly pleaded with them to return to God. He did not heal "the breach of the daughter of God's people disgracefully." Nor did he cry "Peace, peace." He told them plainly that "there was no peace," for the anger of God was upon them.

If God has given me such a friend, I should thank Him much; for then and then only can I grow daily to proper maturity, and advance in saintliness of life. If I have no such friend, with His help I must seek and find one.

It may be a Confessor who will assume care of my soul. To him I shall lay bare the hidden recesses of my soul as best I can and let him read therein the meaning of my temperament and character. And when he has untangled the skeins and has told me what manner of man I am, I shall listen humbly and profit by his advice.

It may be a friend who goes, side by side, through life with me. He knows my comings-in and my goings-out, my likes and my dislikes, my thought-out actions and my instinctive acts. Reading between all these lines, my friend will catch the hidden meanings that betray now this good quality, now that bad trait.

To listen to such a friend is not the most pleasant thing in the world; but why, to escape the hurt, would I want the breaches of my soul to be healed disgracefully?

Dear Lord, try as I may I cannot know myself with satisfying adequacy. Yet, without such knowledge I can never smooth off the rough edges of character, nor develop to the full the good qualities I have. So grant me, please, a true, frank friend who will show me my soul as it is; so that I may daily grow more pleasing in Your sight.

TWENTY-THIRD FRIDAY AFTER PENTECOST

TOO LATE—?

The Lord is good and giveth strength in the day of trouble and knoweth them that hope in Him.

Nahum 1:7.

WHEN a life of sin has reduced all of one's energy, talents, strength, courage to ashes, then may I ask how can it be possible to try to gather up those ashes and create a new being, capable of taking a proper place among those who know not sin?" Thus wrote one who had tasted of the tragedies of life, one who had pulled her life upon her and stood disconsolate on the heap of mounded years. Poor "Mary the Sinner," for so she signed herself, was pleading for help out from the blind darkness of her self-won night, was reaching out gropingly, fearingly, if she might only find someone to lead her out where a gleam of God's sunshine might curtain off the clouds that darkened her soul. "The next world! That has gone out of my life. . . . Next week will bring another birthday for me. Would to God and Mary, the Refuge of Sinners, that it could truly be for me, as a new day wherein I might never again be able to look back! I suppose, some day—when it will be 'too late'." Poor "Mary the Sinner", pre-damned in the reasoning of her own sad heart, had all but lost that last saving thing, her confidence in God.

"Some day—when it will be 'too late' "! How little "Mary the Sinner" knew of her changeless Friend and of His changeless love which never yet waited for us to love Him first! She had forgotten the Magdalene, whose sinful story was once on every lip, yet whose sanctity has been told throughout the ages. She had forgotten Peter who denied his Lord with an oath and swore he never knew Him, yet thereafter became his Master's Vicar upon earth. She had forgotten the scene in Galilee, when her changeless Friend had cried: "Come unto Me all you that labor and are burdened and I will refresh you," for "if your sins be as scarlet, they shall be made as white as snow; and if they be as red as crimson, they shall be as white as wool." Calvary, too, was forgotten and the outstretched arms of Christ and His pleading cry, "I thirst," the Man-God, "Lover of souls," athirst for souls, just such as "Mary the Sinner," souls that had misread life, souls that had been broken on the wheel of life, souls that had followed the phantoms of wealth and pleasure in life, souls that had not spelled out aright just what His love could mean to them. And Mary, almost forgetful of it all, was sorely tempted to cry out: "Too late!"

Oh, there are tragedies in life but none so tragic as that cry "Too late" and none so unfair to our Lord. We may have ripped and torn our lives asunder, we may have foresworn His love, and other, false gods may have had dominion over us unto our harm, we may have spread ruin in our wake, as we plunged wilfully towards the goal whither ambition or pleasure or lust of power beckoned us, but still He calls to us as He did to the Jews of old: "The Lord is good and giveth strength in the day of trouble and knoweth them that hope in Him; for even unto your old age I am the same and unto your gray hairs I will carry you; I have made you and I will bear; I will carry and I will save." Our lives may be strewn in wreckage but "with the tenderness of pierced hands" He will make whole again what is shattered and will heal again what is bruised. The one last sin we must not commit is that fearful cry, "Too late."

Dear Jesus, relentless Lover of my soul, at times I feel it is all quite useless to make another effort. I have tried and tried again and what does it all amount to? But I know it is all too wrong to forget Your changeless love, I know the very worst sin I can commit is to lose my confidence in You. Yet at times I all but lose it. Dear Jesus, never let that be! Just grant that however discouraged I may be, however sinful I may have been, however far I may have gone away from You, just grant that when Your grace comes knocking at my heart I may never, never cry: "Too late!"

TWENTY-THIRD SATURDAY AFTER PENTECOST

A STRANGE LOVER

For whom the Lord loveth, He chastiseth; and He scourgeth every son whom He receiveth.

Hebrews 12:6.

GOD will have some reward for all that. Perhaps He will ask you to suffer a bit more." Thus wrote a priest to his friend—quite prophetically. A good work had been undertaken for another, quite unselfishly, with never the least possibility that any one but God might reward. Yet scarcely had the deed been done, yes, even before the prophecy was penned, God did repay—and in His own coin; for He asked for a bit, nay rather a deal, of suffering and that, too, of the hardest kind—misunderstanding and steel-like hardness from one who should have been the first to read all things aright.

"Perhaps He will ask you to suffer a bit more." What a reward! What strange ways—to *reward* with *pain!* Yet, that is what God has done to many men and women down through the long centuries. He loved Abraham, and rewarded his faith by testing it right up to the altar of Isaac's sacrifice; He loved His Apostles, and gave them martyrdom; He loved the saintly men and women in each generation of the Church, and always is the story of suffering—physical, mental and spiritual—written large across their lives.

And what did He give His own Mother? Surely to her He would give the choicest of all rewards. And what was it? "And thy own soul a sword shall pierce"; and Mary, God's Mother, is the Mother of Sorrows and the Queen of Martyrs.

Physical pain *is* hard to bear, and wounds of the heart still harder. Hard they are even when we have sinned, though then we can scarcely expect special favors from God; but very, very hard when we have been really trying to keep God's law and walk aright where many slip, all the while reaching a helping hand to some other stumbling wayfarer. Then it is that the cry of rebellion stands quivering on our lips: "Is this the reward!"

Yes, strange though it be, it is so often God's way. Anyone can reward with pleasures; God alone dares reward with pain. And He knows best. When I have lightened others' burdens, He may place an extra cross on me; when I have brought calm to other minds, He may have my own grow anxious; when I have brought joy to other hearts, He may darken mine;—just to show He loves me.

Jesus, my God, You are a strange Lover, and strangely do You reward Your lovers. I know well that You have ever asked sacrifice of those who were closest to You; that the penalty of being near You was always pain. Yet, when You act thus with me, I am very prone to wonder why, and even to rebel. Yet, You know what is best for me and I must accept it all as a token of Your love. Just give me strength to accept all pain from You gracefully.

TWENTY-FOURTH SUNDAY AFTER PENTECOST

NO. 1313

For He knoweth the secrets of the heart.
Psalm 43:22.

OH! I guess I am just another 'case'—just one more bit of trouble to you—just No. 1313." That was said half-humorously, whole-earnestly, to God's priest; and he understood. No one wants to be "not a man but a number." Each and every one of us wants to feel that to the one in whom we confide we are each one of us a complete reality, an individual aside and apart from all others. Not one of us wants to be tagged and labeled. Each of us wants to be known as *this* man or *this* woman with *this* specific problem and *this* unsharable and unshared background, with *this* definite group of joys and sorrows, hopes and disappointments. And when we find one who has skilled sympathy enough to treat us thus, we know we have a gift beyond the telling.

That craving to be understood! How deep, very deep God has planted it in our human hearts! And like every other craving that we have tucked away in the inmost fibers of our being, so this He has met abundantly.

And not with sympathetic human friends alone. These He has given us, at least at times—and we thank Him for them heartily. They have read deep within the lines that furrowed our saddened faces; they have caught the meaning of each curve in the smile that lit our countenances; they have touched the silent depths when overwhelming joy or sorrow numbed our lips.

But we did not have them always with us. And there were depths at times they could not sound, and shadows too deep for their piercing.

But He knows us through and through, for His hands have formed us and made us and He has known and knows at every moment the frailness that is ours. To Him no least one of us is "No. 1313," no least one of us *can* be "No. 1313." In the sheerest of isolation we are always before Him islanded off from all others, just as much alone and just as well understood as though no other creature ever existed. At every moment of my existence He is giving me so much attention, that with all His infinitude of wisdom and love He simply could not give me more.

"No. 1313"—maybe at times to men; but never, inevitably never, to God. He sees all—and He understands all. Life would be intolerable were He not to understand so thoroughly and so completely. I want to be known and understood. I want to have all my good qualities sized up correctly, and I want all my bad ones, too, measured accurately; and He does—always and everywhere.

Dear Jesus, I thank You from my heart that You do understand me. Often I puzzle others; frequently I puzzle myself. Such a mass of unfulfilled desires, of stunted good deeds, of half-hearted evil ones. One day so brave, another so cowardly. Today so eager for virtue, tomorrow toying with sin. What a tangled mess! But You understand it all; and I can come to You and know that I am always just I, just myself, and not just one out of unnumbered thousands. Thank You, Jesus, for Your understanding of *me*.

TWENTY-FOURTH MONDAY AFTER PENTECOST

MORE ABOUT GOD, LESS ABOUT SELF

Let thy thoughts be upon the precepts of God, and meditate continually on His commandments, and He will give thee a heart, and the desire of wisdom shall be given to thee.
Ecclesiasticus 6:37.

WE think too much about ourselves and too little about God. Even in our prayers we are largely self-centered, always turning in on self, always taking a hurried glance at God and the things of God, and then a long, long examination of self. Self-examination and self-adjustment and the squaring of self with God's standard are indeed supremely necessary; but these will come inevitably, if our "thoughts be upon the precepts of God" and if we "meditate continually on His commandments." Breathing in the atmosphere of God, our souls must become healthy; feeding on the food of the Divine precepts, they must become strong to live up to all the ways of God. Just as with the body, health soon follows where there is pure air and good food, so, too, with the soul, and with more certainty.

Yet, how do most of us act? When we come to prayer, it is to search unendingly for our faults and to plead querulously for their forgiveness. Undoubtedly, to know our faults is necessary and to ask for their pardon is much needed. But what is more needed is the constant re-vivifying of our principles of action, the constant familiarity with God's views, God's purposes, God's plans. To dwell on these is to bring the flood-lights of Heaven into our souls, and just as the darkness of night cannot linger, when the gates of morning are thrown open, so neither can the darkness of sin tarry where God's brightness is.

Noble thoughts cannot bring forth ignoble deeds; nor honest thoughts unjust deeds; nor holy thoughts unholy deeds. Neither can what is noble, honest and holy long suffer the presence of their contraries. "Meditate continually on His commandments" and then of necessity "He will give thee a heart, and the desire of wisdom shall be given to thee." Fill the mind with the thoughts of God, and a life filled with God will follow. "He will give thee a heart," which will be at one with His, and ever eager to do His will; and "the desire of wisdom shall be given to thee" and wisdom itself will be stamped out large upon every act.

Dear Jesus, of course, I must know myself and for this make the needed self-examination. But I must remember, more than I do, that thinking Your thoughts, and meditating on Your ways is far more needed; for all my actions come finally from my thoughts. If I keep my thoughts noble and honest and holy and attuned with Yours, my life and all its actions will, as a matter of course, become like Yours. So give me grace to spend my time of prayer thinking more of You than of my miserable self.

TWENTY-FOURTH TUESDAY AFTER PENTECOST

A DISAPPOINTMENT TO GOD

My people hath forgotten Me days without number.
Jeremias 2:32.

"FATHER, I'm sorry I've disappointed you after your kindness to me. Your very kindness hurts and makes me feel ashamed," were the words that came piteously from one who was trying to do what was right and yet had slipped again. She had come with her weight of sin to God's priest and come again, and yet again, and never was there a bit of scolding, never a harsh word, but only the kindest of encouragement, only the tenderest urgings to be done with sin and to learn to love God alone. Time after time had high ideals been held out, time after time had the priest's expectancy of nobler living been insisted on and now when once again a slip was made and sin had come anew, one choking thought sprang into that harried soul: "I've disappointed one who touched my soul so tenderly; I've played him false." And into that quivering soul burned deeper and deeper the realization: "I'm a disappointment."

To know that I have failed to live up to the high hopes of those who have toiled unselfishly for my good and to realize that all their efforts have been thrown back on them, makes my head hang low with shame and my heart grow faint within me, and yet I disappoint but a fellow-man whose toiling for me, though great indeed, is but a passing thing of time. But think what it will be to stand before the judgment seat of God and know myself a disappointment to Him! Years have come and years have gone and now when time has fallen away, I come to Him for the last long reckoning and I find Him disappointed. In the long ages ago of eternity, He planned my being and molded the centuries and their peoples for my coming. He hung the stars in the firmament to give me joy, and He poised the sun by day and the moon by night to brighten my way, and patiently through the ages He laid the green carpet of the earth for me and built high mountains and shaped huge cataracts of water for me, and for me marked out with His finger the courses of the waters—and all this that I might learn to know Him and love Him and serve Him with all my heart.

Yet all this was and is the least of His patient kindness to me. When first He placed man upon this earth, He gave him rich gifts to be kept for me but Adam would not have it so and threw away the grace of God for himself and for all his children. But in His love God gave it back again and my Crucifix tells the tale. Thereon, I read the story of His love and I can spell out in His Precious Blood all His pleading to win my heart. Bethlehem I see again and its poverty that would make me love a little less the riches of the world; Nazareth is there and its toil would teach me to shun idleness and the sins thereof; Egypt comes from out its darkness and warns me of an ambition that could drive God Himself away from it lest it murder His young life. I look again and in the nail-dug hands and feet and the spear-rent side I read the awful power of sin and yet the healing value of pain. Patiently and with infinite kindness our Lord has tried to win me to holy living and to utter sanctity, as befits my walk in life. As each day broke His grace was knocking at my heart, and as the noontide came and went it summoned me insistently, and when evening was come it closed my eyes in sleep—and all again that I might know and love and serve Him well. If it pains me to disappoint the expectancy of a few years of mortal man, what shame will be mine if I stand before my changeless Friend and hear Him tell me that His eternal expectancy is doomed to be forever unfulfilled, because I am a disappointment!

Dear Jesus, nothing hurts me so much as to be a disappointment to those who have spent themselves for me. Yet what has any one done for me that I would dare to compare with all that You have done for me? High hopes You have of me that I shall be a saint and love You much and serve You well. You have told me often, so often, of Your hopes; and Your grace has come so richly to aid me to live up to Your hopes. And yet in my heart I know I am not the saint You would have me be. But I must be, Jesus dear, because You have done so much for me and done it all so patiently, so kindly, so insistently too, when I would have done with all the ideals You held out to me. Just give me then a strong, brave heart and give me more richly of Your grace, and never, never let me stand before You and be a disappointment.

TWENTY-FOURTH WEDNESDAY AFTER PENTECOST

KEPT IN MY HEART

I, Daniel, was much troubled with my thoughts and my countenance was changed in me; but I kept the word in my heart.

Daniel 7:28.

DANIEL had seen the great visions of the four beasts and of God sitting on His throne and of the opposing kingdoms of Christ and Antichrist. What it all meant, he did not know; and, though a nameless fear may have crept into his soul, he kept his peace, because he knew God must be back of it all and would straighten things out in His own good way and own good time. And so he did a very wise thing—he kept the word in his heart. No running around hither and thither to tell this one and that one, no sputtering out to any and every willing ear, but the troubling thoughts were tucked away silently in his heart.

It would be a very good thing for me to follow the example of Daniel, when life goes wrong and visions arise that frighten me. Yet often I get fearful then, and my very fear makes me tell my troubles helter-skelter. It may be an impending financial mishap, or a serious difficulty at home, or a threatening sickness. Nervously upset, my one impulse is to run around and talk. Certainly I ought to talk to someone, some one friend tried and true, or to a priest of God, that I may find help in my trial and be kept close to God. That were very wise—but not a general pouring out of my troubles.

But there are other times, when it is more needed to imitate Daniel, and that is when impatience or jealousy or anger eats into my soul with a consuming flame and sets all on fire within. Against the lurid background of my burning thoughts even the most ordinary actions of those against whom I am aroused are distorted into fantastic shapes. Meanings that were never intended are read into words; hurtful significance is given to this glance of the eye and that wave of the hand; all is twisted into fantastic shapes that mock and hurt. Then, above all other times, should I try to think of Daniel and his way of acting, when his thoughts were troubled and his countenance changed. It will do not good but much, very much harm, to broadcast my ill-humor and let everyone see the mess within my soul. To keep it within me—excepting only the talking it out to my trusted friend—is highest wisdom. The hurt will not fester, if it be talked out to one who can be trusted; and it will not infect others, when its poison is not poured out abroad carelessly.

Dear Jesus, I must learn silence, when my soul is troubled. To someone, of course, I must talk. You have so made me that I must confide in someone. But I must learn not to blurt out my hurts or my ill-humor to every passerby. Teach me this self-restraint that is so much needed, and when my soul is pained or troubled let me keep "the word in my heart!"

TWENTY-FOURTH THURSDAY AFTER PENTECOST

"UNDERNEATH ARE THE EVERLASTING ARMS"

No one, O Jesurun, is like to God, who, to come to your aid, marches over the skies, in his majesty upon the clouds. He is a refuge from days of old, and underneath are the everlasting arms.

Deuteronomy 33:26, 27.

MOSES is about to go up to Mount Nebo where he is to die in sight of the Promised Land. Giving his last instructions to the Jews whom he has led for forty years he tells them of God's love and protection. Calling them by the unusual poetic name of "Jesurun," he assures them that though God dwells aloft in the skies He is not far away, for He comes down to earth and clasps them in a fatherly embrace, "and underneath are the everlasting arms." There is no fear that they may fall and be hurt; no danger that harm may strike them for "underneath are the everlasting arms."

What a consoling, strengthening thought for each and all of us! Of course, we all have our dark hours, our days of pain, our days of anxiety, our hours when the bottom seems to have fallen out of existence. Human advice stutters then, and human aid proves a weakest reed whereon to lean. Life will indeed be hopeless at those times unless we know that "underneath are the everlasting arms."

Sickness may have snapped my young strength and blasted into complete nothings all the dreams I had over many years for my life's work. Or maybe false friends have ruined my plans and left me with only their wreckage. It is not easy then to stand erect and face a veiled future with level eyes; but it will be quite simple if I feel underneath the solid support of "the everlasting arms."

Married life may have proved a very storm of conflicting views and moods and emotions; but the restless sea will prove a solid thing if I am conscious that "underneath are the everlasting arms."

Maybe I have given myself to God in priestly or in cloistered life. All went happily along until one day my honeymoon with God came abruptly to an end and the ways of higher holiness seemed blocked with "square-hewn stones." It would be quite natural then for my steps to falter and even halt unless renewed convictions came that "underneath are the everlasting arms" supporting my up-hill journey *home.*

That is where faith comes in, like "a light that shineth in a dark place, until the day dawn and the day-star arise in our hearts" (II Peter i, 19). Moses was able to carry on, because through all the grilling forty years in the desert he was intimately aware that "underneath are the everlasting arms."

Dear Lord Jesus, I get up against it pretty hard at times, but never as hard as Moses. What steadied him should steady me. Days get dark, and the road gets rough and long-kept honest dreams burst into thin air. It is not easy to keep going then unless I realize vividly your supporting strength. So give me, please, an abiding awareness that always and everywhere "underneath are the everlasting arms."

TWENTY-FOURTH FRIDAY AFTER PENTECOST

I OFFERED IT UP, BUT—

Father, if Thou wilt, remove this chalice from Me! But yet not My will, but Thine be done!

St. Luke 22:42.

YES, I offered the headache up, but you bet I took some medicine to get rid of it," was the smiling and frank answer. "That was not very heroic, I suppose, you think, Father." "Well, no, you would never be canonized precisely for that, but you did no wrong." No wrong, of course, rather a deal of good; for while the pain was there it was sanctified and the soul of the sufferer was brought nearer to God.

Was it not in somewhat like manner that our Lord prayed in the Agony in the Garden? He was willing to suffer—it was for that He had come into this world; but, left to itself, His human will felt a great fear of all that was to be and a great revulsion therefrom. "Not My will, but Thine be done!" were His words of complete acceptance, if His Father's will must stand; and yet there was just as unmistakably the oft-repeated prayer: "Let this chalice pass from Me!"

It is quite essential that we have a true realization of what submission to God's holy will means. To accept sickness from His hands and to "offer it up" does not mean that we are to lie down supinely and use no means to recover health. To take remedies is often a clear duty and it would be wrong, were we not so to avail ourselves of what God has sent us in the way of cures. But it does mean that, if and when and as long as the pain stays, I accept it all with God's grace and unite it with the Passion of my changeless Friend.

To accept poverty as a gift from God and to bear the want and privation of even the necessaries of life does not at all imply that we do not use every lawful means to secure a competency of this world's goods. But while we are poor and shorn of what we can so legitimately crave, we kneel beside the Crib and try to realize that, if poverty was good enough for God, it ought to be good enough for us.

To let biased folk "have their say" and talk about us and impute to us things we never did and yet to bear it all in patience and without retort in kind, for the love of God, certainly does not entail the sacrifice on our part of those means whereby we may correct the false impression spread about us and vindicate our good name. But it does mean that while lying tongues wag and knowing heads are nodded, we stand beside our Lord amid the buffoonery of Herod's court and solace our hurt feelings with His.

Of course, if we want to be heroic, if we want to be very like our poor and taunted and crucified King, and if, duty not compelling otherwise, we are of those who "would wish to suffer reproaches, slanders and injuries and to be treated and accounted as fools (without at the same time giving any occasion for it), because they desire to imitate and resemble in some sort their Creator and Lord Jesus Christ, and to be clothed with His garments and livery," let us thank God for the grace He has given us and let us be zealous for the more perfect gifts. Of such there is much need in the Church of God today and every day.

Dear Jesus, I should like much to measure up to the bravery of Your Saints, to be ready to suffer pain, to be in want, to be despised, and even then to cry: "Yet more, O Lord, yet more!" For this I beg Your grace, but at least I must try hard to measure up to the lesser sanctity, and I *will* try hard. When pain comes, I will unite it with Your own and sanctify myself thereby. When the things of this world are wanting to me, I will remember Bethlehem and the hungry days of Your public life, when food was wanting to You. When men say unkind things about me, I will take my crucifix and lessen my heartaches with the memory of Yours. And then, after I have "offered it up," if I pray to have the cross lifted a bit, You will not mind; will You?

TWENTY-FOURTH SATURDAY AFTER PENTECOST

SOMEONE SEES ME

For His eyes are upon the ways of men, and He considereth all their steps.

Job 34:21.

AND you know, Father, you stood right there in front of me—just as vividly, just as really as you now are here—and I simply could not do the wrong to which I was tempted. You just stood there—that was all."

Thus spoke one who had been frequently tempted, but who had learned to seek higher things under the priest's guidance. He was a fine, stalwart young chap, and the world made strong demands on him, and to these demands he had been wont to yield. But now it was different; for everywhere and at all times he was conscious of someone almost visibly watching him, of someone keenly interested in whether he made good or not.

That young man may have had a vivid imagination—for the priest was not really present. But no one of us needs draw on his imagination to realize that God is actually present everywhere. He sees me whether I am in the privacy of my room or out on the crowded street. He sees me when I am at prayer and when I am on the dance floor. His eyes are upon me when I am in church and when I sit at the motion-picture. He sees me—and He is most anxious that I behave myself becomingly at all times in His presence.

And should it not be so? Is not that the way I act when I am with a friend for whose good opinion I care much? Anything that is rude, anything that does not come up to the high standard to which I know he would have me measure up, is simply out of the question while he is with me.

So should the consciousness of God's presence help me. He has told me that He wants me to be holy and perfect as He is; and with all His infinite love He is ever watching me, hoping—maybe "hoping against hope"—that I shall measure up.

If, when I pray, I actually felt that God was right there looking at me as I knelt suppliant before Him, would my prayers be raced through and would my attention be but intermittent?

If, when I walked along with men and the roar of the world was in my ears, I knew that God walked beside me, would I find it hard to listen to His counsels or to carry out His commands?

When I am at work, too, whether it be at home with all its colorless drudgery, or in the shop or office where the routine is quite maddening at times, or in the classroom where my patience is often tried to the limit, if I then saw God with me, would I not find it much easier to do each little thing well, in the way He would have me do it?

Out on the dance floor, or down at the "movies," or out in the auto—if, with the eyes of faith, I saw God really with me, would I dare, could I dare to do aught that was unseemly or to gaze upon aught that was soiling, with infinite Purity so near me?

Is this sheer imagination? Not at all. It is hard fact: God is everywhere. I am always in the presence of God the Father, who created me, of God the Son, who redeemed me, of God the Holy Ghost, who sanctifies me—and in the presence of that Most Blessed Trinity ordinary politeness counsels that I behave myself.

Dear Jesus, I am really glad that no matter where I am, at any hour of the day, or night, Winter or Summer, in youth or old age, You are always there. I want to measure up to all that You expect of me; yet it is quite hard at times. But it helps a lot to know that You are always looking at me and watching my every thought and word and deed. No, not critically—unless I force You to take exception to what I do—but lovingly, expectantly too, for You really want me to measure up to all the ideals You have of me. So, Jesus, give me always this vivid realization of Your presence everywhere, for it helps much to know that Someone sees me.

TWENTY-FIFTH SUNDAY AFTER PENTECOST

THE END IS LONG IN COMING

He that shall persevere unto the end, he shall be saved.
St. Matthew 10:22.

HEAVEN comes at the end, but the end is long in coming." Thus St. Bernadette Soubirous is reported to have remarked, as her failing strength brought her slowly to the grave. Even if she did not actually say it, it is much in line with other things she did say. Years back, at Lourdes grotto, the "Lady" had promised her happiness "not in this world but in the next." That was twenty-one years before, and those twenty-one years had brought their share of suffering—physical, mental and spiritual. "Heaven comes at the end" had cheered her always, and yet, as the years swung slowly by with their freight of pain, her human heart, despite the vision before her, must have kept on saying: "The end is long in coming."

How often do we not cry out as Bernadette did! We know "Heaven comes at the end," we know that God has laid up treasures for us for all eternity, and that no man can even dimly glimpse what will be our happiness at home with Him forever. But the clouds grow darker and the darkness comes thickeningly on, and the vision is blurred. It is hard to push on, reaching a steadying hand to rest upon the future that seems to be as distant today as it was yesterday. And then the thought may well come: Is it all a mirage—a will-o'-the-wisp? Are we just plain fools counting on a future that never comes?

Father and mother may feel this way when they face a future made black and bare by the ungratefulness of children. Friend may have known and loved friend, and life's path may have been less fatiguing because of mutual aid; but now friendship's bond is sundered and life's path must be traveled alone. And never did the way seem so wearing and so long.

The young are told to keep their lives clean and fresh and pure, and that when God comes to seal all with His final judgment the clean of heart will be very near and dear to Him. But that "Great Assize" is far away, and the world of sin is an appealing world that finds full response in newly awakened lives.

For some, the years have brought more than their share of sorrow and pain, and yet there seems to be no surcease. The vision of Heaven has been kept bright over many and many a dark day; but it may grow hard for dimming eyes to catch it afresh as of yore.

"But the end is long in coming." And God knows we find it hard to wait and to tarry till He come. And so He understands, and will have patience with our impatience, and only asks that we too have patience with ourselves—and with Him.

Dear Jesus, thanks to You I am assured that "Heaven comes at the end." And for that sure knowledge I am very grateful. But it comes only at the end, and often I get so tired of trying, so weary of plodding ahead in the dark. I know I ought to keep the vision bright; but when darkness comes, and pain afflicts me, it is very hard. And then it seems to be so dreadfully true that "the end is long in coming." But, Jesus, stand by me, please, in just those hours when the vision is dimmed, and hold my hand lest I stray aside—for I do want to keep on the way to Heaven, no matter how far it be away.

TWENTY-FIFTH MONDAY AFTER PENTECOST

TRUSTED IN

And the Lord said to me: Behold I have given My words in thy mouth. Lo, I have set thee this day over the nations and over kingdoms, to root up and to pull down, and to waste, and to destroy, and to build, and to plant.

Jeremias 1:9, 10.

I WOULDN'T mind, if only I felt she trusted me." That was the remark that came from a young teacher, who was of the great army of those who really needed the kind word kindly spoken and the warming assurance that the one over her really placed confidence in her and did not regard her as a child. She wanted to do much good and she could do much good and she actually was doing much, but she needed the spur of the encouragement and thrill that comes from the given approval of those above.

So often we work ahead in this unthinking world and we wonder much what others think of us. If we are sensible, we do not work for their praise nor let the lack of their approbation unduly depress us, but we would so like to know whether or not we are managing things aright. We are not so anxious to please them, as we are to know from them whether the thing is well or poorly done, whether it is worth our while to keep at it any longer. In no sense of pride or of smug self-complacency we want to know that we are shouldering responsibilities aright and so are trusted.

"If only I felt she trusted me!" Do we ever think in our moments of darkness that that doubt can never arise in our minds about our Lord? "If only I felt He trusted me!" And why cannot it arise? Why?

The first great trust He has put in me is to bring me into being with an immortal soul that belongs to Him more than it belongs to me, and so I must return it to Him untampered with. The intellect that is mine and His must not be tainted with error and the will that is mine and His must not be soiled by grasping forbidden fruit. He has trusted me with the gift of faith and all the crowded treasures of grace. With infinite generosity He has trusted me with His own Body and Blood, so trusted me that He comes most really and truly and substantially to dwell within me, whenever I care to have Him come to me.

He has trusted me maybe with the young lives that I have helped Him to bring into this world through a wedlock hallowed by His Sacrament. He pleads with me to form their little minds to know Him and mold their tiny hearts to love Him. He is very jealous of them—and yet He has trusted me with them.

Or it may be that the children He has given to me come from other homes and are confided to me in the classroom. "Suffer the little children to come unto Me" is the charge that He lays upon me, and it is for me to help father and mother—or ofttimes in their stead—to tell the children of their God "who loveth souls," and loves their fresh young souls in an especial way and wants them to be kept always fresh and young with the eternal youth of grace.

To each and all of us, now in this wise, now in that, He has shown His trust in us. There are tasks of eternal pricelessness that must be done and He looks to me for some of them. There are human lives to be swayed and molded, and He has trusted me to sway and mold them, now in the home, now in the classroom, now in the chance meetings of friendship or of business. But the trust is there—and it is a great and sacred one.

Dear Jesus, I am very glad that You have shown such trust in me. Often, so very often, I know not what those who are over me think of me or how they judge my action. It may be I ought to be above such craving—but I wonder. Have You not made my heart, and is not that craving rooted in it? And so it is very good to know always that You, at least, trust me, and show that trust so evidently. Just give me the grace, both in my life and in the lives of others, not to betray that trust.

TWENTY-FIFTH TUESDAY AFTER PENTECOST

SPOILING EVERYTHING

And whereas I have all these things, I think I have nothing, so long as I see Mardochai the Jew sitting before the king's gate.

Esther 5:13.

AMAN had been advanced to the highest place in the kingdom and was favored by the king, Assuerus, before all others. Great wealth was his, and honor beyond all others, and before him every knee in the whole land bent—except the knee of Mardochai the Jew. This bit deep into the soul of Aman and quite spoiled everything else. To his friends and Zares his wife "he declared . . . the greatness of his riches, and the multitude of his children, and with how great glory the king had advanced him above all his princes and servants." He told them, too, in his joy that Queen Esther had invited him to a banquet to be given only for the king and himself. But it was all spoiled—"and whereas I have all these things, I think I have nothing, so long as I see Mardochai the Jew sitting before the king's gate." And in his envy and anger he plotted the massacre of all the Jewish captives—only to find that he had accomplished his own ruin.

Aman's story—if not in its ruinous outcome, at least in its envy—has been repeated in the life of many a man. Honor or wealth or power may be had, singly or all together, and yet they mean nothing because of some trifling thing that is not had.

Sometimes it is a trinket that I would possess, but another has it. At times it is a position just slightly in advance of my own that I would have, and yet another holds it. Sometimes it is a bit of work that I should like to do, but it is given to another. At times it is the approbation of a certain definite individual that I want to have but which I do not get, or—worse—which is deliberately withheld.

And this single "fly in the ointment" spoils everything for me. All the fine things are blurred, all the beauties of friendship are marred, all the peace of life is gone—over a trifle.

What fools! To be upset just because in all the large scope of even the humblest life one little thing cannot be gained. Shall a splendid banquet be counted as nothing just because no after-dinner mints are served?

Am I allowing my life to be clouded over by some such trifle? Is the generous array of good things given me by God quite overlooked just because I have not some trifling thing on which I have set my heart unweaningly?

Dear Jesus, please give me common sense. No matter how poorly endowed my life may seem to be, there are manifold riches therein, all given me by Your love. Yet, often I do want something that is not there, and which I cannot get. If so, please do not let me spoil everything by wilfull attachment to something You do not see fit to let me gain. And even if it be another's wilfulness that cheats me of it, let me have sense enough not to let it sour me on all the many other good things I really have. Thanks to Your good graciousness, I have more than enough with which to fill my life and make me happy.

TWENTY-FIFTH WEDNESDAY AFTER PENTECOST

STANDING SUCCESS

But when he (Ozias) was made strong, his heart was lifted up to his destruction, and he neglected the Lord his God.
2 Paralipomenon 26:16.

WHY is it that, so often, when a man is appointed to an office, he begins to preen his feathers and lord it over all? Why is it that, instead of continually trying to make himself worthy of his high position, he acts with readily recognized self-assurance that he is supremely fit for it? Why?" There it was, the frank, age-old question about small folk in big jobs. And the answer? Only one: "Most of us cannot stand success."

"Most of us cannot stand success." How true and yet what a pitiable commentary on our smallness! No matter what our positions be in life, the one thought uppermost in our minds should be how we may daily fit ourselves for our work, how we may daily do our work better, how we may daily learn from others new ways of doing old things, new approaches to old problems, and unseen angles to new problems. A sad day for us and for our work will be the day when we begin to think ourselves fit in every way for our task, and the saddest of all days will be that day when our self-assurance will have grown so habitual that we have become unconscious of it.

But there is no danger for me herein! Is there not? Ozias of old had long been a good king, and he had long done "that which was right in the eyes of the Lord"; but the day came that spelled his ruin, for "when he was made strong, his heart was lifted up to his destruction, and he neglected the Lord, his God."

My position may be lowly or great, but there is a task ahead of me. I may have pledged my love to another a few months ago or many years back, and it is my daily duty so to interweave our lives that we both live happily here and win Heaven together. My task only began at the altar-steps.

It may be that God has confided to my care the little ones, whose love and service He wants here and hereafter; and so it will be my task each day to make myself more worthy of my parenthood.

It may be that my tasks lie in the classroom or in the office. There again, since my life touches on so many others, inevitably for weal or woe, I ought to take special thought how my influence may be always for good. No preachments, no; just the thundering appeal of a true life.

And if my days are spent within the cloister or near the sanctuary lamp, I can never, even remotely, be worthy of my privilege. And so each day, nay rather every hour, I should try to render myself at least less unworthy to be one of God's servitors within His courts.

Dear Lord, You have deigned to give me certain tasks in life, and I must do them well. When the tasks are lowly and hidden, there is little fear of my losing my poor head. But let there be the least bit of honor or of glamor attached, and straightway there is danger that my little head will be turned and that I shall forget my native incapacity. So please give me grace to remember always that I must fit myself each day for each and every task; for if I do this humbly and self-distrustingly, then I can stand success.

TWENTY-FIFTH THURSDAY AFTER PENTECOST

A CONSTANT VISITOR

Blessed is the man that heareth me, and watcheth daily at my gates, and waiteth at the posts of my doors.
Proverbs 8:34.

OUR hearts are hungry for friendship with the good, the noble and the true. There is a craving within us, which only years of lowest degradation can banish, for friends whose every word and work may lead us one step nearer the ideal of our lives. We may seem very self-sufficient in many lines. We may be sought by our fellow-men for cheer and heartening in all their manifold trials, but each and all of us need an inspiring friend. Hither we seek him and thither our quest leads us on, and most of us know the poignancy of fruitless search. Such friends are few and far between, and maybe we wander always in the intervening wastes alone.

But this need not be, nor, even if we have happily missed the loneliness of isolated ways, have we to rest our tiring weight on human shoulders only. Noble friends are good, yes, very good, but there are times when the noblest of them is but a broken staff, a helpless fellow-exile. They fag beneath the burden of their own great cross or maybe there is no human strength that can lift in any way the cross we bear. Then it is that he is blessed who has learned to watch daily at the gates of the home of Christ and wait at the posts of his doors. To school myself just to turn aside and steal but a hurried moment to greet my changeless Friend, who is ever a-listening for my footfall on His threshold, will bring new sunshine into my shadow-flecked life. Most cheering of friends, most secretive of confidants, I may run in to have just one word with Him, but when I leave, somehow I see the sunshine now and not the shadows, somehow I find a music in my heart that is but the echo of cheering words I heard Him speak therein. A moment's tarrying and yet my heart unburdened itself, a moment's tarrying and yet my cross was lifted or else my Friend gave new courage to bear a burden He would have me carry a little while longer. Thus it is each day whether sunshine or shadow play upon my heart, and then the day comes, as come it always does, when storm-clouds break and I find myself aghast at what seems to be the coming wreckage of my life. Then it is that our Lord will hear me drag my leaden steps within His home and see me throw myself before Him in full terror at the storm. Yet withal my heart will have an unshaken confidence that, as of old, so in these later days, His words can stay the winds and waves, though mountain-high.

Dear Lord, no man can know what Your Real Presence means, save only he who comes and watches daily at Your gates and waits at the posts of Your doors. No other comfort is there in this land of tears like unto this, whether it be that joy or sorrow moves our souls. To You I come, to You I tell my heart's own story, from You in ways, which You alone could tell, I draw fresh courage for life's battles. "For, though I should walk in the midst of the shadow of death I fear no evils, for Thou art with me, Thy rod and Thy staff, they have comforted me."

TWENTY-FIFTH FRIDAY AFTER PENTECOST

SEEKING HELP RIGHTLY

I thirst.

St. John 19:28.

WE sometimes deem it a decided weakness to let another know of our interior suffering, whether of body or of mind. Should we not be strong enough to bear it alone and to whisper no least word to anyone? Would it not be wiser, nobler, so to act? Well, it may be in itself, but for most of us there is a true need to talk it all out with someone, to tell some-one of our pains and our sorrows, even though we know beforehand that there can be no lifting of the cross.

That tendency is rooted in our very nature; and may we not say that our Lord sanctioned and put His all-wise approval on this, when He cried out on the Cross, "I thirst"? He sought no relief, for there was none save in the drugged wine with which He would not dull His pain; but was it not good of our Lord to show us this truly human trait that in His agony He would cry out His suffering? He suffered long in silence to show us that it is very good that we bear all patiently and without murmur; and even when He did call out in His agony, there was no complaining, no rebellion, no pleading for false sympathy.

Let us take our trials to our Lord, of course; always, and first, and last. Let us look to Him and Him alone for the ultimate help of His grace without which all other help proves but a broken reed. But let us remember, too, that we can, yes and at times should, show the wounds of soul and body to some kind friend in God, who will lead us gently but firmly back to the same dear Friend to whom we have gone of ourselves. Pent-up sorrow or shut-up pain gnaws away at body and soul and it helps a deal to pour it all out into a willing ear.

Only let us be certain that we tell our trial to a friend in God and of God. Not to the worldly-minded who would have us drown it all out with the music and pleasures that sweep us out of ourselves into a witless way of living. Not to rebellious men who, like the wife of Job, would have us curse God and die. Not to the proud who, counting not on God's grace, will throw us back on our own will-power, and have us grin and bear it pagan-wise. No, to none of these; but to one who is at home with the things of God, whose mind is attuned to the thoughts of God, whose will does really strive to beat in unison with God.

Dear Jesus, I am glad You have taught me that it is well not to keep my load of sorrow to myself and to stumble ahead unaided. I know I must come to You, if I am to be really helped; and yet I realize that, knowing this poor heart of mine, You will be glad to have me tell my crosses to another pilgrim in this vale of tears, another pilgrim who has learned to carry crosses, too, by looking up and beyond the mists that cloud our vision here to our home above. And I would ask You to send me such a friend always, that my weary and perhaps wavering steps may be led more surely back to You.

TWENTY-FIFTH SATURDAY AFTER PENTECOST

I HOPE I DIE BEFORE YOU

Even to your old age I am the same, and to your gray hairs I will carry you; I have made you and I will bear; I will carry and will save.

Isaias 46:4.

"WELL, I hope I die before you do. Life would be too hard without your support."

Thus spoke one friend to the other. He really meant it, even though it might sound foolish or sentimental. He had learned to lean heavily on his friend, for his road through life had always been a hard one, and the shadows were long and dark. Push ahead he might so long as he was conscious of his friend's nearness and ready help. But the future would be too bleak and too forbidding were that friend gone.

To many of us that thought of dreaded isolation has come with all its chilling fear. Each one of us needs help in some one way or another. We may be strong intellectually, yet need the support of another to make us morally strong. Moral strength may be ours, and yet we may find another's help quite needed to carry the cross of impaired bodily vigor.

All earthly friends we may lose, and yet an abiding friend we must have—one who will be with us tomorrow, and tomorrow's morrow—on, on, until earth's pilgrimage is ended.

And God has met that need.

My best Friend will never leave me, can never cease to be my Friend. Life may run on for only a few days or a few weeks more—He will be with us. It may stretch out over years—He will be with us still. At home in our wonted ways, or far afield in strange lands—there He will be at our sides. In youth or old age, in times of gladness or of sorrow, in riches or in poverty—no matter; He will be with us always and everywhere.

For "even to your old age I am the same, and to your gray hairs I will carry you; I have made you, and I will bear; I will carry and I will save." Never need I fear to lose Him—except by sin. And even then, I may regain His friendship at once, if only I will to have it again!

Dear Jesus, You have been very, very good to me to be my changeless Friend—one who will never, can never, leave me. I fear the loss of earthly friends upon whom I lean heavily. Some are gone already. Others may go—and then! Oh, You know the loneliness of it all, the sense of helplessness that grips me in my isolation. Yes, You know it so well that You have given me Yourself to be my Friend—today, tomorrow and up to the hour of death. Thank You, Lord, for being my changeless Friend here—and may You be such for all eternity, too!

TWENTY-SIXTH SUNDAY AFTER PENTECOST

GOD IS NOT A SPY

And because you are sons, God hath sent the Spirit of His Son into your hearts, crying: "Abba, Father!"
Galatians 4:6.

DO you think God is a big policeman, just watching and waiting to catch you in a sin, so that He may send you to hell?" This was the only answer to give the poor soul who found no joy in serving God, but was ever wracking her soul for fear lest there be sin there, was ever sieving that tortured mind to find out whether there was anything that God might almost eagerly pounce upon so as to thrust her out of His sight for all eternity. Sin here, sin there, sin everywhere—and always very close at hand was God, spying and scrutinizing so as to catch her in a fault no matter how slight it might be.

What an injustice to God! What an insult even to an earthly parent! Yet many a man and woman acts so towards God. Of course, God will punish sin; and if it be mortal and unrepented, He will punish it for all eternity. But God does not want to punish sin, even when I have committed sin. He wants me to repent. He is far, far more anxious to forgive and forget than I am to repent.

The proof? Just take the crucifix and look at it. God is nailed there to the Cross for one purpose only—to save me from my sins; not from the sins I never committed, but from the sins I have actually committed, no matter how vile and loathsome and repeated they may be. If God wanted to catch me in my sins, why did He take all the trouble to become man, and live a hard life and end it all by the horrible death on the Cross? I was already in sin, and so He could easily catch me in my sins. Utterly unreasonable was it for Him to die to save me, when He actually did not want to save me. Can I accuse God of such nonsense?

Yet that is just what I do when I fret and fume and keep my soul in continual torment lest God find the least thing wrong therein. Yes, I ought to avoid sin, even the least; but I must not turn into a fretful ferret, and be unfair to God in the bargain.

St. Paul tells me clearly that this is not what God wants. God is my Father, and He would have me carry this consoling thought with me everywhere for "you are sons," yes, and, to have us act as sons, "God hath sent the Spirit of His Son into your hearts, crying: "Abba, Father!" That is the cry of love, of confidence, and I am to call Him Father at all times, and most of all when I have sinned seriously. For He is still my Father, then, pleading for me to give Him back my love, begging me to repent of my sins so that I may once again be His child. And when lesser faults have come into my life—even with full deliberation and consent—though I know they displease Him, I know, too, that He is Father, just waiting to forgive me if only I be truly sorry for my wilfulness.

Dear Jesus, I know sin is hateful to You and that You punish unrepented sin. But You are merciful, too, and most anxious to spare and save. That is what Your whole life on earth meant, that is the one reason why You were nailed to the Cross. Please keep me from sin, of course; but if I do sin, don't let me add insult to injury by thinking of You as though You were a spying tyrant, eager to find me in a sin. Let me be fair to You, even when I have offended You, and let me always remember that Your mercy is above all Your works.

TWENTY-SIXTH MONDAY AFTER PENTECOST

MAKING GOD FORSAKE US

Why transgress you the commandment of the Lord which will not be for your good, and have forsaken the Lord, to make Him forsake you?

2 Paralipomenon 24:20.

WELL, my dear man, how can you expect from God the great graces you need when you are not playing straight with Him? You know what you ought to do, but you simply will not do it—and the result is sin on your part. And then you turn around and ask me why God does not help you." Even as the prophet Zacharias of old to the Jews, so, too, though in other words, God's priest smote the soul of the young man: "Why transgress you the commandment of the Lord which will not be for your good, and have forsaken the Lord, to make Him forsake you?"

And so maybe with us. We want God's help because life is driving hard against us. Yet all the while we doggedly refuse to give up something that we know we cannot keep and have His love.

It may be something that in itself is a trifle. But the veriest trifle can hold us back from nearness to God, even as the tiniest pebble can make us limp along a highway. For we may be of those who cannot give God only part of our love, but must give Him all, or else a large unhappiness is ours. Deep down in our hearts we know what we ought to do, but do it we will not. And then we blame God if we are not happy.

Again it may be something that robs us of God's love by leading us into serious sin against Him. Perhaps we really do not want the sin, and yet we refuse to do away with the occasion wherein, as our own sad story in the past tells us, sin will almost always come. Then when sin has come, and remorse and shame fill our souls, are we not prone to accuse God of lacking in help in our time of need? Yet in all truth, we ourselves have so forsaken God as to make Him forsake us.

Dear Jesus, I want Your love, and to have it I would serve You well. Nothing must come between us and I must not steal from You any share of my love, but give it all to You when and how and as You want me. This is my real wish, dear Lord, and yet at times I may grow weak. But never, please, never let me so forsake You that I make You forsake me.

TWENTY-SIXTH TUESDAY AFTER PENTECOST

EVEN IN JUDA!

For even in Juda there were found good works.
2 Paralipomenon 12:12.

DAVID had reigned and had "died in a good age, full of days, and riches, and glory." Solomon had reigned and "he slept with his fathers." Then Roboam in his haughtiness caused Israel to part from Juda, and, when his kingdom "was strengthened and fortified, he forsook the law of the Lord." Still, when the prophet Semeias came to him, he had prudence enough to humble himself and God tempered His punishments; "for even in Juda there were found good works."

"Even in Juda there were found good works." How strange these words!

Why, in Juda, more than anywhere in the whole wide world, there should have been much good! To the people of that land God had shown plentiful mercy: in Egypt, at Mt. Sinai, in the desert when they came into the Promised Land. He had been pleased to call Himself the God of Abraham, of Isaac and of Jacob; He had made them His chosen people. And yet "*even in Juda* there were found good works"!

What a lesson for all of us who have been favored of God, and for me in particular! I look back over the past and I see His mercy written large everywhere: in infancy; in childhood; in youth; in mature years. I find His gifts plentiful in the order of nature: health and strength of body; kind parents; good opportunities in life. And in order of grace, I know I am one of God's spoiled children: Baptism; Confirmation; Confession; His Sacramental Presence on our altars; His Sacramental Presence so often within me.

And yet—"even in Juda there were found good works." Is that what I know of myself? And is that what others think of me? I ought to be a saint, but—!

Where is my prudence? Where is my self-restraint? Where is my patience? In view of all His gifts to me, my life should be one long prayer; and yet what of my prayers? He has aked me for my heart; yet how it is tied down to the miserable things of time! He has asked me to love my neighbor as myself; but what of my gossiping tongue and my ill-concealed dislikes? Even in God's spoiled child are there found good works?

Dear Lord, what a disappointment the Jews of old were to You! You gave them much; they made such scant return. Yet what of myself? To no one have You been more generous than to me; and yet what a niggardly return I make! I ought to be a saint, but—! Give me grace, please, soon to be much ashamed of myself; for it must not ever be again that *even in me* You will find good works.

TWENTY-SIXTH WEDNESDAY AFTER PENTECOST

GOD'S

And now thus saith the Lord that created thee, O Jacob, and formed thee, O Israel: Fear not, for I have redeemed thee, and called thee by thy name; thou art Mine.

Isaias 43:1.

THE fundamental loneliness and insufficiency of each individual human life is well shown in the fact that we all want to "belong" to something or someone. To stand and face life alone is the starkest trial in all life's many problems. So we join with others and seek their companionship. We "belong" to a club, to a literary group, to a bridge club, to an athletic association. We give ourselves to a "cause" and labor with others in seeking to promote it. We seek enduring, intimate friendships and, when this need of other human love is strong, we give our lives each to each in the highest terms of human love—the marriage bond. Then in very truth each belongs to the other, rounding out their individual selves.

For other some, the sense of loneliness and inadequacy is just as real and just as poignant, but by God's grace they face life without the joys of human love that they may work untrammeled for God alone. For to them as "to the tribe of Levi he gave no possession, because the Lord, the God of Israel, Himself is their possession" (Jos. 13:33).

But whether we travel through life accompanied by shared-and-sharing human love, or without it, for each and all of us the deepest depths of our craving to "belong" to some thing or someone other than ourselves can be adequately satisfied by one and one alone—God. And truly we do belong to Him, in so real and necessary a sense that God himself could not have us not belong to Him. His right of ownership is worked into the very fibers of our being and we simply could not exist unless we were His. From the very moment we came into existence on now through time and unending eternity we are His. We belong to Him, and He Himself cannot give us away to another.

"Thou art Mine." And so whether human love be rightly mine or whether I have freely deprived myself of it for God, the loneliness and inadequacy of my poor self has been met by God. Small I am, yes, but I belong to Infinity; unwise I am, but I belong to Omniscience; weak and frail I am, but Omnipotence guards me. Apart I am and sundered from all others in the deepest things of life, but He has created and formed me and no least corner of my being can be hidden from His eyes.

"Thou art Mine!" I belong to God—and that gives a meaning to life and makes it really worth while. I belong to God—and that gives me a sense of security that robs life of its fears and death of its terrors. I belong to God—and that spurs me into knowing and loving and serving Him as the only One truly worthy of the best that is in me.

Dear Jesus, what a consolation it is to know that I belong to You, wholly and irrevocably. Other human loves may be mine, but that does not satisfy completely, even when given unstintingly. And so it means everything to belong to You. Only Your infinite self can satisfy this craving which You Yourself have crowded into my small self. Thanks, dear Lord, for making me Yours.

TWENTY-SIXTH THURSDAY AFTER PENTECOST

TAKING IT FOR GRANTED

> **Is it then to be thought that God should indeed dwell upon earth? For if heaven, and the heavens of heavens cannot contain Thee, how much less this house which I have built?**
>
> **3 Kings 8:27.**

WE take so much for granted during life. When anything first comes to us, it makes some kind of impression on us, and then, inevitably, as we get used to it, we take it for granted. Thus young folk in love are overjoyed at each meeting; but, when the years go by over their wedded love, each meeting is a commonplace thing. So, too, in Religious life, the first few years are thrilling years and after that there is much of the dull routine of long campaigning, even though one is campaigning so close to Christ the King. So it is in regard to the lesser things of life—food and drink and dress and play. A new garment sets us a-walking like a peacock, but only for a few days. Yes, to modernize an old, old adage: "We get no thrill out of things we are used to."

This thrill of newness seized on Solomon, as he stood at the door of the just completed temple in Jerusalem. God had shown His approval, for "it came to pass, when the priests were come out of the sanctuary, that a cloud filled the house of the Lord." God was once more abiding by a visible sign amid His people and Solomon cried out in wonderment: "Is it then to be thought that God should indeed dwell upon earth? For if heaven and the heavens of heavens cannot contain Thee, how much less this house which I have built?"

It was, indeed, a remarkable and a very gracious thing for God to give a special sign of His presence. But it was only a sign. That cloud was not God. But we in our churches have God, really and truly and substantially present. God whom "heaven and the heavens of heavens cannot contain" is there, dwelling on our altars, concealed behind the appearances of bread. A marvel? Such a marvel, that if this miracle could be witnessed by us only once in a lifetime, we would journey to the ends of the earth to be present, we would live in hopes of that miracle-visit, and memories of it would lengthen out over all the days that would follow it. But now God is living in the same city with us, on the same street with us, yes, oftentimes in our very house. And do we ever stop in amazement over His presence? Or rather is it not just an ordinary every-day fact like the presence of our breakfast on the table or of a companion at work in the office?

Is it not a numbing thought that we take God's presence so much for granted? We speak with reverence, do we ever get a thrill out of the consciousness of His nearness? Would it make one iota of perceptible difference to us, if every altar were without Him tomorrow?

Dear Jesus, what a gracious condescension on Your part to be with us! And what a miracle! It takes all Your omnipotence to be thus really present in the tabernacle, and each day You renew this tremendous miracle! Yet, day in and day out, I take it all for granted, just as I do the ordinary, commonplace things of life. This should not be, dear Lord, and yet in a way it is hard to have it otherwise, for You are with us always and I get accustomed to things so easily. But I shall try to be less inattentive to the greatness of Your presence and not take it all for granted.

TWENTY-SIXTH FRIDAY AFTER PENTECOST

I FORGIVE

Father, forgive them! For they know not what they do.
St. Luke 23:34.

IT wouldn't have been safe to ask that months back, Father." "No, Mary, but months back we did not have all these fine long chats. And what do you think our Lord would ask of you?" Slowly her eyes were lowered to the ground, those eyes that months back had flashed fire at the very thought of her brutal assailant; far forward bent her head, and a tense silence as of brooding Angels come down upon them. Then slowly the head was lifted and quietly, but firmly, came the deliberate words: "He'd ask what His priest is asking. Father, get the lad off all punishment, if you can. I forgive."—And the silence then was a sacred thing, the sanctifying atmosphere of a great forgiveness.

That young girl had been bitter, so bitter that blasphemy fell easily from her lips, but nearer and nearer had she brought her bruised torn soul to our Lord and the healing was inevitable. Standing beneath the Cross, she heard Him cry aloud: "Father, forgive them!" At first that seemed to her a mocking cry, but soon the selfless gentleness of it pierced deep into her soul and her answer, too, came full and strong: "I forgive."

"Father, forgive them!" There was a needed lesson our Lord wanted to teach us from the pulpit of the Cross. There is nothing our poor sensitive souls find harder to do than forgive. "What, forgive that man who stole from me my very livelihood!" "What, forgive that vicious tongue that has tarnished my good name!" "Forgive that self-willed upstart who lords it over us and admits no views other than his own! Do you think I have lost my mind?"

Is not that about my way of acting, when forgiveness is proposed to me? Of course, I know it is grand and glorious and noble to forgive. Oh, yes! But not in *this* case. *This* case is different. The offending party must be brought to his senses; he must be made to realize he cannot walk roughshod, this way, over people's feeling. "I'm going to teach him a lesson!" Yes, and all the while precious little do I care about the improvement of his character. I am just nursing my spirit of revenge.

Dear Lord, it is hard for me to learn Your spirit of humble forgiveness. There are times, of course, when justice must be meted out, even as You Yourself punish unrepentant sinners. But it were far, far better for me to sin by over-forgiveness than otherwise. It heals my own bruises more quickly and brings peace swiftly into my soul. Then, too, I pray every day: "Forgive us our trespasses *as* we forgive those who trespass against us." I would not have You use short-measure of forgiveness for me, and yet, if I short-measure others, I daily ask You to treat me in like manner. But over and above all this, yes, and best of all, to forgive makes me more like You.

TWENTY-SIXTH SATURDAY AFTER PENTECOST

THE EYES OF FAITH

But he (Eliseus) answered: Fear not! For there are more with us than with them. And Eliseus prayed and said: Lord, open his eyes, that he may see. And the Lord opened the eyes of the servant and he saw; and behold the mountain was full of horses and chariots of fire round about Eliseus.
4 Kings 6:16, 17.

AGAINST the city, wherein dwelt the prophet Eliseus, the king of the Syrians had "sent horses and chariots and the strength of an army." By night they came and camped, besieging the city and, when morning was come, the servant of Eliseus saw the embattled hosts. Fear smote his heart and he cried out in anguish to his master: "Alas, alas, alas, my Lord, what shall we do?" It did look hopeless, and yet the prophet of God had eyes of faith and saw beyond what the eyes of flesh could see. "There are more with us than with them," was his answer and by his prayer God showed this to his servant.

The eyes of faith! Would that we might see with them always! Many a day in this land of pilgrimage we are hard beset and the odds against our souls seem hopeless. Every incentive seems present to violate God's law; every motive to obey seems weak and worthless. The call of the world to be done with traveling along the narrow path is most insistent, and most appealing, too. Those who violate God's law prosper: the sinfully childless couple; the business man who does not hesitate to cheat; the lawyer who resorts without scruple to sharp practices; the doctor who willingly helps others to violate God's command. "Alas, alas, alas, what shall we do?" Yield and follow the ways of men against God's known will or fight ahead a losing battle?

No, not, decidedly not, a losing battle. "Fear not! For there are more with us than with them." The Angels of God, victorious of old against God's enemies are with us; the saints of God who, having the very same battles to fight, fought the good fight and won; Mary, our Mother, who crushed the evil one beneath her heel. These are all with us, unseen, yes, but strong beyond the might of all the powers of darkness. And, more than they, God Himself is with us to help us win the battle which is His, to nerve our hearts when they would faint and fail—and, when the day of battle is over, to reward us unendingly with His infinite Self. "What though tonight break you and me, if so tomorrow save?"

Dear Lord, the battle for right and virtue grows very hard at times. It seems all so hopeless, all so useless. Men violate Your law and yet they prosper. I try to keep Your law and look where I stand! Without Your help I cannot win the fight, and my heart will fail within me, unless I keep full consciousness of Your unseen help. So give me much grace always to see with the eyes of faith, beyond the enemies of my soul, that "there are more with us than with them."

TWENTY-SEVENTH SUNDAY AFTER PENTECOST

GOD EVERYWHERE

> **If I ascend into Heaven, Thou art there; if I descend into hell Thou art present. If I take my wings early in the morning and dwell in the uttermost parts of the sea, even there also shall Thy hand lead me, and Thy right hand shall hold me.**
>
> **Psalm 138:8-10.**

TO be away from a friend whom we love much is a distinct pain. To be always with such a friend is a privilege and joy that we count finest and truest in life. It is good to share our joys and to tell of our successes; it helps much to share our sorrows and to lift each other's crosses. To plot the morrow's work, and to re-scan what has passed makes each of us stronger to play straight and true and fearlessly the game of life. Rightly the Scripture says: "A brother helped by a brother is like a walled city."

If human help means so much, what of God's ever-present help! For

He is with us always. No hour of the day, no moment of the night will ever come when He will not be with us—unless we deliberately thrust Him away from us by mortal sin.

In youth He is with us to help us run along the way of life merrily yet holily. In maturing years He stands by us that we may face life's sterner realities and manage them well. When age comes on apace, His arm supports us that we may walk joyfully towards death's gates that will usher us into His unveiled presence.

With us He goes when hours of relaxation are ours: in the auto, as we speed over hill and dale; on the beach, as we frolic in the waves of His own making; in the theater, if only the play be proper; on the dance-hall floor, if no unseemliness be ours. Each pleasure is sanctified by His nearness; each bit of relaxation makes us dearer to Him if only we take it as He would have us take it.

With us, too, He tarries when work is the order of the day: down in the business world helping us to fight a true man's fight and to play the game hard but fair; in the classroom that we may form aright the minds of the little ones so dear to Him; in the home that the daily chores may not grow irksome, but that each may be a labor of love.

God everywhere! Out in the wilderness where silence alone is heard; and down in the milling crowds that jam our city streets. On land—on sea; on the mountain—in the valley; above the earth—down into the very hidden parts thereof. But best of all—in the innermost sanctuary of my soul, those secret chambers which are hidden from even my dearest friend and oft stay locked even against my own prying.

Dear Jesus, I almost feel like asking whether You Yourself know what it means to have You with me always. But of course You know because You are God and know all things. Yet I must tell You how much it means to me to have You with me always: sanctifying my pleasures and making holy my sorrows; helping me over rough places, and with me when I swing merrily along life's path. Dear Jesus, thanks—yes, thanks a thousand times that You are with me everywhere!

TWENTY-SEVENTH MONDAY AFTER PENTECOST

THE INCENTIVE OF THE GRAVE

And Joachaz slept with his fathers, and they buried him in Samaria, and Joas, his son, reigned in his stead.

4 Kings 13:9.

AGAIN and again, only with a change of names, do we read this verse in Sacred Scripture. The good king or the bad king, the rightful ruler or the usurper, each and everyone of them "slept with his fathers and they buried him," and then someone else "reigned in his stead." A day of labor, a day of triumph, a short period of well-spent or misspent activity and then—"they buried him." After a bit of pomp and power, the grave—and then somehow or other the world went on without the man who strutted so noisily across the stage of life.

A very necessary lesson there for me, while "life's fitful fever is upon me." At times, I seem so important and I am told that I am so necessary for the work in hand. Or, again, at times life seems so real, so essentially a part of myself that it is immeasurably hard for me to realize that one day it is to be severed from me. Yet a writer has said very truly: "Trust me, Today's Most Indispensables, five hundred men can take your place or mine." My passing hence may provoke a slight ripple on the great lake of life, but the greatest ripple ever made on that lake was soon, very soon smoothed out.

A depressing thought? Yes, if this world were the only place in which we were to exist. Then, indeed, the futility of it all might rightly numb us into inactivity. But if there is a life beyond the grave, and if that life is to be measured exactly by each and every action here, then the fact that the grave lies ahead and that others will take our place quite easily, is a blessed thought.

Today, labor and toil; tomorrow, rest and reward. Today, by an act of faith working ahead for God and as He wants us; tomorrow, an eternity with God in return for our fitful labors. That thought spurs us into action and has us up and doing, so that we do all we can for God and in every way we can and for everyone we can. That thought drives us on to spend ourselves in right living and in right doing towards others.

Now is the time to show God we love Him; beyond the grave He will requite our love. Now is the time, sometimes by word, but always by example, to entice all others to love God and to serve Him well. "The love of Christ drives us on" will be our cry, even as it was Saint Paul's.

Dear Lord, it is a hard and most depressing thing to face an open grave and to convince myself that one day I shall lie within. But it is also a spurring thought. I have but a short time, a very short time, wherein I can work for You and do good for You among my fellowmen. And on this short while will depend my eternity with You. So I must be up and doing always, first by making myself holy and, after that and only through that, helping others on to love and serve You. So grant, dear Lord, that the open grave may be for me not a thing to fear but a spur to constant action!

TWENTY-SEVENTH TUESDAY AFTER PENTECOST

INTO A DESERT PLACE

And He said to them: "Come apart into a desert place, and rest a little." For there were many coming and going, and they had not so much as time to eat.

St. Mark 6:31.

THERE is a deal of hurly-burly about our lives. They are, indeed, "like a fitful fever." The consciousness of life's shortness seems most subtly to drive us relentlessly into action. Now this, now that, must be done; now hither, now thither must we rush. Always "on the go"—and rarely arriving anywhere!

There are, indeed, demands on our time, and these can become quite exacting. Thus they became for our Lord and His Apostles; so much so that "there were many coming and going, and they had not so much as time to eat." So what did our Lord do?

Quietly but firmly, He dissociated Himself and His Apostles from all, with the simple command: "Come apart into a desert place, and rest a little!" Out from the whirlpool of activity into the quiet waters, out from the crowded ways of men "into a desert place, and rest a little."

Splendid psychology; more splendid spirituality, such as only our Lord could give. "Come apart into a desert place!" Yes, the crowds needed them, but to give out always and never to take time to replenish one's spiritual forces is faulty technique. The reservoir that always tumbles forth its waters and never receives any within it, soon will run dry.

So with us. Mother busy at home with its many little cares, father ply-ing his daily bread-winning tasks, teacher in the classroom, nurse at the bedside of the sick, clerk in the daily grind of the office—each and all of us must "take time out" and go "apart into a desert place and rest a little." It may be only the isolation of our own chamber or the solitude of the home of our Changeless Friend, but have it we must; and the more insistent the demands of men and women upon us to heal their wounds of soul or body, the more imperative the need for this solitude. The old monks said with truth: "Silence is the bath of the soul," as those best testify who know how invigorating and refreshing the solitude of silence is.

Nor will this solitude be lonely, if we heed the invitation, *"Come apart!"* Into the solitude we go with our changeless Friend and, apart from the raucous world, we listen to Him alone and drink in deeply of His words of eternal life. It may be for just a few moments daily; for, after all, need the bath of the soul of necessity be longer than the bath of the body?

Dear Lord, my life is such a hurried, fitful thing! Having only a few short years wherein to live, I seem to rush helter-skelter into action. To be active in the service of my fellow man is much needed, and is my plain duty according to my sphere of life. But always and everywhere there is an equal need that I should "come apart" into solitude with You and replenish my soul, that it faint not by the way. This lesson I must learn; and and when, as in Your life, in mine, too, there are "many coming and going," call my soul into solitude, there to "rest a little" in Your company.

TWENTY-SEVENTH WEDNESDAY AFTER PENTECOST

SADNESS NOT FOR MAN

The vineyard is confounded, and the fig tree hath languished; the pomegranate tree and the palm tree and the apple tree, and all the trees of the field, are withered; because joy is withdrawn from the children of men.

Joel 1:12.

SADNESS was never made for man. God crowned His creation with a creature, made to His own image and likeness and in God the light is never darkened by shadows. Thus would God have man. The light of the sun is to cheer and guide his mortal feet, and the light of God's grace and supernatural friendship to throw unflickering rays on the path that would lead his immortal soul back home. Darkness there may be for the soul, even as night falls on the body; but both darknesses were meant for respite, not for irritation.

This is the ailing of many a soul. When God in His wisdom is kind enough to shed refreshing darkness, we read things quite amiss and then "joy is withered from among the children of men." Death comes to those we love and we let the shadows lengthen out across our lives and grieve as those that have no hope. Sickness checks our merry chase for time's poor phantoms and we tug hard at the unwelcome bonds. A disappointment here, a setback there, and there again the vanishing of long-kept dreams leave a blight upon our souls and the fruitage of our virtues is no more. Yet it could and should be otherwise. The shadows that fall upon our lives must leave them sweet and smiling as the shading of the passing cloud upon the hills' green slopes. With the eyes of faith, we look about and above and beyond, until we see God's grace so manifoldly on our lives, that we smile on the gathering clouds and our hearts beat on merrily, when all the way seems dark and drear.

And why not? There is One always by our side to pour this oil of gladness into our hearts and to dry the tears before they ever fall, One whose love knows no overclouding, into whose welcoming presence we can always hurry and hear the Voice that was music to Mother Mary's ears and kept joy there even beneath the Cross.

Jesus, Giver of all good gifts, oh, give me the joyousness of Your saints. It means so much to keep Your sunlight in my heart and I am so prone to miss the silver lining of the clouds You send my way. A foolish child I am, without a child's glad heart. But make me a happy-hearted child and keep me so in all the darkness of this vale of tears until the morning of Heaven comes and in the morning You will "wipe away all tears from our eyes and death shall be no more, nor mourning, nor crying, nor sorrow shall be any more, for the former things are passed away."

TWENTY-SEVENTH THURSDAY AFTER PENTECOST

GOD'S TIRED MAN

Love is strong as death.... Many waters cannot quench love, neither can the floods drown it.

Canticles 8:6, 7.

HE was not such an old priest, but he had been ailing long and death was now all too evidently close upon him. Some one falsely tried to hint that he would get well again, but the firm, strong answer came: "No, I'm tired, very tired—and I want to go home." Even this was misunderstood as meaning his own home, but his quick reply left no room for doubt. "Oh, no, I want to go home to God. I'm very tired." Tired he was, indeed, for no one ever called upon him at any hour of the day or night but that he came at once to help. Long had he pushed himself to the limit of human endurance to win every soul he met—and a very, very tired priest of God longed for eternal rest. And it came soon.

Tired for God! What a wonderful thought! So many people get tired chasing the almighty dollar; others get tired running from one pleasure to another; others get tired doing nothing worthwhile at all. All of which is very worthless, and silly, and in the end leaves us tired uselessly.

But to us who know God, and how He loves souls, and how He died for them, and how He longs to have each soul at home with Him for all eternity, it ought to be a real privilege to get tired, at least sometimes, for God. We may not be called upon to give ourselves and our energies entirely to God's service, as that priest was called; but to each and every one of us come frequent opportunities to do something extra for God.

It may be that in my own home there is need of extra generosity and extra help because sickness or financial difficulties have come. It is so easy to be selfish and wriggle out of the unpleasant task; yet God then clearly wants us to get tired for Him.

It may be that, at school or in the parish, volunteers are asked for work that is really work and has no flash or publicity about it. Of course I can easily "duck it." But if the work is really for the good of my schoolmates or fellow-parishioners and thus really for God, is it not quite a privilege?

I get tired from dancing or from playing games or from late parties; and I don't mind it a bit. Why? Precisely because I love what I am doing. If

I were forced to dance or to play games or to go to a party, I would come away exhausted. Love makes all the difference in the world.

So, too, it will be when I get tired for God—I shan't mind it a bit, if I really love God and really want to bring others near to Him. That is the secret of a mother's love that never grows tired. That too will be the secret of my work for God—a desperate falling in love with God.

Dear Jesus, I often get tired from doing things that are useless, or at least of no permanent value. That is not always wrong, because life must have its hours of ease and recreation. But I know I could be tired more often from doing things for You and for the souls You love. In the past I have not often been tired for You, and I fear it is because I do not love You as I should. So give me much grace to fall desperately, absorbingly in love with You—and then I really will begin to work for You as I should.

TWENTY-SEVENTH FRIDAY AFTER PENTECOST

WHEN IDEALS TUMBLE

Therefore turn thou to thy God; keep mercy and judgment, and hope in thy God always.

Osee 12:6.

BELIEVE me when I say it is *not easy,* when you are tempted, and what you want wars against what you ought to have, what you've the right to take; and when the pain gnaws away and gets the better of you and the inner man cries out for relief, one's ideals seem to tumble down and sit on the ground in a heap." What a true picture for most of us, when the fight for life goes hard against us! Our ideals seem to "tumble down and sit on the ground in a heap." Just a little while back we were so eager for all that is highest and best in life, so quick to sense another's pain and to reach thereto a helping hand, so careful to do the right and avoid the wrong, so considerate of another's slightest wants. Our ideals were bright then and towering, and alluring, but now? "On the ground, in a heap."

Of course, it were senseless to let them rest there, yet of ourselves we cannot make them rise again. Today all that is low and mean and petty entices us; today the unkind word hangs a-trembling on our lips; today it matters little what others may like; there is only one to be consulted now.

Yesterday the highest reaches of sanctity beckoned us on enticingly and our springing souls leaped to the heights, today leaden feet find the ways of ordinary decency of thought and word and deed quite too hard for traveling. What fools we were to attempt to scale the heights! Far, far more wise the down-grade where we may coast and watch beautiful scenery go by.

What must we do then? Just coast? Well, hardly! Yet of ourselves we shall never attempt the heights again, never lend willing eye to the ideals that would lift us up. To our Lord we must go and we must beg Him to make His worthwhile things more real to us, and to fill us full of a strong will to dare the upward path that leads to Him.

And He will help us. That is precisely why He came on earth and led His life as man here as one of us, that we might have His life as a pattern of our own. He will speak to us through the story of His life and He will strengthen our will by His inward grace. Then when temptations come, as come they will, and "the inner man cries for relief," we shall be strong enough to face the up-grade and plod ahead to the heights.

Dear Jesus, what a changeling I am! Up today and down tomorrow, "one day eager and brave, the next not caring to try"; one day knocking for entrance at the gateway of the stars, the next day "of the earth, earthly." One day I want very much to be like You; the next day I care little whether I am quite a decent human being or not. Such a changeling! And so I need You, dear Lord, that I may not take the down-grade that calls so appealingly at times.

TWENTY-SEVENTH SATURDAY AFTER PENTECOST

INDISPENSABILITY

So you also, when you shall have done all these things that are commanded you, say: We are unprofitable servants; we have done that which we ought to do.

St. Luke 17:10.

SOMEONE, who had a keen sense of humor, superbly pilloried the self-importance we all are at times prone to feel:

"Farewell! I'm fading," cried
A hailstone, earthward pelted;
"How will the earth abide
Without me, when I'm melted?"

Funny thought? Yes, exceedingly so! But are we not just as funny, when we take ourselves too seriously?

Unless I am quite worthless, it would be foolish for me to deny that I am doing some good or am of some real value. Humility does not consist in lying, even to oneself. But no matter what I am doing, and no matter what position I may hold, and no matter how indispensable I may seem to be, the solid rock-bottom truth is that one of these future days this world is going to get along without me, just as it got along without me during many a long day in the past. And to think that no other human being can take my place or fill it adequately is sheerest self-delusion.

This should be a curb on any pride and a sobering thought, when my forward position or the praise of men would entice me to strut about on life's stage. "How will the world abide without me, when I'm melted?"

To my own little circle I may be of definite help, and for them and with them I should do all the good I can. They need me, and I should do wrong to stint them. Yet all the while, as I labor, I must keep my poise and my conviction that, if and when I go, God will still protect that group of near and dear ones.

Out on the larger group of men and women my influence may be exerted through printed or spoken word, and it may rightly be that many are helped over life's hurdles by my counsels. But other tongues have been stilled and other pens laid aside and yet the world survived.

Will this discourage me or numb my energies? Not if I have a proper sense of values or look down the corridors of time into eternity as God does. Rather will it spur me into action that here and now, "whilst it is day," I may do all the good I can for "the night cometh, when no man can work."

Dear Jesus, I am apt to have a distorted sense of my importance. Certainly there is work for which You have deigned to need me and that I must do, and I want to do it. But let me not exaggerate my work or think myself indispensable. That is a sad, sad state of mind. I will try, dear Lord, to work hard for You and to do all the good I can for You, realizing all the time that I am by no means indispensable.

LAST SUNDAY AFTER PENTECOST

HATING TO BE REPROVED

He, that hateth to be reproved, walketh in the trace of a sinner.

Ecclesiasticus 21:7.

NO, it will do no good. He has gone beyond the stage where you can tell him anything."

That was the reply given to one who wanted to tell "the man higher up" that all was not going as well as he thought it was. Affairs were, indeed, quite awry in his office and his business was by no means going the way it ought but—. He "knew it all" and, though he was not conscious of his omniscience, none could tell him anything except with studied prudence. And the result? The same as always: a failure in the long run.

How well the Wise Man puts it, "He, that hateth to be reproved, walketh in the trace of a sinner"! The day that we fail to listen to suggestions, the day that others feel that any least correction, no matter how kindly or delicately given, will be brushed aside, that day is a sad one, nay, rather, the saddest one in our lives. As long as we lend ear to those who chide us for our good, there is large hope for us, no matter how seriously we may have fallen. But, when we have reached that lofty eminence from which we survey the world better and more competently than all others, well—the loftier the eminence, the harder the fall back to the ground.

Against such a day we should all pray; but, if God has gifted us with talents out of the ordinary or with a will that is strong or with power to sway and mold other lives, then our prayer must be all the more insistent against that day. We need someone to point out our mistakes. And if, on the road of life, God sends us a friend who is frank enough and fearless enough to tell us the truth about ourselves, we should thank God much.

Dear Jesus, that would, indeed, be a sad, sad day when I would resent correction. It is not easy to have another tell me of my faults; and yet I know from all human history and from my own short past that the road of life is filled with pitfalls, when one runs along it without a guide. So please protect me against a self-sufficiency which would wall me off from the advice and correction of others! Until You call me home, let me keep common sense enough not to hate to be reproved. Then I shall not walk, or at least not for long, in the trace of a sinner.

LAST MONDAY AFTER PENTECOST

THANK GOD, I KNEW HIM!

> **This woman (Dorcas) was full of good works and almsdeeds which she did. And it came to pass in those days that she was sick and died. . . . And all the widows stood about him (Peter) weeping, and showing him the coats and garments which Dorcas made them.**
>
> **Acts 9:36-39.**

THE old priest lay dead. Far, far away a young man waited for the message that would tell him that all was over. It came—and down the street to the neighboring church he went, that he might pray for the man of God who had helped him over many a rough spot on the road of life. But, when he had genuflected and knelt to pray, quickly, before all else, the words came straight from his heart: "Dear Lord, thank You for his friendship! Thank You that I knew the man; for he brought me nearer You." Then, and only then, did he pray that God's mercy would be plentiful in pardoning whatever was amiss in the life that was over.

What a thought for each of us! Suppose I were to die this minute, would any kneel down and forcefully thank God that they had known me? Would they swiftly think of this, even before they had thought to pray for my soul?

Mother lies in death and, around her silent form, father and children kneel. As they look back over the years, despite all their sorrow, is there a deep, abiding joy that she was wife and mother to them, because of her vital nearness to God? Father has folded tired hands and the roar of the world is hushed for him now. Does mother thank God from her heart that years back she placed her hand in his "for better, for worse—until death do us part"? Do son and daughter feel that they "are the children of the saints" and that father's care over them was but an image of God's care?

A teacher has laid aside the books and closed the desk for the long last time. As pupils come now to bid a last farewell, is there a conscious sense of loss, a gripping realization that the one, who has now gone home to God, always looked on them as little friends to be led by word and, far more, by example, to know and love and serve Him better?

A friend has died, and as the mourners come, does each one go back over the years and find here a kindly word, and there a helping hand—and everywhere the wordless exhortation of a life that lifted them up to higher things?

Again, I ask myself: If I were to die now—what? The answer can be clearly read, if only I have eyes to see it. Let me look to my daily actions, and see how they affect the lives of others. Let me listen to my words and put myself in the place of my listeners and ask myself would I be helped or hindered by such words. Let me look to the ideals I harbor in my mind, for they are being slowly but surely stamped out on my character. Are these ideals high and holy? If so, when I am gone, men will thank God they have known me. If not——

Dear Jesus, I should like to leave a rich heritage of holy memories, when I am gone. To have so lived that men and women will be the better for my fleeting presence is a desire I ought always to keep fresh in my heart. I want it to be so. I want my life to be such that, through it and by it, each one I meet will be drawn nearer unto You. And so, let me live each day in thought and word and deed, that all will thank You that they have known me.

LAST TUESDAY AFTER PENTECOST

NOT TOO CLINGINGLY

By the word of the Lord they pitched their tents, and by His word they marched.

Numbers 9:23.

THE Jews had left Egypt and were out in the wilderness that borders Mt. Sinai. They had come from out of the land of their captivity and were now on their way to the Promised Land. God was their leader, and their marching or their tarrying was wholly at His command. "At the commandment of the Lord they marched, and at His commandment they pitched the tabernacle. All the days that the cloud abode over the tabernacle, they remained in the same place. And, if it was so that it continued over it a long time, the children of Israel kept the watches of the Lord and marched not. . . . If the cloud tarried from evening until morning and immediately at break of day left the tabernacle, they marched forward. . . . By the word of the Lord they pitched their tents and by His word they marched."

The one great solvent of life's difficulties is resignation to the will of God. Life is a maze of some happiness and much trouble and, strive as we may to arrange it aright, our best laid plans frequently go amiss. It is hard to make it all out; it is such a puzzle. When we have tried hard and done our best, defeat awaits us, or misunderstandings or wrecking jealousies. Then, at other times, when we have done practically nothing to warrant it, all goes splendidly.

What fools we are, then, to let our hearts cling to anything so that we grow impatient, if it is not ours! Of course, we must inevitably and by an inner force of nature set our hearts on many things, but not too clingingly. There must be love, the love of husband and wife, parent and child, friend and friend. There must be an eagerness to do well and succeed; else our work and sports, our social position in life, will go awry. There must be a wholesome self-respect and a desire for the legitimate goodwill of other men, lest our work be thwarted through their disdain for us.

But all the while—not too clingingly. If those we love are taken away from us, then we must let God have them, nor complain, when He takes them home. If friends no longer welcome us but treat us coldly, then we must stand on Pilate's porch and hear the cries, "Away with Him!" from the very ones who just five days before had raised their voices in Hosannas. Failure comes after the best of efforts. Well, where better can we betake ourselves than out to Calvary to stand beneath the Cross whereon the outcast Christ dies a placarded failure?

Not too clingingly—yes, but in no gloomy, morose way, but because we leave everything to God. Happiness or failure may come direct from Him, as they sometimes do, or they may come through the thoughtlessness or plottings of fellowmen. But in the last analysis they come to us because God wills it so or, at least, allows it so—and He really does know what is best for us.

Dear Jesus, this tangled scheme of life proves almost too much for me at times. Naturally I must love others; naturally I must try to succeed in what my station in life demands that I should do. But the hard and trying thing is to do all this in such a frame of mind and heart that I am willing to let it all go, if You want it so. Give me, then, much grace to be resigned to Your holy will, so that I love what I ought to love and seek what I ought to seek—but not too clingingly.

LAST WEDNESDAY AFTER PENTECOST

A CHILDISH FAULT

O that all the people might prophesy, and that the Lord would give them His spirit!

Numbers 11:29.

MOSES was surrounded by the seventy, standing about the tabernacle and "the Lord came down in a cloud and spoke to him, taking away of the spirit that was in Moses and giving to the seventy men." Suddenly news is brought that Eldad and Medad in the camp behind have won like gift of prophecy from God and Josue forthwith cried out: "My lord Moses, forbid them." But Moses, rising far above the usual level of jealousy among men brooked not the words of even his trusty follower and cried: "Why hast thou emulation for me? O that all the people might prophesy and that the Lord would give them His spirit!" Moses desired naught save the good of Israel and self and selfish aims were all lost sight of here.

Is it quite so with us? Rather does not a deal of trouble come into our lives because of jealousy? From reason we know it is a childish trait and

God Himself tells us in the Book of Job: "Envy slayeth the little foolish one"; and again in Proverbs: "Envy is the rottenness of the bones." It is emphatically not the fault of a grown-up person. Yet few there are, who are quite freed from its tangles.

The gift of making friends is ours and though they crowd about us and give us of their affection, we are too often fretful, when another gains like hold upon them. It may be that we are skilled in the ways of study and stand well forward among our companions or perhaps even leave them far behind. Then, if one comes who dares win equal or greater laurels than our own, our hearts are sorely tried and rendered all unhappy, as though this great grand world had not room within it for another pigmy intellect like our own. Again we find a companion placed above us in authority, one younger in years and, to our manner of thought, less endowed with fitting qualities than we have, and then a storm brews which makes peace of soul impossible. Again in minor, yes, trifling matters. A little favor shown to another without our sharing in it, a small wee word of praise that leaves our own name unmentioned, a bit of failure to notice us as we pass by—what pangs of heart do not such trifles cause! And yet we claim to have come into maturer years and to have a broad and healthy outlook on the world and to be above the petty littleness of the common crowd! Poor fools! With shortened focus we cannot see beyond ourselves and in those miserable selves each slightest good quality is magnified until we are quite convinced that we and we alone must be the recipient of all good gifts nor must any other receive like favors, lest our supremacy be not recognized by all.

O Jesus, dearest Lord, the child I am! If fault there must be in my life, ought these not be the faults of grown-up folks! It is all so pitiable, all so immature! Your great creation is quite large enough for many another being as wonderful as I often think I am. And even here is a more unseemly fault since based on what is more unreal, for am I after all so wonderful? Would this world be as beautiful as it is, were there no one more endowed than I within it? My dearest Lord, give of the spirit Moses had, and when I feel the grippings of this jealousy may I ever cry out with him: "O that all the people might prophesy and that the Lord would give them His spirit!"

LAST THURSDAY AFTER PENTECOST

TAKEN NOTICE OF

Well done, good and faithful servant.
St. Matthew 25:21.

TO be taken notice of is one of the strong cravings of men and women of this world. That is why we strut about and show off on life's stage. The splurge of wealth, of rank, of talent is the goal of everyone's desire. The old Roman poet, Horace, had his soul-thirst slaked when he was pointed out by the noting fingers of passers-by. So it was before his time and so it is today. Fortunes are squandered, health is shattered, lives are wrecked, so be it the poor folks may hear the sound of flattering whispers in their ears or gloat over glaring headlines that tell the world of their prowess. Thus they work and thus they slave. And for what? To win an applause that will sound tomorrow for another idol, to secure praise from lips which tomorrow will cry as did the Romans years ago, when another favorite was pushed from off his pedestal: "While he lies upon the river bank, let us tramp down Caesar's enemy." Yesterday Caesar's friend and so the plaudits,—today discarded, and so the hissing cries!

Is life then futile? Is this craving of my heart, "to have someone notice me," to go uneased? To play to the galleries is a losing game, and yet I cannot lead my life alone! I cannot fight the fight of life aright, if I feel it makes but little difference to anyone whether I live or die, succeed or fail. By an inborn law of my very being, I must be conscious that my thoughts and words and deeds are noted by some friend. But is there such? Yes, thanks to God there is, and He is a friend who will not throw me aside, when talents decline or beauty fades or riches fail. To win His applause is to win life's sweetest guerdon, that never can be stolen by another. And may I lawfully, holily strive to win His praises? Nay rather, I must, for failure to win them means that I have really failed to play my part in life aright, and that means utter worthlessness. I do not have to be learned or strong, nor wealthy, nor heralded abroad for any deed of high emprise. No, none of that; nay quite the contrary, for I can win His approbation only by lowly-mindedness and prayerfulness, and other-worldliness and charity and all the precious traits of soul that make a worthy man. No least applause will come from Him for petty earthly ways wherein the things of time or self are sought. But only when I have lived my life as well becomes a man who has not here a lasting home but is a-pilgrimaging on to God, then only will He say: "Well done!"

Jesus, my God, I do so want someone to notice all my ways, and yet I dare not ease this craving by the quest of the praise of men. That were not right nor can it ease my heart. And so I look to You. As You love my soul, do ever let me realize that You are taking note of all I think or say or do, whether sunshine dances all about my path or hours come that leave scars upon my soul. But most of all when the curtain is drawing across my little stage and my departure is at hand, let me hear Your final praise: "Well done!"

LAST FRIDAY AFTER PENTECOST

KIND PEOPLE

A brother that is helped by his brother is like a strong city

Proverbs 18:19.

THANK you for your kindness, all these long months! What would the world do without kind people?" Thus spoke the dying soldier of Christ, who had fought lustily the battles of his Captain, year in and year out over the span of many a year. But now "tattoo" had sounded and he had stacked his arms as manfully as he had shouldered them in the long campaigns—and waited for "taps," that would mean for him rest in Heaven unendingly. Yet his heart was human, very human, and the stalwart soldier, though he never asked for it, found consolation and help from his younger companion as weeks of suffering were told off into months, and months into years. Kind he had been to everyone and his message always was: "Be kind!" And thus his dying words were fitting: "What would the world do without kind people?"

What would it do? It would become a place of torture and of bitter unhappiness. Kindness is the touchstone that unfolds the human heart and makes it pour out all its misery unto its own healing. It lifts the weary head up to look once more to the stars above and to God beyond the stars. It nerves listless hands, which have been struck down in the fight of life, to reach out again to catch hold of the daily problems that surround us.

When father and mother are kind, the child will come to them trustingly, nor be afraid to let them know that it has slipped, as it walked too bravely ahead, or that it finds itself puzzled as the mysteries of life crowd themselves in on its growing years. When teacher is kind, the pupils will know that they have not a taskmaster but a friend, eager and willing to help, seeking only their good in everything. Let the one in charge of office or factory be kind and understanding, and there will grow a loyalty and a spirit of service among all those under him that all the money in the world could not buy.

Yet kindness does not mean weakness, nor does it imply any softness or sentimentality. That never does any good to any one, and frequently does much harm. But it means an understanding of the human heart, which comes from the ability to put ourselves into the place of others and feel as they feel, and think as they think. And so it comes to pass that, when we talk to them and when we deal with them, we are really dealing with ourselves put over into their place. And the poor old world needs much of this understanding kindness, which is gentle enough to win, yet firm enough to strike hard and tellingly, if correction must be given. Gentle firmness and firm gentleness is the kindness that heals the wounds of men.

Dear Jesus, let me be kind! The men and women about me need my kindness, just as I need theirs. You Yourself were always kind with that gentle firmness that made all flock to You and love You. You did not break the bruised reed nor quench the smoking flax. So let me learn from You how to be gentle, and firm, too, so that I may do my part to dry the tears of men and to make the sunshine brighter in this vale of tears.

LAST SATURDAY AFTER PENTECOST

COMPARATIVE LIVES

Take heed to thyself.

1 Timothy 4:16.

"NO, we shall never get anywhere, if we lead comparative lives. We must do, each of us, his own work, and let others do theirs." Such were the words of the wise priest of God, as he and his companion talked over the interplay of human lives. Here this one was in a position of authority unworthily; there, one, gifted beyond the mass of men was detailed for work that any man could do. Here disappointment was eating a heart away, because another was preferred; there unseemly self-contentedness marked an inferior, who had gone beyond his merits. There it was, the old, old story of the roller-coaster of life: some up now, some down now; and then the "ups" go down and the "downs" go up—until all come to the end and die.

Comparative lives! What a goodly phrase! Always matching myself up against someone else! Always measuring what I have with what they have! Always making comparisons! And the result—discontent, murmurings, and a general peevishness with life and maybe with God Himself that I have not gotten "all that is coming to me"—as though anything really *ought* to come to me!

What a profitless way of spending one's time! Another may have more wealth—what of it? The answer I need to know is how I am using what I have. Another may be blessed with more health of body—but that is neither here nor there. What ought to concern me is whether I am using the bit of health and strength I have for God. Another may be in a higher position than I, and I may be tempted to chafe thereat. But what I should find out is whether I am fumbling the job I have or throwing my whole self into the work assigned me here and now. My class may be a low one, and another, maybe less gifted, has a higher one. But, really, what difference does it make? My task is to turn out pupils who get to know God better, whether through spelling or rhetoric, through the multiplication table or calculus, through the scales or counterpoint and fugue.

Comparative lives! What a world of unhappiness therein! My work is *my* work and another's work is his, and we are both to travel well the road of life and get back home to God. Do we want all the roads to be exactly alike? "Take heed to thyself!" No, not in a selfish, isolating way; not in a way that separates us from other men and makes us unwilling to help them in their work. But let me take heed to myself, so that the work I have to do is done well without repining that it is not some other work; so that the duties of my station in life are all fulfilled without complaining that they might well have been different. To take in hand the tasks that have been assigned to me—high or low, in the public eye or shut far away therefrom—that is the way to play the game of life straight, the way God wants us to play it, that means taking heed to myself.

Dear Lord, I am so foolish at times. Instead of attending to my own self and my own work, instead of trying to do in the best way possible, all the tasks assigned me, I keep comparing myself and what I have and what I am supposed to do with others and their tasks. What a profitless business! I must learn to take heed to myself and all I do and to think always of how to do it better. That is what You want me to do, and I ask Your grace to do it by always taking heed to myself.

END OF VOLUME—II

INDEX OF TITLES

TABLE OF BIBLE REFERENCES

(Figure (s) after . . . are the page numbers)

Other References